LEARNING TO BE

The Cambridge University Press which as Assistant Secretary to the Syndics manly and almost unchanged since the war. He had to invent the jobs he was doing, first as Education Secretary in charge of schoolbook publishing, travelling extensively in Africa and Asia to explore new markets and discover new authors. He was appointed to the new title of Chief Editor in 1965 and was responsible for creating a team of bright young professionals, including women, whom he trained in editorial roles. New subject lists were created. In the USA a whole editorial department had to be developed, to produce a major flow of books and journals. The pattern became a model for other territories.

MICHAEL BLACK reflects on his personal interest in the subjects that meant most to him – especially literature, including his warm relationship with F.R. Leavis and his development of the Cambridge Edition of the Works of D.H. Lawrence – up to his retirement from the post of University Publisher in 1987. The narrative is informal, personal, and has its lighter moments.

LEARNING TO BE A PUBLISHER

*Cambridge University Press 1951–1987
Personal Reminiscences*

MICHAEL BLACK

© MICHAEL BLACK 2011

This publication is in copyright. Subject to statutory exception
and to the provisions of relevant collective licensing agreements,
no reproduction of any part may take place without
the written permission of the author

First published 2011

Printed in the United Kingdom at the University Press, Cambridge

ISBN 978-1-107-40180-8 Paperback

Copies available from:
Cambridge University Press Bookshop
1 Trinity Street
Cambridge CB2 1SZ
UK

Contents

List of figures		*page* vi
Acknowledgements		viii
1	Prelude	1
2	Joining the Press	4
3	The Syndicate	16
4	From Pink Order to Blue Label	23
5	The Bible: the Privilege: the history of the Press	41
6	The English list at the Press – 1	50
7	Education Secretaries	70
8	Africa and stations East	92
9	Dick David as Secretary	109
10	Chief Editor 1965–78	136
11	Migration	168
12	*Scrutiny* and after	174
13	The English list – 2	194
14	Other literatures	211
15	Getting the Lawrence Edition started	224
16	Lawrence and literary biography	241

Figures

1	Ruth and Billy Kingsford among guests at my wedding in Barnsley in 1953. Cambridge University Press.	*page* 7
2	Bentley House: the library. Cambridge University Press.	14
3	The Pitt Building, 1833, by R.B. Harraden. Cambridge University Press.	24
4	A forme of Monotype-setting in process of correction, at the proof-stage. From the Ramsey & Muspratt Archive/Cambridgeshire Collection.	28
5	John Dreyfus. From a private collection.	31
6	Reynolds Stone's engraved emblem for the *New Cambridge Modern History*.	35
7	Reynolds Stone's emblem for the New English Bible.	44
8	Oscar Watson. Cambridge University Press.	71
9	Philip Harris.	93
10	Bentley House. Cambridge University Press.	115
11	Dick David and Colin Ecclesare at 'morning prayers' in Bentley House. Cambridge University Press.	116
12	The Oriel Room in the Pitt Building, with a Syndicate meeting in progress. Cambridge University Press.	122
13	The new Printing House building, opened in 1963. Cambridge University Press.	139
14	The quatercentenary celebrations, 1984. Cambridge University Press.	154
15	Geoffrey Cass, my wife Fay and myself at a quatercentenary evening event. Cambridge University Press.	155
16	The Edinburgh Building. Cambridge University Press.	170
17	F.R. Leavis in his garden at 12 Bulstrode Gardens. Reproduced by permission of the Centre for Leavis Studies.	176

18 Book-jacket for Odette de Mourgues' *Racine*, by
    Peter Branfield.   217
19 A volume from the Lawrence Edition with Reynolds
    Stone's phoenix-symbol.   235

Acknowledgements

I have had help and encouragement from friends who were former Press staff-members, notably Jeremy Mynott, who read it all and made helpful comments. It has been pleasant to deal with present staff, especially Kevin Taylor, Gillian Dadd and Elizabeth Davey, who have secured the passage through the contemporary production process, which was instructive for me, an elderly survivor of the old ways of doing things. It has given me a glimpse into the future. I am also grateful to Chris Jackson, skilled subeditor, who made many helpful suggestions. Alison Harris kindly provided the photograph of her husband, Philip, for which I am very grateful.

I am particularly grateful to Jacques Berthoud for allowing me to reproduce the long letter in Chapter 13. This is an important aspect, little known but well worth recording, of the literary history of the English-speaking world in the recent past.

MB

CHAPTER I

Prelude

At various moments in the past I have found myself writing some account of my time at the Cambridge University Press. The first occasion was in 1984 when I wrote about the reissue of *Scrutiny* and my relationship with F.R. Leavis for the book *The Leavises*, edited by Denys Thompson. In retirement – since 1987 – I have written further pieces, for instance for the memorial volume for Dick David, former Secretary. These, modified and expanded and with others added, are here incorporated into a narrative.

The first incentive to bring these things together and add more came when in January 2001 I found myself asked to go back to the Press building and look through a pile of old files, helping to decide which should be preserved as of historical interest. I found myself thinking, 'I am one of the few living people for whom any of these old documents have a meaning, for I was there and remember what they were about.' And then it occurred to me that in September of that year it would be 50 years since I joined the Press. Having written its history for the quatercentenary in 1984 I am aware how long it has been going, and how much it has changed. Even so, 50 years – and now 10 years more – is a sizeable proportion of the total. There was a further incentive when David McKitterick began to work on the third volume of his official history of the Press, and showed me draft material. This sent me back to my own memories. I also found myself recovering and looking at things like lists of telephone numbers, other printed forms – the sort of ephemera which don't even get printed now and got rapidly thrown away then, but which happen to record what otherwise one would easily forget, like names and functions. I talked to former colleagues, especially Jeremy Mynott, and we found ourselves pooling what we could remember. Jeremy has helped me since to compile this book.

When I first came to the Press in 1951, I met people like S.C. Roberts and Walter Lewis, who had retired not many years before as Secretary to the Syndics and University Printer, and were still about and sociable.

I represented 'After the War' and the future: they represented 'Before the War' – though Roberts could also say that he represented both before and after the 1914–18 War. He had been appointed Assistant Secretary (my first formal title) in 1911 and was in touch with the first generation of recognisably modern Cambridge publishing, which had begun in the 1890s. So in that contingent way I feel – I suppose people of my age always do – that I am a link with things of nearly a century ago, am in touch with almost the whole twentieth century.

And the story implicit in what I record is that of an institution which moved in my time, and partly as a result of my activity, from a quite small, even quaint, traditional entity to a much larger, modern one; and while it remained in touch with its old self – which I begin by recording – it passed with increasing speed into a series of modern transformations. And in the process a traditional technology, hot-metal printing, which went back to Gutenberg, began to disappear, and some traditional kinds of book disappeared as well.

I had the sense, coming to the Press so soon after the War years, that the world was divided between those who were thinking 'Now we can get back to how it was' and those who were thinking 'Now we must move on.' In the years after 1945 things remained more difficult than they had been during the War itself: just as it took the War a year or two to take hold of everyday life, so it took at least five years for things to recover – in some ways they never did. My appointment in 1951 marked the point when my superiors, notably R.J.L. Kingsford, then Secretary, had decided that it was possible and necessary to make a concerted effort at catching up and moving on.

There is another dialectic that I was not aware of at the time. What I was told during my first years could be summed up as 'This is what we do, and this is how we do it.' Of course, one has to learn that. What I came to realise, especially when I had to write the single-volume 1984 *History* of the Press, is that the people Roberts had known and worked for, the people he succeeded, had had quite different preoccupations, namely: '*What* are we going to do, and *how* are we going to do it?' They were pioneers, initiators, and had to make a lot of it up as they went along. From what I learned about them, they had been successful. They had had to discover and invent. My immediate predecessors and superiors inherited from them a going enterprise which looked well-ordered and successful in its own terms, but there was a danger that in the 1950s and after the impetus to innovate and develop would be exerted within the framework of the known in a world which was changing faster and faster.

'What we do and how we do it' came too easily. I found that I had to go back to the earlier questions and find new answers.

Perhaps I ought to give an outline of my own background before I start. I had been brought up in Cornwall, and lived through the whole of the 1939–45 War as a child – but very conscious of what was going on, and deeply affected by it like everyone else. I was excessively bright at school, and came up to Cambridge in 1945 having just turned 17 but having already spent three years in the sixth form. I read English, was shocked and disappointed not to get a First Class in Part I of the Tripos, changed to Modern Languages and was similarly shocked and disappointed not to get a First in Part II. Salutary for me, having once always been top of a small class. It is relevant that as a mere bright boy straight from school I was competing with men who had served through the War. The man in the next room to mine in College had lost both legs at the landing at Anzio. The few years of age-difference concealed a lifetime (deathtime) experience. I was in 1948 called up to do two years' National Service in the Army. I went into the Intelligence Corps and served in a Field Security Section in occupied Austria. In 1950 I managed to get back to Cambridge, and did Part II English.

Readers unfamiliar with Cambridge need to know that the University governs its institutions, including the Press, by electing a supervisory committee traditionally called by the old name Syndicate, so that individual members are Syndics. The professional officers who served the Syndicate in the Cambridge publishing office were then called the Secretary to the Syndicate and his Assistant Secretaries, had official status as University Officers and could expect to become Fellows of their colleges. And the old Press used to be on a picturesque and inconvenient site in the heart of the University town, the whole fronted by the magnificent and impractical Pitt Building.

In what follows I have allowed myself a light touch or two: it stops me being too solemn and I hope it makes it readable. This is not formal history, but reminiscence and reflection.

CHAPTER 2

Joining the Press

I got my First, at last, in June 1951, and the question was, what next? A few months earlier I had visited the CU Appointments Board and had interviews with the Secretary, Colonel Oswald Guy, a friendly officer-type with a soft, deep, creamy voice, who spoke to me benignly, as to a young officer seeking a posting. His first idea was that there was a, er, branch of the Foreign Office, you know, who were looking for people ... He had looked at my file and seen that I had done my National Service in the Intelligence Corps. I thought well, maybe, let's see, and allowed him to put my name forward. I think this was in the Lent Term.

In the Easter Vac I was invited in an official letter to attend a weekend affair in residential London, a largish house which drew no attention to itself. The event was like what used to be called a Wosby, or War Office Selection Board, a device for selecting officers now being adopted for other selection procedures. You found yourself in a group of applicants, might be divided up into teams and asked to perform acted-out situations (I could never take them seriously), would have interviews with psychiatrists, would address the group on a chosen topic, and things like that. I forget what I said to the group: I do remember a passionate address on the recent communist takeover of Czechoslovakia, and thinking '*He's* a crusader.' Rather a contrast with the rest of us. At the end I seem to remember an interview with a board at which someone asked me if I remembered a cousin of my mother's. I had never met him, had not even heard of him, but I learned some time later that he had been in the Navy after the First War and had caused trouble in a mutiny – had been Left Wing. I hardly registered the question at the time, but when I was politely rejected it came back to me. But I was not sorry; the weekend had shown me – and them – that I was not keen enough. One could say that it was one of their more sensible decisions. Reflecting since then on my own earlier glimpses into the intelligence world, it became clear to me that it is a realm with a natural appeal to the outsize or unstable personality with a great absence of critical sense, and much of what goes on, when it is not necessary routine security work, is pointless and silly, indeed damaging – but self-gratifying. I should never have tried.

Well, that was an escape. By June I was thinking hard about doing a Ph.D. and becoming an academic. I took advice about this, had drafted a research application and was thinking of studying the Warton family, the pre-romantic scholar-poets who did a good deal to create the taste for what we now call romanticism. It wasn't a bad idea, but hardly likely to be a great moment in modern scholarship. Then there came a message from Guy: there was a job going at the Press, and would I like to try? 'Why not?' I thought. In fact it seemed a good idea: it was a job, in a respected organisation, would actually pay me a wage and would give me scope for my intellectual interests.

I might say here that, like most young people of that time and since with an idealistic or intellectual bent, I had acquired the idea that the world of work – of business – was somehow sordid. You had to sell things (there was a cliché about 'selling soap') and make money that way: it was profit-oriented, and then as now 'profit' was a dirty word. Stupid, really, since if you are not making a profit you are not making a living. I suppose this was the end-result of a century and more of serious profit-making by the British, and if you went round the country and looked at the results you couldn't be altogether happy about it, and that is how the clichés arose. I had always had a bit of a dread that, since I was not in one of the professions, I was doomed to be in commerce or industry. I was a pure romantic then about the academy, so it was not clear to me that it was for many such people a bolt-hole. Was the Press perhaps a brilliant alternative, with the advantages of both worlds?

So I had my first interview, with Kingsford, the Secretary. Being interviewed doesn't permit any but the iciest minds to reflect on what is going on and how they feel about it, but I had the sense that I liked him, and we got on. I do remember making one response which may have been conclusive. He had made the necessary remarks about the Press being a publisher which had by its constitution to publish scholarly books which the ordinary publisher would shun as not profit-making. I took this in and liked the idea, but, more sensibly than I realised, said that all the same it had to be run like a business, hadn't it? Yes, he said, and I think he gave me a mental tick.

In the Long Vac I was called to a second interview, and took the train from Cornwall again. This time it was not in Kingsford's pleasant office, but in the old Syndicate Room – pretty intimidating, with its hollow square of long tables and an appointments committee of Syndics sitting round it. The Chairman of the Syndicate was the then Master of St John's, Ernest Benians. He sat in the middle of the head-table, as chairmen do, and I sat in the middle of the table on the other side of the square. So he sat facing me, full face, and what most struck me was that he had enormous tufts of hair growing out of his ears, like a misplaced moustache. I gazed transfixed. I must have answered the questions all right. I was asked why I had changed my Tripos to Modern Languages after Part I English, and I replied that if you couldn't be profound or brilliant you could at least be versatile, and that went down quite well. From their point of view a breadth of interest was a good thing. Stanley Bennett asked me a trick question: did I notice anything about the imprints on Faber books (they used to use roman numerals for the year of publication). I was floored, but it didn't seem to matter.

Back home, quite soon, I got my letter of appointment. I was to be an Assistant Secretary to the Syndics, at a salary of £550[1] a year; 5 per cent of this salary was to go to the FSSU (Federated Superannuation System for Universities), and by virtue of the office and my appointment by the Syndics themselves I was a University Officer. Lower grades of staff were appointed by the management, so there was this mystical divide. So, on 15 (I think) September 1951, I walked from my digs to the Pitt Building, or rather the Secretary's Office, and met my colleagues. I might mention that in those days people in that sort of job started in the morning at 10 a.m. (to allow the secretaries to open the mail and put it on the desk with the file, but mainly because it was hallowed Civil Service practice). Lunch was at 1 p.m., and one resumed from 2.30 to 5.30. One had to work on Saturday mornings, though one might leave at 12, to go off somewhere for the weekend. There were six weeks' holiday (I almost said 'leave') a year.

That indicates that I had joined not just a business, or a university department, but a class – indeed a caste. It's dead now, or transformed, but I respect it in memory. I could not have said this at the time, because I didn't realise it, but the small group of men (they were all men) that I had joined were mentally and spiritually at one with other groups which were running the country, the services and the colonies. They had a common ethos as well as common habits. One most striking thing about them is that although to their enemies they seemed class-ridden, they were in fact open to talent, knew that they depended for success and continued

---

[1] Just over £11,000 in modern terms (2000 values). I seem to remember that I had a net income of £18 a month, after rent.

Joining the Press

Figure 1. Formally attired, Ruth and Billy Kingsford among guests at my wedding in Barnsley in 1953

life on getting it – or the cleverest of them did. I was a grammar school and scholarship boy, but that itself was a Cambridge thing, and I was accepted – provided of course that I performed and to a reasonable degree fitted in. It was not difficult to fit in with people I liked and respected, and who had everything to teach me. This ethos meant that the Officers of the Press, like the principal Officers of the University, had a natural affinity with civil and colonial servants, who had nearly all been to Oxford and Cambridge, and regular service officers who had nearly all been to public schools.

Frank Kendon, Arthur Gray (one of the Assistant Printers) and I were the non-public-school men on the senior staff, though Frank's school, Goudhurst, was private and rather special. Billy Kingsford was a Governor of Sherborne and cared very much about it, but was not a snob. He was in fact a perfect gentleman, very good at the job but modest and kind, so it was possible not to notice how good at it he was. When he retired in 1963 he absolutely refused to have any ceremony to mark it; it was just that at 5.30 p.m. one Friday he went round all the offices, shook hands and said a friendly good-bye. When the door closed I gazed at it astonished, and surprised myself by bursting into tears.

The other Officers of the Press, or those in Cambridge, were Charles Carrington, the Education Secretary, Frank Kendon, first Assistant Secretary, Owen (called 'Oscar' for very mixed reasons) Watson and myself, the new third Assistant Secretary, appointed mostly because there was a backlog of work from wartime and post-war shortages and restrictions, and someone had to pile in and help shift it. In the London office at Bentley House, the Officers were Dick David and Colin Eccleshare, Manager and Assistant Manager. Officers all had their names printed on the official letter-head: I was there, from the first day, as M.H. Black BA.

Perhaps I should say that the titles Secretary and Assistant Secretary were traditional old-university styles, derived from centuries of national government, where a Minister is also a Secretary of State. Secretaries were the permanent officers who served official or elected bodies, like the Press Syndicate, or chartered bodies like the Royal Society. Originally they did the paperwork, or saw that it was done, kept the files, made minutes, did the ensuing correspondence, reported back, ran the office and so on. The titles are part of the mystique I have been outlining: a civil servant or a colonial officer would know that a Secretary with a capital S was not a typist. Conversely, words like Manager applied to the other world, the one I had been not too keen to join.

As for the people, Charles Carrington was the most representative of the world I am evoking. A public-schoolboy and Oxford graduate, he had taught history at Haileybury. He had fought in the First War, and was honest enough to admit that he had half-enjoyed it. He wrote a book about it: *A Subaltern's War*, under the pen-name Charles Edmonds. He had survived it, it was exciting, part of the nation's active (or violent) history, a great adventure for an 18-year-old, and he had come out on the other side proud and undamaged. He fought in the Second War in the RAF – though I think it was a staff job. He had co-written a successful school history of England, and a big book *The British Overseas*, both published by the Press. He was a historian of empire, and did not apologise for it: refreshing, really. He left to become Professor of British Commonwealth Relations at Chatham House in the 1950s, and wrote a good biography of Kipling. Like my other colleagues, he was good for me. I had my fixed ideas, acquired mostly at university. I had loved Kipling as a boy – raced through all the volumes in the public library. I had then discovered he was an 'imperialist' and that the Empire itself was a Bad Thing, so allowed my acquired opinions to overrule my actual knowledge and feeling. Charles was a man who knew and had really thought about these things. (And later, I was to see bits of the Empire as they were disappearing. What I saw was creditable.)

He was a remarkable man, though he lent himself to self-parody, and one could imagine him as a character-part in a TV drama: peppery ex-colonel. He was tall, thin, handsome and rather imposing. He did have a formidable temper: one noticed him sort of standing at ease with his hands behind him, the parted feet would then start to beat alternately in a rising rhythm, he would go up on his toes, the face would go red, and then it would come – or he would rush out. There was a story, quite credible, about his entering his office one day in a bad mood, seeing an accusingly full in-tray and emptying it out of the window onto the astonished undergraduates in Mill Lane. I have an odd memory of being at tea once in the Syndicate Room when he was reminiscing about his travels and I wasn't really listening. 'You know that part of Toulon', he was saying, 'You know, the red-light district . . .?' 'Yes', I said, automatically, and then thought 'Good God, what am I saying?' and went very red. But he was going on, and nobody noticed me.

Charles's function was to get good schoolbooks which would sell large numbers, in the UK and in the British territories overseas, which then had educational systems based on the British one. Schoolbooks were unlike the rest of the Press's publishing, in that they had to be commissioned. In order to get the books, he had to travel a lot, which he liked, especially overseas, and no-one could know how much of the travel was productive. I dare say it was productive for him because his intellectual interest was fuelled.

Frank Kendon was as unlike Charles as it was possible to be, since he was a meditative pacifist and a poet. I say more about his editorial activity in a later chapter: it was this which made him valuable to the Press, and a model to me, though I found him hard to get my mind around, since his views of literature and mine were opposed. More exactly, I felt he was a survival – as indeed he was – but of something else I had thought I despised – the old literary world. His bearing was anything but military: I see him in my mind's eye, also in the Syndicate Room at tea. It was an institution: we all came down at 4 p.m. and stood round a table in the corner. There was a huge teapot, thick willow-pattern cups, and Mr Rumsey bore in a cake from Fitzbillies, the shop across the road. We stood and chatted for twenty minutes or so. It was our equivalent of being in the Mess. Frank stood there in his old tweed jacket and his old flannel trousers which naturally bent at the knees. He rolled himself a cigarette without using one of those little machines. It was done by deft, caressing finger movements, finally sweeping the little packed cylinder across the tongue-tip to wet the edge of the paper. The fingers trembled a bit as he held a match to it, the few protruding shreds of tobaccco burst into flame and shrivelled, and the fragrant smoke emerged. He was being watched by an interested cat which had come in to see what was going on here. It was a sandy cat. 'A Syndi – cat!' Frank said. Curious, what one remembers.

We were joined most days at the tea ceremony by the equivalent officers on the Printing side: Brooke Crutchley, University Printer, and the two Assistant Printers Arthur Gray and John Dreyfus. Arthur was really the Works Manager, and might even have been thought of in those days as a ranker officer – no Cambridge degree, though he got one under Statute B III 6, by virtue of his office. He was a good manager; a bit limited, I thought. He was territorial, and wouldn't have liked to see me wandering into the Works to have a word with someone or to pick up a copy of a jacket. John Dreyfus was a star, and I say more of him later. So when we were all there, the officer or administrative class was united in one room: eight of us in 1951, or ten when the two London Managers, as it were posted overseas, came to Cambridge for meetings. I should add Ronald Mansbridge in the New York Branch – *really* overseas.

Frank was failing slowly and finally had to leave. I later inherited his office and his desk (there was a hierarchy of offices, and I think I must have become Education Secretary to get there). As I sat at the desk I could look out to my right into the very peaceful court, like a great cube of silent, motionless air going up behind the Pitt Building. I derive that figure from Frank, who had looked at it too, especially one winter afternoon:

> Long lost in paper work, in paper thought,
> At last I looked up from my masters' table –
> Window to window across the ancient court.
> Air is a moving net of flakes of snow,
> All small alike, silently interlacing,
> Wandering, waving, moving, delaying, turning,
> Filling the great cube of space above the grass.[2]
> Often in spring, often in crystal summer,
> Or in all clear seasons, as if the eyes were wings,
> From a tedium of task have I resorted

---

[2] So it was, before the court was tarmacked over to make a carpark. There was even a walnut tree in the centre, once.

> To that wide well of still and resting air,
> It motionless, its motionless attendance there,
> For rest, refreshment, veritable example,
> Of peaceful stillness, patient clarity.
> But these small snowflakes tell, of that deceptive air,
> A different character: the lines they weave
> Are not a very movement of their making:
> Innumerable and never-ending eddies
> Trouble invisibly the air's transparency
> Even in height of summer – even the innocent air
> Deceiving me: never, never so still,
> Never of that character which in my lack,
> Searching widely through nature, I
> Had forced upon her of my spirit's greed . . .
> Perhaps there is no rest: no air is ever still:
> No air no heart no stranger ever still.

That comes from *The Time Piece*, Frank's poem-cycle published by the Press in 1945, one of the little Cambridge books I have picked up second-hand because they were pretty. But back to that desk, the old-fashioned pedestal sort. When I opened the central drawer, as it came back towards my waist, the top edge of the front panel revealed a strip of paper fixed upon it with sellotape, so that you could read it as the drawer opened. On it in Frank's characteristic cursive was written:

Let not ambition mock their useful toil

A valuable reminder.

Oscar Watson was in India in the Army at the end of the War, and then read Modern Languages. He is still alive as I write, living in France as a very distinguished potter, keeping goats and making goats' cheese in a cottage in the Loire valley. Following Charles Carrington's departure he became briefly Education Secretary. He left Cambridge and the Press because his marriage failed; his wife went back to France, and he wanted to be near her. He had always been more keen on his talent as potter than on his work as editor. But in 1951 he was there as my immediate colleague: we had adjoining offices on the top floor of the Pitt Building, and he taught me the ropes – see the next chapter on Pink Orders and so on.

So within a year or two there were newcomers. Frank had to be replaced, Charles left, Oscar became Education Secretary, and in September 1954 Tony Becher joined as Assistant Secretary. He had read Maths and Moral Science at St John's, was a friend of Jonathan Miller, Freddy

Raphael and the whole *Beyond the Fringe* group – he helped write the scripts while remaining on the fringe. He and I co-edited *The Cambridge Review* in 1955–6.[3]

Perhaps the most significant appointment was Anthony Parker as Assistant Secretary. He had read Natural Science (it went without saying that we were all Cambridge graduates then), and he was brought in specifically to look after the science books. So he was the first specialist editor: he could talk to authors of his books in their own terms and could understand the books he was dealing with. This was a departure, an innovation, one of Kingsford's quiet forward moves. I had myself until then handled books in every subject: indeed I got some of my education by reading books in the biological sciences, such as Macfarlane Burnet's *Natural History of Infectious Disease* or Arthur Ramsay's *Physiological Approach to the Lower Animals*. But with Hilton and Wylie on topology I had simply to pass the book to the printers (though I designed it an innovative jacket). Anthony was conscientious and effective but naturally gloomy: in Bentley House he was referred to as Eeyore.

The rest of the staff in the Secretary's Office were mostly secretaries with a small 's'. The office manager was the rather grand Miss Hampton, who only became Peggy after ten years or so. She had been to secretarial college, ran the team of secretaries and supervised important matters like the organisation of post-Syndicate business, minutes of meetings, book-files, recruitment of secretarial staff. Miss Barlow (one of *the* Barlows) was Kingsford's personal secretary, Miss Ward looked after Frank and Oscar, Miss Short after Tony and me. They mostly lived in the big office just opposite the door of the Secretary's Building.

Mr Woods ran the little showroom in the entrance hall of the Pitt Building, acted as receptionist and had some vague administrative duties. He was a contact with the University and the world: dons bought their *Reporter* from him, and occasionally a book. The Cambridge booksellers hated the idea of the Press selling direct to the public, so this was almost furtive. But at least the latest books were on show, and occasionally

---

[3] The now dead but historically important *Review* then appeared eight times a term – twenty-four issues a year, including a special May Week number. It was a lot of work, with a recurrent natural cycle. There was correspondence, with a pigeon-hole for letters at Heffers' shop in Petty Cury, since many of the articles were commissioned, especially the book-reviews, and then we had to produce it by going over to Heffers' printing works, reading the proofs and passing for press on the spot. We introduced some illustrations and specially designed covers. We aimed to be a bit controversial. When I asked Geoffrey Kirk for something once, he said 'Something to make the old men angry, you mean?' There was a small editorial fee, and we sold unused review copies to the shop.

Mr Woods could oblige booksellers with a copy of a book they had not ordered or had sold out.

Mr Woods – I think he was Charles, or even Charlie, but if you knew people's first, or as we used to say Christian, names then, you never dared use them unless you were friends and equals, or colleagues – was a charming figure: small and neat with a rather melodious voice and a totally bald, polished, nut-brown head. He and Mrs Woods, a lady very grandly dressed, attended every first night at the Arts Theatre. I think she had been on the stage, and he in amateur theatricals, where, I gather, he displayed a music-hall entertainer's manner which was the obverse of the showroom suavity.

So there we were: five, or later six, Officers of the Press, supported by four or five secretaries and a showroom manager. That was the Secretary's Office, a nest of strange birds lodged within the framework of the Printing House, and now intruding a couple of fledgelings into it. Indeed there was something anomalous about the Secretary's Office, referred to a bit dubiously as 'The Syndics' by the other parts of the Press, the big, real parts – the Printing House and Bentley House. In his autobiographical record S.C. Roberts tells how before 1927 the Secretary's Building had only one storey. When the second was added he was able to house a private secretary. One might speculate that before 1927 the Secretary sat and worked either in the office on the ground floor that in my time housed the secretaries, or else in the Syndicate Room itself. Given that there was also an Educational Secretary and an Assistant Secretary, they either shared that office, or one or more of them camped in the Syndicate Room. When the second floor was built, with three sizeable offices on it, the three Officers could have an office each. That left little room for the secretaries with a small 's'. One even hesitates the thought: did the senior staff, did Waller, use the office full-time? They all had fellowships, and presumably college rooms, and all of them did a little lecturing for the English Faculty when it came into existence. Was their attitude to the work that of a Cambridge academic: one looked into the office to see if anything needed attending to, picked up the mail and went back to college? Perhaps a historian could tell us.

As for the Printing House, that was not so much a house as a college-like set of buildings of various dates, with differences of level and inconveniences of access. In it worked some 200 craftsmen, who walked or cycled in every morning and out every evening, causing a momentary traffic jam in Trumpington Street. During the day large lorries with loads of paper or machinery laboriously backed into the narrow entrances in Mill Lane.

Figure 2. Bentley House: the library

Conversely, in Bentley House there were the two Managers, the beginnings of a publicity department, a fully developed marketing machine, and some 200 salesmen, clerks, warehousemen, secretaries and so on. From Cambridge Bentley House was reached by private telephone line, a regular exchange of memoranda carried on the daily van, or by going down to the station, getting on the Liverpool Street train and taking the Underground to Euston Square. There, at 200 Euston Road, London NW1, you walked into the centre of a UK-wide and increasingly a worldwide marketing office: the headquarters from where the travellers, as they were then called, departed and returned, where twice a year there were sales conferences attended by representatives from overseas, and where on the first Thursday in January the London Manager held a lunch-time reception which was thought of as the best publishers' party of the year. People from what is now called the media were there, once even a Prime Minister (Edward Heath), distinguished writers and journalists, literary editors, star reviewers. It happened in London, not Cambridge, because London was where everything centred.

Bentley House had been built in Roberts's reign, but was organised and designed by Kingsford, the first Manager, who also started the tradition that the London Manager became President of the Publishers' Association. It was the only purpose-built publishers' office in London, had a quite grand (though to my prejudiced eye rather too 'Georgian') façade with the University shield in the middle, a handsome staircase, a really large and elegantly panelled and ceilinged library-showroom, and three floors of offices and meeting-rooms above a ground-floor warehouse with access for vehicles at the back. It was hard not to see it as the real centre, the hub of the empire. What went on in Cambridge, the 'Syndics' mystery which generated the books by some metaphysical process – that was rather shrugged off by the people who, like the printers, did the real work.

CHAPTER 3

The Syndicate

Nowhere was the continuity with the past more evident than at Syndicate meetings. They were still held, as they had been since 1894, in the Old Syndicate room in the former Secretary's Building on the Old Press Site, and then (as they have been since 1963 and are today) in the refurbished Oriel Room in the Pitt Building, at 2.15 p.m. on alternate Fridays in term. I have fond memories of the old room, with its Morris carpet, its hollow square of tables, its open fire with a screen in front of it to protect the Chairman's back, the white-painted bookshelves all round up to the ceiling, full of Cambridge books published since 1870, with one shelf reserved for recent publications. I used to acquire some sense of the Press's history by browsing among these shelves.

By age-group and inclination the then Syndics were naturally men of the 1930s and even earlier. They sailed along Kings Parade to the meeting, gowns billowing over their well-cut tweeds and polished shoes. To a man (it now seems) they smoked pipes. They sat around the hollow square in their appointed places as they still do. There were sixteen of them: the Vice-Chancellor's Deputy as Chairman, the University Treasurer ex officio, and fourteen Syndics elected for a seven-year term, once or exceptionally twice renewable. So a good Syndic could do 21 years.

They had before them some sheets of plain paper, blotting-paper, a steel pen, a well-sharpened Venus pencil, a large pewter inkpot regularly refilled, a glass ashtray and a virgin box of matches (which they were apt to pocket). As they sat down, they lit up, and the fragrant cloud went up to the ceiling. By teatime at 4 p.m. it had descended to eye-level.

Now that I think of it, one later Syndic, the biochemist Frank Young, smoked a cigar, and a very few abstained. One such was the Reverend Professor C.H. Dodd, noted theologian and scholar of the New Testament, successful author and Director of the New English Bible project, then under way. He was a tiny, white-haired cherub in granny-glasses, with the voice of a very intense and rather charming elderly child. He twinkled. Two things about him struck me as observer: wonder that he could get his feet, tiny as they were, through the bottoms of his Edwardian trousers, and the Assyrian boldness and complexity of the pencil doodles which he made during the meeting and which were reverently collected at the end.

Another, a few years later, was Dom David Knowles, whose truly great work on the *Monastic and Religious Orders in England* was being completed at the time. Another slight figure, he sat there in his worn and faded but neat clerical black, withdrawn and austere-seeming with his shorn head, burnt-out eyes and tight-shut, downturned mouth in an ashen face. He was sharply aware of the world, however little he was of it, and would quietly drop lapidary remarks, also collected for future display, such as 'Anything can be written at any length.' Once someone talking about the writing of history in a gushing way turned to him, saying, 'Don't you think, Professor Knowles, that history has to be rewritten in every generation?' A mild inner convulsion was seen to take rapid place, and he breathed out in his exhausted monotone, 'Oh, yes. *And by everybody.*' My italics convey a resigned disgust which, to his surprise, produced a roar of laughter. Seeing that he had made a joke, he gave a tight little smile.

His successor, ironically, was the historian of *The Tudor Revolution in Government* (a book I had to see through the Press soon after my arrival). Geoffrey Elton was a paradox, since he was a good Syndic by making with some panache the opposing case to almost everything. He was regularly voted down, and would occasionally ask the Chairman to see that his dissent was recorded in the minutes – the historian's instinct. He remained on the Syndicate for many years, and in Geoffrey Cass's time in the 1970s a lot had to be got through the Syndicate which was radical and didn't brook much delay or any dissent. I remember once going up the stairs to a meeting and trying to console Geoffrey Cass for the other Geoffrey's role by saying 'Yes, but he's a great little trouper', which seemed to put things in an acceptable light for a moment.

Other Syndics I remember from that time were Richard Braithwaite, the philosopher, Austin Robinson, the economist, and the tiny, owlish mathematician F.P. White of St John's, whose pipe seemed to prevent all communication by speech, but permitted him to shake it up and down to indicate yes, and wag it from side to side to indicate no, with a faint mooing noise. Others were George Salt, the somehow well-named biologist, and Wilfred Mansfield, the Director of the University Farm, who was useful on the Business Sub-Syndicate and sensible at all times. The

Chairman was at first Paul Vellacott, Master of Peterhouse, but he was ill and died, and Stanley Bennett took over. More of him below.

At an early stage, before I went to meetings, I came to have a low opinion of one Syndic, Lewis Harmer (good name), the Drapers Professor of French (and Drapers seems right too). The harm in him was not obvious: he seemed genial, if rather talkative. He was the merest linguist, spoke French better than the French and enlightened them about their usage. About their literature his views were worth nothing. Having read Part II French after Cambridge English Part I, I had been startled at first to find how antiquated the teaching was. One of the people who reformed it was Odette de Mourgues – later Harmer's successor as Professor. She had come to England in 1946, in her 30s, already qualified in Law, but wanting to turn to Literature. She was Research Student, then Lectrice, then Fellow of Girton, and in 1951 became Assistant Lecturer. Importantly, she had been supervised for her Ph.D. by Leavis – until Queenie became jealous of her and made him exclude her. (Odette told me this herself. There had been no impropriety; the jealousy was purely intellectual.) She had been introduced to Leavis by the friendly Henri Fluchère, then Director of the *Alliance française* in London. She learned a lot from Leavis and from Cambridge English, and in 1951 or 1952 offered the Press her revised thesis, 'Metaphysical Baroque and Précieux Poetry'. This was presented by Oscar Watson. To Oscar's horror, Harmer talked against it, and the Syndics were too polite to overrule the Professor. It was stupid and disloyal of him. The book went to Oxford and was published in 1953, when I bought it and saw what we had missed. More: the refusal set back the cause in Cambridge, though she went on and acquired allies, and the department became creditable and influential. I got books from her later – as I say in another chapter.

Harmer's successor as Modern Language Syndic was Edward Wilson, Professor of Spanish, who had been a friend of William Empson and James Smith of *Scrutiny* fame, and was open to the new approaches. He made an impression at Syndicate meetings: called on to speak, he too would wag his head from side to side, to indicate not dissent but gathering mental momentum, and would sometimes conclude by saying his last phrase three times, three times, three times. This chiming effect always produced a respectful silence, as if to endorse the *Snark* dictum: What I tell you three times is true. More about him too, later.

Tea was at 4 p.m., and on Syndicate days there were two enormous teapots and something good from Fitzbillies – a Dundee cake or almond ring. For a year or two I did not attend meetings, but waited outside the door until the drone of one voice was succeeded by a burst of general conversation, and then went in, took a piece of cake and a cup of tea, made a little conversation and left. Business resumed at 4.30, and usually finished before 5.30.

With Frank's decline, Oscar began to attend the meetings as Minutes Secretary, and at some point I came in too. I need to say something about the organisation of the business. I carried into the meeting the Minutes Book, a very big, very heavy blue volume bound in leather, in which the minutes were at first entered in ink, in longhand (Mr Woods's?). The first item on the agenda was my moment: I had to read the minutes aloud, very fast, in a clear voice, balancing speed against comprehensibility. Certain items were lists: of print-numbers and prices fixed, or of books declined. These were abridged for reading, in that I had to shout out in the vocal equivalent of square brackets: 'The following books were declined: [eight items].'

The Syndics sat down to a printed agenda; I don't remember that it was pre-circulated, though they did have sent to them a little printed notice reminding them of the meeting. On Thursday mornings the Secretary drew up the agenda and sent it in his neat pencilled writing across to the Printing House. It was proofed in the afternoon, printed on Friday morning, and at 2 p.m. on Friday afternoon laid round the table as a folded four-page crown quarto sheet printed in Scotch Roman. It might have as many as thirty items and might be accompanied by a typed set of minutes from a Sub-Syndicate. This was the only paper presented at the meeting. It was the Secretary's function, turning from time to time to a pile of papers and files beside him, to guide the meeting verbally through the items, reading or summarising referees' reports (he had marked the relevant passages), and reporting his own conversations and correspondence. The gently puffing Syndics received this information, and then the discussion began.

This procedure was, you could say, delightfully antiquated. But it chimes with the ethos I have been outlining. At 2.15 p.m. on Fridays the Secretary, up in his handsome office, with a partners' desk facing a good coal fire tended from time to time by a man in a green baize apron, would get up, put on his gown, collect his pile of files, go down the stairs to the Syndicate Room and, when the Chairman had called the meeting to order and the Assistant Secretary had read the minutes, would light his pipe and to his fellow senior members of the University say, in effect, 'Now, here are this week's proposals. What shall we do about them?' It was collegial. The people were all equals, and the us-and-them as between Officers and Syndics was minimal. The smoking was a tribal rite.

Books at the beginning of the agenda were usually accepted: it was no accident that they were placed there. Books at the end got revolutionary justice, being as it were bundled into a lorry, taken to the edge of town and machine-gunned after a rapid trial. These were the marginal or unsuitable books. The Secretary had himself rejected out of hand the religious and other maniacs who, then as since, regularly offer their measurements of the Pyramids, speculations on the lost tribes of Israel or the casket letters of Mary Queen of Scots, the authorship of Shakespeare's plays, how to square the circle, and so on.

I did have one relevant function from the beginning: this was to keep the long printed list of Syndics' Commitments, an innovation, which was now tabled at every meeting. I had been taken on in order to speed things: there were actual MSS in the safe which needed to be dealt with now that paper could be got again. Some had been waiting a long time, I suppose. There was also this list of books which had been accepted, many of them years before, and which might turn up needing to be handled – or might not: some never did. It was one of my jobs to write to these authors asking them if they could forecast a date for their completion: if they did, I entered it on the list. I also added, after each Syndicate meeting, the books which had just been accepted, placed an asterisk against those MSS which had been delivered, deleted those which had been put in hand. The list itself, on the inside of a four-page folio sheet, was printed from standing type, and I had it corrected before each meeting. On the front page, under the title SYNDICS' COMMITMENTS in a large size of Perpetua caps, there was a table showing what had been added and deleted since last meeting, leaving a total which was in three figures. It was also cumulative, and showed the trend over the year. My recollection is that it contained some 200–300 entries almost evenly divided between 'books in the press' and 'titles accepted'. The intention was that the total, which had been increasing, should now steady, as books, including the MSS already in the safe, were put in hand as fast as titles were added.

The Syndics had other kinds of meeting, for certain groups. Once a term (I think) there was a meeting of the Business Sub-Syndicate. This was manned by the more practical, capable or business-minded Syndics, such as Mansfield, who ran an organisation, or Robinson and Reddaway, who understood finance and accounting. A special meeting in the summer considered and approved the annual accounts, and was attended by the Press's London Officers, members of the University Financial Board, and the Press's auditors. The Sub-Syndicate would also consider major business decisions: for instance it approved the epoch-making decision to buy from Clare its unused playing field, on which the whole Press now stands. The decision was helped by the fact that Kingsford, Reddaway and the University Treasurer were Fellows of Clare, and no doubt also sat on the college committee on the other side of the transaction. This enabled Kingsford and Crutchley to organise the building of the new Printing House and the transfer from the old one in 1963, just before Kingsford retired.[1]

The continuing or humdrum role of the Sub-Syndicate was to approve Kingsford's figures for voting grants to 'unprofitable' books. That is to say, the books accepted by the Syndicate were divided into three categories: 1. 'Profitable' (i.e. printed in large numbers and likely to reprint); 2. 'Cover Costs' (i.e. printed in numbers not fewer than 1,500, and showing a 10 per cent surplus on the working); and 3. 'Grant' or 'Unprofitable' (i.e. works of serious scholarship, often complex setting, printed in smaller numbers, expected to take even longer than others to sell out, and needing a subsidy in order to make the standard notional profit on turnover).

This was one of those metaphysical trinities which the Press of its nature generated. The advantage of the grant system was that in their annual report the Syndicate could point out that during the year they had voted a total of £x thousand pounds to scholarly publishing and were thus visibly doing their duty. The less obvious disadvantage was that at the acceptance stage the predictions were mere predictions, and were to some extent regularly falsified. Evidently, a 'profitable' book could flop and make a bigger loss than any grant. 'Cover cost' books could spill into the categories above or below. And history proved that 'grant' books could become classics, reprint and over time make a respectable surplus. It remains the case that the categories did broadly represent what we published. It would have been better to make the analysis after the event – but that would mean waiting for 10, 20 or even 50 years.

There were other meetings. There were a Scientific and a Literary Books Committee which met, I think, twice a year, with half the Syndicate on each. Their function was to entertain good ideas for commissioning large enterprises, series or profitable books. The Officers or individual Syndics put forward proposals: I remember George Salt proposing the Cambridge Studies in Experimental Biology, which he went on to edit. It must have

---

[1] Retired seems appropriate: he was a retiring person, but extraordinarily effective, and likely to be underestimated in consequence. Roberts might seem to deserve the credit, but it was Kingsford who turned the American office into a Branch; he had built Bentley House; and now he had initiated the transformation of the Press, which David hesitantly continued and Cass triumphantly completed.

been a Literary Books Committee recommendation well before my time that G.N. Clark should be invited to be General Editor of the *New Cambridge Modern History*, an editorial board be appointed, and its recommendations for volume editors and chapter-contributors accepted. I would guess that most of the series that were operating when I came had been similarly instituted. I frequently used the Literary Books Committee later, when I was getting the Syndicate to enter new subjects, sometimes against Geoffrey Elton's opposition. It helped to have got the idea past the Committee, so that it could be sent on to the full Syndicate as a formal recommendation of one of its own bodies – they could hardly decline, and Geoffrey had already had his say. So the machinery was also the politics.

I think it was Boris Ford who set up the Schoolbooks Committee on this pattern. Charles Carrington had had an odd, uneasy relation with the Syndicate: he had to get their approval for what he wanted to publish, but did it very awkwardly, suggesting to them that he was a bit of a nuisance, wasn't he, and they didn't want to know about this bit of the business really, did they, but it was just a schoolbook, and they could take it on without much pain and let him get out of the room (which he did) and get on with his real work. Boris Ford was a smooth operator with a good public presence, and as his successor I wanted the Syndics to take this part of their business seriously as natural and important and as a reputable intellectual and academic function – as I think they must have done after the Education Act of 1870 had produced a very large market for schoolbooks which would either be good or bad. There had been a perceived public duty, and they began to publish for the market in the 1870s. The University at that time had also founded examining bodies and a teacher-training department. The Schoolbooks Committee actually co-opted an observer-member who was a teacher of some standing.

CHAPTER 4

From Pink Order to Blue Label

Printing and publishing staff, we all worked on the old Press site, a block, in American terms, fronted by the Pitt Building and stretching back down to the river, with Silver Street on one side and Mill Lane on the other. The Secretary's Office, headquarters of the publishing side, was in the little Syndicate Building on the Mill Lane side of the court with its curved bridge high up across to the Pitt Building. All else was the Printing House. Actually – sign of the times – there now wasn't room for all the Secretary's staff in the old building, and we had a foothold across the bridge. So at first I had a small office in the Pitt Building on the top floor at the Mill Lane end, and if I walked down the corridor into the body of the building I came to the tower, and in it the Oriel Room – originally intended for the Syndicate to meet in in 1833, but now used as the Printer's reception desk for work received, enquiries and progress-chasing. In the Tripos season it was a busy place: examiners could be seen leaving their papers for printing, and the publishers would sigh, knowing that that work had to take priority over what we were doing. The room seemed to be presided over by Eddie Toller, bright and quizzical like a blackbird.

So I was sort of in the Printer's territory. The notional divide was both real and easy to cross, and it was as if I had a foot on each side, as well as being some kind of intermediary between Cambridge and London. (There was a sort of theology here, another trinity, expressed in the imprint. At the foot of the title page you would read CAMBRIDGE: AT THE UNIVERSITY PRESS [date], as if that meant something quite clear. On the verso you read that for practical purposes this meant Bentley House, 200 Euston Road London NW1 and 32 East 57th Street New York NY 22. At the foot of that page you would read: Printed in Great Britain at the University Press Cambridge. So, all was revealed, but it was quite complicated. I was the title-page bit.)

Correspondingly, on the river-side of the ground floor of the Secretary's Building there was a green baize door: go through that and you were in the bindery, and beyond that in a small machine-room. The whole

Figure 3. The Pitt Building, in a pen and water-colour sketchbook made just before the opening in 1833, by R.B. Harraden: one of two pages detached and sold to me by Milo Keynes, Maynard's brother, and now in the Press's archive.

atmosphere changed: there was the sound of people working actively, and the sharp scents of ink, paper and cloth. If you walked up or down Silver Street, as I had done in my undergraduate days, you heard the rhythmic sound of the big printing presses, crashing like quick mechanical waves. For the people of Cambridge, that was 'the Pitt Press'.

What Assistant Secretaries did seems primitive, in modern terms. Mostly, we 'saw books through the Press'. We were a mixture of editorial assistant, progress controller, copy-writer and designer, so we did a little of everything; the main task was to keep authors happy, or at least informed, from the point when the book came in for production to the point when it was printed and bound and delivered to the London Office, Bentley House, which took over, held the stock and did the marketing. Meanwhile both Bentley House and New York had to be made aware that there was a book coming their way eventually.

Typically, there would be a telephone call from the Secretary, and I'd go down across the bridge to his room. An author might be there, and I would be introduced. He (usually it was a he) had his manuscript with him, and I would be asked to take it on and look after it. Back in my room I would turn over the pages and see what it was all about, perhaps grasping enough at this stage to draft a blurb. The book had been accepted by the Syndicate, but initially I had nothing to do with that process: it was a matter of getting it produced.

So I would reach for the Pink Order Book, so nicknamed for the obvious reason that the order forms which it contained had a top or tear-off copy on pink paper. It was, for no particular reason, a tall crown octavo (I think – sort of A5 in modern terms). The format, but much more the colour, distinguished it from the White Order Book – properly speaking, the Printing Order Book, which was a royal octavo (I think – more like A4 or an American quarto). Both types of order were headed TO MR CRUTCHLEY in a pleasantly formal way, and the pink one went on to say 'Please receive the accompanying manuscript [author's name, title] for specimen/estimate/subediting (delete as appropriate). Estimate for [blank] copies/run on [blank] copies'; and one would fill in the numbers, starting at 750 for a very learned book, but typically 1,500 or even 2,000 for a monograph, and for a school book 5,000, 10,000 or even 20,000 – in which case one would ask for a figure for making stereotype moulds and plates for the reprint, or even printing from plates.

Did we specify a format? I think we did. If the book was in a series, then the format was prescribed, but for an individual book the Assistant Secretary would, subject to advice from the Printer, specify crown octavo, tall crown, demy octavo, medium octavo, royal octavo, or the same range of quartos. Exceptionally, there might be a folio – usually for a bibliographical subject.

If we did specify the page size, we expected to be advised if the choice was inappropriate. Our own suggestion was mostly based on publishing reasons, especially cost, which led one to assume that the 'normal' book would be a demy octavo, which was an economical format in terms of paper and machining cost, and, to the purchaser, apparent value for money. A short book would be a tall crown; a schoolbook a crown octavo (but that came later when I was Education Secretary and it began to be expected that schoolbooks would be illustrated, and I fostered a number of quartos).

So the typescript went across the metaphysical divide into the Printer's domain, where first of all it was looked at by the subeditors, for good reason. Cambridge subeditors were Brooke Crutchley's invention. They didn't just copy-edit in the modern way. Even at this preliminary stage they got quite deeply into the book, examined and analysed the typescript in order to identify its purpose, structure and distinguishing features – the things which affected or even dictated the design, the things which needed to be expressed in type. These were not just obvious features like chapter-headings, page-heads and so on. Rather, they were aspects of the text, its fine structure, and things inherent in the subject and its treatment by the author.

Those subeditors were rather powerful people. I remember, of course, Peter Burbidge, extraordinary all-rounder;[1] the formidable Australian Isobel Gawler, a very strong-minded person whom some equally strong-minded authors loved and others feared; and a mild scientist. I remember vividly that Miss Gawler once made a report to me on those aspects of a series of lectures by a distinguished Dutch professor of history which she felt needed treatment – her diagnosis. He was not used to being criticised (or that is how it seemed to him), and he wrote a letter of complaint to the Syndicate. Kingsford presented the letter to them, and they backed their staff. The author withdrew his book.

These three advised the design department, and this is where John Dreyfus would come in, since he, more than anyone else, was responsible for this process. It seems extraordinary now, but for every book not in a series there would be produced a one-off design, set in type as a four-page (or as many pages as would be needed) printed specimen, in the typeface and on the paper specified, and showing the typographical treatment of every feature.

---

[1] He joined the Printer's staff in March 1947, six months after demobilisation. When I joined he was the Chief Subeditor, responsible for formulating the process and the standards, as well as organising the work of a department which grew over the years.

The estimators would use this as the basis for an almost ludicrously precise estimate of the composition and machining and paper cost, producing a unit printing-cost and a run-on cost (the lower unit cost of printing further copies). The estimator, usually a former keyboard operator, would reckon every character, spaces included, so that the cast-off (the term for the detailed calculation of the extent and complexity) was accurate to within one page, and the cost itself calculated to the nearest penny. I would take the estimate, on a small printed card with the figures entered in copperplate pen, together with the specimen, to the Secretary, and by the simple process of guessing a unit binding-price, adding it to the unit printing-cost and multiplying the whole by three or by five according to trade terms, he would come up with an approximate price which would be used in announcements. The White Order would now be given, and the manuscript sent off for setting.

When one did the Printing Order, the book was said to be 'put in hand' – an old term of trade. At this moment one was supposed to fill in and circulate to the sales offices a form familiarly called the 'put-in-hand form', though I think it had a more formal name like 'advice of forthcoming publication'. It was headed by author's name and book-title, gave the details of length and price derived from the estimate, listed the contents and incorporated a first draft of a blurb. It was the standard vice of Assistant Secretaries with a putting-off-till-tomorrow tendency to half fill in the form and then put it on one side while waiting for some detail. Then Michael Black, who needed the blurb in order to compile the seasonal list, would, if he actually knew of the book and realised it ought to be included, come round and dun the culprit.

The book was then subedited, a process which could take weeks. The subeditor worked through the text in detail, not simply advising the copy-preparer of the incidence of the conventions and their typographical treatment. The text would be read, quotations checked and finicky things like footnote-convention, bibliography and similar matters made consistent. In doing this, other features would emerge, and the subeditor, perhaps through the Assistant Secretary, would engage with the author. Local authors could come in and do it face-to-face. It was a real service, and most authors were grateful, seeing it as help.

But it prolonged the production time, which was never short. There were some books which had to be published for the Christmas season (i.e. published not later than October, but preferably in July or September), and these got a 'programme' with dates for proof and return, and machining. Those books, given priority, held up the rest.

Figure 4. A forme of Monotype-setting in process of correction, at the proof-stage. The gleam of silver shows types inserted as corrections; the others are black with ink from the proofing process.

In due course a proof, usually already made up into page, would go to the author, and he would return it through me with corrections. One had to warn them not to expect the galleys that the older ones had got used to before the War. The change meant that the index could be compiled on first proof and proofed with the revise; it also assumed that subediting of the typescript had, as it was designed to, identified and solved all the problems which in the old days had been pointed out by the press-reader and expensively corrected on the proofs. Galleys were still used in a very few cases. I seem to remember that they were used for editions: the text was proofed in page-on-galley (i.e. paginated but not imposed, or made up into sixteen-page sections) so that the editor could give page- and line-numbers in the notes. This meant that editions were in the press for a long time: Walter Lewis had complained that the type had grown whiskers. I found myself dunning Peter Laslett to return the proofs of Locke's *Two Treatises* which he had had for years.

A notorious case of long parturition was R.B. Onians's *Origins of European Thought*, published very soon after I arrived. It had started life well before the War as a prize essay of under 200 pages, and after years of proofing, revising and reproofing had reached over 400. It was known in the Press as *The Golden Twig*, because it seemed to spring from Frazer; actually it is profoundly original and explains a lot, in literature especially, and ought to be better known. But Onians would not let it go: it was his life's work, and he kept finding more material and needing to put it in. It became expensive, and he was made to pay, allegedly using his wife's money. Kingsford would write him exasperated letters, and I remember an occasion when Onians came in to see him and, in his quiet desperation, refused to go until he got his way. 'I threw him down the stairs', Kingsford said – and I believe he really did use force. But Onians won by simple obstinacy.

When I returned the proof to the Printer 'For revise' I would send it across with a 'Yellow Label' which asked for a dummy (a set of folded sheets of the paper to be used, to the exact make-up of the particular book) and a final cost, including corrections. The dummy went off to Bentley House with a Binding Order; when it was cased and blocked it not only showed how the binding would look, it supplied an exact format for the jacket to fit. I would specify a binding-material: those were the days in which one had a choice between a fine-textured cloth like Sundour (guaranteed not to fade), buckram for big scholarly books with a long life, canvas for 'arty' subjects and 'crash' – a very heavy-textured canvas – for big art-books. The top edge might be coloured, and head-and-tail bands added for special books. We hardly ever used cloth-substitutes, except for schoolbooks – and when we did, it had an overall printed design. The brass was often blocked on a black or coloured foil in a panel which might be decorated. Very occasionally the front board would also be blocked, blind (no gold or ink) or in gold.

With all the costs, including the binding-price, I could do a working (cost, receipts, overheads, royalties) and ask the Secretary to fix the price. Then I could pass the jacket for press with an English and an American price. Meanwhile the final proofs had gone back to the Printer with a

'Blue Label' which said, firmly, 'PRESS: Print 1,500 [or whatever] and Keep/Mould/Disperse the type'. One never said 'dis' because a quick reprint might just possibly be required; so standing type was reviewed regularly and moulded or dissed as the sales suggested. One also sent back the jacket-proof for press, with the English and US prices at the bottom and top of the front flap. All this assumes that one had done all the right things at the right moment earlier.

The working was done in yet another book of forms, the 'Costs and workings book'. It had a formulaic structure – a set of printed outlines of a two-sided account. On the left, printing-cost including corrections, binding-cost, jacket-cost (guessed), royalty on copies sold (check with the contract), working expenses (one-third of turnover). On the right side, x copies free, and then print-run minus x copies sold – the majority at UK price minus English discount (one-third off for A terms (to general bookseller for popular sales), 30 per cent off for B terms (for university book-sales)) and the American order sold to the US Branch at 60 per cent off. Balance in favour required was 10 per cent of total turnover, this figure being made up by the Syndics grant in the case of books accepted as making a loss and so being sold at less than the economic price for a short run. These were the days of pounds, shillings and pence, and before the days of calculators, so one's first purchase on joining the Press was a ready reckoner. This was like a dictionary, but what one looked up were fractions, percentages and multiplications: one-third off 22 shillings and sixpence was ... and this multiplied by 1,450 was ...

Prices were expected to come out at about £1 per hundred pages, so a 400-page book would be 4 guineas, and the book-buyers would groan at Cambridge prices – a sound which echoes down the ages. But in my first years English prices seemed low in the USA.

But to go back to that early or Pink-Order stage, and the important business of the specimen. In producing an original and considered design for nearly every book, the Printer was as it were proclaiming an ideal. All authors know that every book is different: they have made it so. But for every book actually to come out *looking* different, not just popped into a uniform, shows at the least an attempt to realise the fact: and to make the identity a real and considered one; and to take the process so far was to take one's function with proper seriousness. It was also to recognise, at that point in printing history, that the Monotype process and the Press's long apprenticeship to it had blossomed into this superb capability and this seemingly effortless skill. I would say that Cambridge books of the period are one of the great achievements of hot-metal letterpress printing,

Figure 5. John Dreyfus

and partly because they don't advertise it and you have to know quite a lot to see it. And this was John Dreyfus's work. I mustn't overlook the contribution of those who worked for and with him; but he led the team and did a lot of the thinking.

I had reason to know this. I started new and ignorant, and could become either an ally or a nuisance, so John would quite often come over to my office with the returned typescript and go over the specimen with me, so that I should get the point. He would start with the basics, explaining the choice of typeface, and about line-length and leading. I gathered that leads were metal strips between the lines of type, which separated them by a point, a point and a half, or even two points (72 points to the inch), so that the eye didn't double back to the beginning of the line but descended easily to the next. Text set solid in long lines was hard to read. I learned that a text with a lot of proper names in it required a face where the capitals weren't too black and busy: one wanted an even texture. Fournier had a set of capitals which were lower than the ascenders, and the weight was uniformly light. It also had a related Greek; so Moule's *Idiom Book of New Testament Greek* was set in Fournier. And so on: fairly basic stuff, really.

But also, quite early, I found myself looking after books of great complexity, at least one of them epoch-making. This was Ventris and Chadwick's *Documents in Mycenean Greek*. Ventris had deciphered the Mycenean Linear B script, and shown the language to be an archaic form of Greek. The bulk of the book gave sample texts and deciphered them. The fragments were clay tablets incised in characters which represented a syllabary. John got the Monotype to make matrices of the characters, so that the texts could be keyboarded; but that was only one aspect of a triumphant performance – the whole big book needs to be seen and analysed.

Not that it or any of the books I dealt with produced what was ordinarily thought of as 'fine printing'. It's not hard to despise all that – the classical text, the illustrations, the drop initials, the use of colour: all meant to be stroked after a good dinner, cigar in hand; to be collected, but not actually to be read, still less *used*. There is this important distinction between the beauty of the collectors' book and the much more stern, un-self-advertising but extremely strenuous fineness of the well-designed book meant to be really hard-used by professionals: to be re-read, to be continually referred to. Such books have to work. You may not – actually should not – be aware of what has had to be done to make them work.

Cambridge books of the time will in due course be collected – perhaps they are already. I do myself collect, in a modest way, Cambridge books of the 1920s and 1930s. They are often surprisingly small: crown and tall crown octavos. People who knew Walter Lewis could be amazed that he and his foreman compositor Nobbs – robust people, to put it mildly – could print such dainty books. There is a sort of aura of antique paper, swash italic and little ornaments. Just after the War paper was still scarce, so had to be used to the full; it was thin and hard, and there had to be as much on the page as was consistent with readability. That period had a kind of after-effect, in that Cambridge books went on looking slim and even a little stern. If in the pre-War period slight books were bumped out, after the War big books were packed in.

I remember getting the *New Cambridge Modern History* off the ground. It was a set of big volumes – 500 pages-plus, and straight setting. I remember John coming across with a four-page specimen. It was a 6-by-9-inch medium octavo (recently introduced as the most economical format) and was in Times: quite a long line, set solid. John was pleased with it. 'It's madly readable', he said, and so it was. You have to be sophisticated to do something apparently so simple. (We printed 15,000 copies and sold them at 2 guineas, or was it 45 shillings? – anyway, a bargain. He had helped to make the low price.)

I can see him now. I had a stand-up designer's desk in my office, and used to work at it. We'd stand side by side with something before us to discuss. He'd put his left elbow on the desk, and rest his cheek on his hand. He would cross his left leg over the right, and rest it on the point of his well-polished shoe. Pen in right hand, he would point to the features of the specimen, or to something in the text. No overt teaching or indoctrination, but what a lot I learned! There was an occasional tiny historic moment. 'What's this?' I might ask. A new typeface, or new to me. I remember meeting Ehrhardt for the first time, I think its first use in a Press book (*Locke's Travels in France*, I seem to remember). It had a supremely close set, and made a very controlled page, with its narrow vertical accent, and somehow I remember it now as typifying the ethos I am trying to represent: elegant, rather severe.

Since John was an exceptionally sweet-natured person, I never had a cross word with him – I don't think anyone else did either. But actually we were both in a slightly awkward situation; not of our making, but it could have turned sour.

This had to do with the constitution of the Press and goes back to that relationship between the two businesses, printing and publishing, and their interpenetration. Given that in the 1950s the Press was principally known as a supremely good printing house with unique skills, some authors came to it for that reason. What I have suggested about the design process – its depth, its grasp – meant that a Cambridge book was designed from the inside out, and the printed form was for that reason a profound harmony. This printed form was then taken by the publishers, who – it might be said – slapped a binding and jacket on it which might or might not bear any relation to the inside. My role.

For historic reasons bindings were organised from Cambridge, which gave the order and specified the design, through the London publishing house. In Bentley House the binding department was run by a tiny, mysterious figure with a drinker's nose called Mr P. O'Neill (few people had Christian names in those days). He was in touch with a network of small binderies in the home counties, and with a brass-cutting firm in London, which made all the binding-brasses – and very bad they were, I came to think.

As for the jackets, since Roberts's time as an Assistant Secretary with a taste for design, they were designed in Cambridge, by the successive Assistant Secretaries. They had until recently all been done by Frank Kendon, the Senior Assistant Secretary and the nearest thing we had in those days to an editor, in that he did do things to texts that needed work on them. He was ageing fast and getting tired. He had been very good at over-all picture jackets, but his typographical jackets had become very sketchy and now looked amateurish by contrast with the interior of the books.

In consequence of all this, one could imagine the Printer picking up the early copy of a new book rather gingerly, looking sadly at the jacket, taking it off and looking at the binding, and putting the thing down with a sigh. To do him justice, one could imagine the Secretary, Billy Kingsford, doing the same, since he had in his time done better jackets and commissioned really fine bindings. However, one couldn't imagine him saying 'All right, let the printers do it.'

So, to my astonishment, I quite soon found myself being told that I was going to do the jackets for my books. On my saying that I knew nothing about it, the answer was 'Then learn.' I found myself sent, one day a week, to the Central School of Arts and Crafts in Holborn to learn design in the department of printing. The School's title may have suggested to Kingsford the happy and appropriate heritage of Morris and Emery Walker and their successors; but actually the course I was on was run by Anthony Froshaug, a hairshirt Bauhaus devotee (had not Pevsner suggested that the modernists were in some unexplained way the lineal successors of the Arts and Crafts movement?). He turned out to be friendly and pleasant, a good teacher, and he positively lusted after my Cambridge Type Catalogue, but so far as I attempted to represent a Cambridge tradition with everything centred in inscriptional caps and the whole art in the spacing and the choice of type-size, I was gently derided. Everything had to be ranged left, in upper- and lower-case, and of course in Gill Sans. In effect I learned to do prospectuses for Lund Humphries – not what had been proposed for me. But you learn something from every experience: it was a good thing to discover this other fierce tradition, which had the advantage then of seeming 'contemporary' (key 1950s term) – and to see my own tradition from the outside.[2]

Anyway, I bought myself a layout pad and, with my type-measure and a sharp pencil, standing at my desk for a whole afternoon at a time, laboriously produced very detailed layouts, tracing letters from the type-catalogue. It was murmured that I left nothing for the comp to do, in terms of spacing. At first I didn't feel sure enough of what I was doing – in the way that Morison had been – to leave anything to the comp, and later I didn't want to. I was similarly remorseless with brasses: I sent the brassmaker a block-maker's

---

[2] Very early I was sent for several afternoons to the 'Tech' (the College of Arts and Technology, now Anglia Ruskin University). It had good departments of English and Art as well as printing, and newcomers to the Press staff went there to grasp essentials like handsetting type from the case into a composing-stick, proofing it and dissing back into the case.

Figure 6. Reynolds Stone's engraving of the University's coat of arms for the *New Cambridge Modern History*

proof of type I had had set up and said 'Follow this exactly.' They didn't seem to mind, and the bindings improved.

Here too, on this rather sensitive ground, John was friendly and helpful. He was willing to suggest a typeface ('How about Romulus?') or would say 'I've just bought in these ornamental rules' or 'You might like to try these borders.' I really was trying to get the binding and jacket to harmonise with the books' interior, so that the Printer might say, on looking at an early copy, 'Well, at least that's an improvement.' Word did come across the divide once, to the effect that my jackets started off looking too much like title-pages: could I make them more like posters? It was nicely put; Kingsford undertook to tell me. I think it must have been John who explained to me the concept of the tint-block, which applied a weight of flat colour; and that you could either overprint the type in black or reverse a title to print in white or the base-colour of the paper, and so get three colours with two inks.

My jackets became respectable in quite a short time, and I came to love doing them. I was also asked to do jackets for reprints of classic books, so that I devised something austere and impressive for Whitehead and Russell's *Principia Mathematica*. There were incidental pleasures like commissioning a new Cambridge shield from Reynolds Stone for the *New Cambridge Modern History*, which gave me the opportunity to visit him in Dorset on return from holiday in Cornwall. I am quite pleased to see, forty-something years on, that my basic jacket-design goes on being used in various modified forms in subsequent *Histories*.

But as the 1960s succeeded the 1950s we had a kind of boom; most books sold rather well, and it made sense to give them jackets which were not merely neat and appropriately identifiable as Cambridge, but which 'sold' the books in the shop, in competition with all the other books with *their* 'selling' jackets. It became my job to commission jackets with a strong graphic element from professional designers, for 25 guineas a time. Here again John's advice was invaluable, since he had spotted the good designers, had got to know them and had used them in other contexts. He was doing them as well as me a good turn in passing on the names.

I think Madeleine Dinkel was the first I used. She sometimes did the binding-design as well, so one had a real harmony; but then so did Michael Harvey. Peter Branfield did pen-portraits of classic authors which came out like etchings. Will Carter and David Kindersley went on doing bold calligraphic jackets, as they had occasionally for Frank Kendon. Most of all I remember Cecil Keeling, whose very original jackets and bindings combined type or lettering with the most extraordinarily bold woodcuts: with the layout he would actually send in the block, on end-grain of box. We had commissioned it; it was ours. I hear that some have survived. There was a kind of grotesque power in them which might have frightened children.

I suppose one appropriate upshot of this whole process was that, when I graduated to being a real editor and started to commission books, I got John Styan to write *The Dramatic Experience: A Guide to the Reading of Plays* (1965), and then, with an introduction from John, got David Gentleman to design and illustrate it, lay it out and do the jacket and binding, so that the book was really through-composed, to borrow the musical term. On the other hand, since it was printed by litho at Jarrold's I don't think that it looked like a Cambridge book, nice as it was. A touch of Bauhaus, even. A moral there, somewhere. And I should say that my model here was Frank Kendon. One of his last triumphs was Sir James Gray's *How Animals Move* (1953), based on Christmas Lectures at the British Institution. The lectures had used sophisticated visual aids, especially film. Frank found an appropriate equivalent by getting Edward Bawden to illustrate the book and to do the jacket and binding. Bawden wrote to Frank saying that at first he had feared he might have been rather wasting his talent, but now that he saw the book he realised that the Press had done him justice. In 1955 Frank produced *The Suburban Child*, by James Kenward, with illustrations by Edward Ardizzone – another little gem.

This was a very odd book for the Press to have published. Some of the books in this class can be referred to a tradition, especially the 'country crafts' or 'condition of England' category which the Press had quite impressively developed. But how to account for H.W. Tilman and his books, except that they were fun? He was an English type – officer and gentleman, explorer, mountaineer, single-handed yachtsman: he did all those things in places from China to Chitral (a title, actually) or sailing with 'Mischief' (his boat) to Patagonia (another title), or just climbing the Alps and Himalayas (*Where Men and Mountains Meet*). He wrote these breezy but very literate books, illustrated with his own photographs; and people who did a bit of climbing and sailing, or just stayed at home but liked to think themselves adventurous, bought them in sufficient quantities. The Press published them because it wanted (and I suppose I am saying that the people in Bentley House particularly wanted) to show that we could handle that sort of book too: the travellers liked them and so did the booksellers. They made a Christmas-season title to go at the front of the Autumn List. Frank looked after those books. It was his advocacy which made the Syndics accept Ronald Searle's first publication. Searle became famous as a cartoonist and comic illustrator, but this book was of drawings he had made in a Japanese prisoner-of-war camp – very harrowing. Similarly the Press published Christopher Fry's first verse-play because Frank thought the old dramatic tradition should be maintained.

So he had been a real editor, in his own very idiosyncratic way. I started to be one when I worked on two books with Tony Becher. The first was *The Shakespearean Ciphers Examined* (1957), by William F. and Elizabeth (not a mis-spelling: her mother had been determined that nobody should call her Eliza) Smith Friedman, two American authors. He had started life as a mathematician, and was early into computing; he was also a famous cryptographer who had cracked the Japanese code and been made rich by the State for inventions he had not been able to market commercially, for security reasons. In retirement he had amused himself by reviewing all the attempts to show that Shakespeare, or whoever wrote his plays, had advertised his authorship by concealing ciphers in them. He had fun blowing all this out of the water and, since he was a professional destroying the merest amateurs, can be said to have done it definitively. Mrs Friedman had started as his assistant. They lived in splendour in Washington DC, and on my first visit to the USA in 1956 I was invited to a reception at which very distinguished Negro retainers in white gloves said 'May Ah replenish yo' glass, Suh?' (Negro with a capital N was the required form then. I had been told one must use it.) This was my first glimpse of capitalist splendour: my second, also in Washington, occurred years later when Betty Eisenstein showed me her home, and I was very struck by the quality of the reproductions: that Renoir, for instance … I looked again and saw it was not a reproduction; nor were the others.

The Friedmans could not write anything but laborious officialese, and their humour was leaden, so Tony and I had to rewrite the book, every word, inserting witticisms and occasionally even correcting the logic of the arguments. It was quite fun slaughtering all those loonies (one of them, actually called Looney, naturally could not allow a thing like that to influence him). Although a sort of joke, the book is definitive: the standards can be applied and the arguments re-used in any future Shakespearean episode, and applied to other mad crusades.

The other book was John Chadwick's *Decipherment of Linear B*, the popular exposition which Kingsford had very shrewdly commissioned alongside the big book. Here Chadwick was an entirely competent writer. Our function as editors was to tell him when we could not quite follow the argument because he had assumed that readers were better informed than they really were. This is the problem of the experts: because things are clear to them, especially an implicit logic or a standard technical knowledge, they assume it is clear to the reader. We went through the book more than once, writing notes about the places where something needed to be spelled out, and then reading the new version until all was clear. The book, published in 1958, is still in print. I did not know it, but the exercise was crucial for me: the technique of writing for the general reader applies, only slightly modified, to the editing of schoolbooks and of books for readers of English as a second language. One has to move from 'Can I understand this?' to 'Can they understand this?'

I also found myself reading a typescript called *The Elements of Drama*, by an unknown J.L. Styan, published in 1960. Dick David read it too, since he was our authority on drama. He said it was all right but did not tell him anything he did not know. I knew less than Dick, and so found it interesting, informative and well presented. Our odd little exchange had actually defined the difference between the scholarly monograph and the potential textbook, and fortunately I prevailed. It turned out that Styan and I had it in common that he had taught for a while at my old school. He had become an Extra-Mural Lecturer at Hull – a number of important authors from Richard Hoggart to Raymond Williams started that way. Teaching intelligent but not academically qualified adults by lecture courses provided a basis for well-structured expositions, which could start simple but become sophisticated. I read the MS with care, and made some notes and suggestions. The book was a success, is still in print, and John Styan became a productive and valuable author. I had founded the Press's post-war drama list without knowing it.

In June 1961 Tony Becher moved on to the Nuffield Foundation, where he became involved in large projects for curriculum renewal in English schools, and I met him again in my own new capacity as Education Secretary.

Questioned about the Press's output, people would say 'Oh, we publish about 120 books a year.' This was presented as a norm, without implications. That is to say, nobody in 1951 would have said 'We have decided to expand our output' – or the opposite – because that would imply a conscious policy, and we were in a state of nature. I suspect Kingsford had a modest expansion in mind, if only to deal with the backlog of old acceptances. But I had no sense that the new acceptances were themselves increasing: the Commitments List was first of all a device for seeing that the backlog did not get any bigger.

It was certainly the case that my emptying the safe and sending over the old commitments for production (abetted soon by Tony Becher) produced a lump of new work that the Printing House had suddenly to deal with. Moreover, we only had a partial claim on the Printer's capacity. The Printing House did a good deal of work for London publishers: going up to Bentley House on the Fenman, if I saw Arthur Gray in his bowler hat I knew he was on the lookout for trade and groaned, for the other publishers got priority. This new pressure from us was met by subcontracting some of our work to other printers: an office was established in the Printing House to deal with this, and staff employed to handle the administration. A small number of respected printers were accepted as just good enough for us; they were given our house-style manual and told about subediting. Crutchley naturally had to add a handling charge to their bill, so it was not an economising device, more a way of dealing with a perhaps temporary surge, which actually turned into a one-way tide. The University Printing House was never thereafter the publisher's sole supplier, and the proportion of new books handled by them steadily diminished from then on – but that was not grasped then, still less foreseen.

The Cambridge list even in those days was a large one – I guess some 2,500 titles. Arithmetically, a steady yearly output of 120 (or so) books produces a list of 2,400 in 20 years if nothing goes out of print, and Cambridge books were expected to be in print for at least 20 years – that was scholarly publishing. Moreover there were some classics which had been in print for 50 years or more, since they had reprinted, some many times. Some had become text-books because of their range and quality; others were actually accepted as likely to be adopted. So I was aware – if only because I had to do a new jacket for them as they reprinted – of Baldwin's *Dynamic Aspects of Biochemistry*, Borradaile and Potts on *The Invertebrata*, Jackson's *Machinery of Justice in England*, Chambers's *Beowulf*, Kenny's *Cases in Criminal Law*, Hardy's *Pure Mathematics*, Tanner on the English Constitution, and so on. These books sold well and regularly. The Press was the leading publisher in taxonomic botany: Clapham, Tutin and Warburg's *Flora of the British Isles* came out early in my time, to be followed by the *Excursion Flora* and the *Illustrations* volumes. In the sciences and mathematics the Press's reputation was inseparable from the University's: from the turn of the century and especially since the 1920s it had been a Golden Age. And this was continuing: fluid mechanics and the plastic theory of metal structures were post-war innovations, and we were the publishers of the classic books. It was an impressive list: the economic consequence was that 75 per cent of the year's turnover was from backlist sales, and this was so steady that it seemed a law of nature.

It was like a self-balancing system. There was a steady but not large inflow, into a long-lived, slow-growing mass. The characteristic sales-pattern for a monograph was that (if you got the number right) half the edition sold in year 1, 25 per cent in year 2 and the remainder over the following years. If the end of the edition came quickly, the annual sale might justify a reprint. Already by the end of the 1950s we had become aware that there was a boom in the academic market, especially in the USA, so books sold quicker than expected, and this happened even when we raised print-numbers, so that the standard became 2,000, then 2,500 or even 3,000. Actually we began to establish a range of print-numbers depending on subject, so one had to find the right slot in a range increasing upwards. The Press's expansion therefore first came in the numbers printed and sold rather than the number of titles published – a healthy state of affairs soon to disappear.

Throughout the Western world universities, having recovered from the War, were expanding their student intakes, then themselves increasing in number. It was said that at one time a new university library was being founded every day – needing to build rapidly a stock of books, and getting the money from central funds. There were also moves to broaden and diversify the curriculum: new subjects were being instituted, and they needed textbooks and monographs – and journals.

In the USA the 'egghead' paperback made classic highbrow books available cheaply and in numbers. Pressed by Mansbridge, Cambridge took up the idea in 1959, and started to reprint classics in the new form with smart covers: Moore's *Principia*, Coulton, Dodd, Bennett, Dover Wilson and so on. Importantly, the idea was extended to new books: with a university textbook it became common to print a first edition of 2,500 in cloth and 10,000 in paper.

This was also the moment at which the output of new titles itself began to expand. To some considerable extent this was my doing, first in 1960 as Education Secretary (but I never confined myself to schoolbooks) and then in 1965 as Chief Editor.

CHAPTER 5

The Bible: the Privilege: the history of the Press

One aspect of my portfolio of acquirements or duties was unusual or personal to me. Quite soon – I would guess in about 1953 – Kingsford called me to his office and said he had a job for me. It seemed that Stanley Morison wanted to write something about the history of Bible-printing, and needed someone to devil for him – to do the basic research. I was to be his devil. The Press had a century and a half of relations – as supplier – with the BFBS (British and Foreign Bible Society) in London, and the Society had in the Library of its Queen Victoria Street building an unmatched – outside the British Museum – collection of Bibles old and new, British and Foreign. So I was to go to the library one day a week, Thursdays I think, for as long as it took, and it took a year or two. Bible House was near St Brides and Blackfriars Bridge – so the site of Shakespeare's theatre – and Printing House Square, then still the site of *The Times*. It was the heart of the old printing and bookselling quarter round St Paul's, heavily damaged by bombing, but now being tidied up and rebuilt. There was still a certain historical atmosphere about it: some of the old alley-ways and street-lines remained, and the College of Arms was just down the road (Sir Anthony Wagner, Garter King of Arms, had just revised St John Hope's old Cambridge Manual on English Heraldry, and I had seen it through the Press).

So I took the Fenman and the tube to St Paul's, and introduced myself to Miss Christmas, the Librarian's assistant, who said, more or less, 'Help yourself.' I did. It couldn't happen now, and not just because the BFBS collection is safely in the Cambridge University Library. I was freely handling books worth hundreds of thousands of pounds; cheerfully and without asking permission I took a good few of them home with me and got them photographed in Cambridge, returning them the following week. They were in more or less open cases, very dirty, and by the end of the morning my hands were black with sacred dirt. They had not been touched for years, since they bore no relation to the Society's daily business. There was a disbound and much interleaved copy of the old catalogue, by Darlow and Moule, and I used it to identify the books. It was logically arranged, by language and date, and contained a good deal of background information.

It was clear that I had to start, as Gutenberg did, with the Latin Bible – the international object of trade, and at first the only Bible there was in the West. It grew equally clear that format became important: after 1491 there were octavos in smaller type-sizes, and you had an economical and portable object for private study. It was also clear that after roman type was introduced, in the late 1520s, you were in another age. I came upon the great scholar-printers, Froben and Estienne in particular, and marvelled at their ingenuity and boldness, their range of types and sizes, and the beauty of the great folios – unexcelled since, and only matched by Baskerville and Bruce Rogers in the English Bible. Then I had to follow the Reformation: Luther's New Testament and Bible, and the French and Swiss versions. In their train one came to the English: late, derivative, provincial and contributing nothing to the story – at least as far as the design was concerned.

It was a wonderful way of discovering how that peculiar long and complex text could get treated typographically: how national traditions are instituted and evolve; how nations copied each other or refused to do so for theological reasons. It was an introduction to the history of printing, of the Reformation and of course the Bible itself. Necessarily I had to read a lot about all three subjects.

It was relevant that on my first visit to the USA in 1956 Ronald Mansbridge had taken me to the Folger Library in Washington, and there was Charlton Hinman using a collating machine developed during the War to study aerial photographs, and demonstrating that no two copies of the Shakespeare First Folio were absolutely identical: the printers adjusted or corrected the type during the course of printing, so that proofing and impression were not strictly distinguished, as they became later (one reason why you couldn't insert a cipher message in the text and be sure it would survive). I had produced Elizabeth Armstrong's *Robert Estienne: Royal Printer* (1954), a piece of book-design and production worthy of its subject, and bought Febvre and Martin's monumental *L'Apparition du livre* on its appearance in 1958; in 1959 I sponsored Fredson Bower's *Textual and Literary Criticism*, and talked to him about the whole subject, so I was becoming informed about such matters.

At the BFBS Library I filled many notebooks, and then wrote up my notes in a form which could be typed (my poor secretary!) and passed on to Morison. I found that I was tracing a set of evolving typographical treatments which varied with format and with national tradition, with the Latin Bible as the original international standard. The arrival of vernacular versions first represented a national variant and then a doctrinal breaking of the mould. The development and spread of roman type (except in Northern countries which went on using blackletter) and the increasing range of type-sizes permitted conventions of articulation and referencing. One could sum it up by saying that what we had come to accept in our time as the way the printed Bible naturally looked was actually a freezing of a long and complex process which had had stages much more interesting than the final result. The rather modest but practical upshot, the point at which the evolution virtually stopped, was the Geneva Bible, itself an international product, in Latin, French, Italian and English, which crystallised about 1560. And that is why the first Cambridge Bible of 1591 looked as it did.

Paradoxically, but not surprisingly to those who knew him, Morison received my notes and made no use of them that I could see, beyond an interest in the Geneva Bible as such. But he complimented me on them, urging me not to be 'weary of well-doing'. In the end I was doing it for its own sake, and my own education.

I was glad to have done it, and still am. I got two articles out of it, in *The Library*, on 'The Evolution of a Book-Form' – one on the octavo and one on the folio; and also an article in the *Gutenberg Jahrbuch* on the design of Luther's Bible and its influence. The *Library* articles were pioneering, and I get satisfaction from seeing them listed in bibliographies nearly half a century later.

Another thing I was doing at this time was attending the meetings of the Literary Panel of the NEB (New English Bible). Frank Kendon went until he became too ill; he had been expected, as poet, to play an important part in Englishing the Psalms. I took his place as new boy: Kingsford told me that I should act as full member and take part in the discussion, but I got a massive and frigid snub from Roger Mynors when I tried. Dreadful silence all round. It was a curious body, doing curious work. The Translation Panels circulated typed drafts to the Literary Panel, which was supposed to add the 'style'. The style added tended to be, inevitably, twentieth-century English, upper-class, classically educated, with an occasional gentle lurch towards what was thought to be interestingly idiomatic. It could also be pedantic: for 300 years it had been understood that tares are what an enemy sows in your corn. Now it was darnel. Could you identify darnel if you saw it? No, nor tares, but at least you knew what they signified.

Figure 7. Reynolds Stone's emblem for the New English Bible

So we were producing the features of the NEB which literary-minded unbelievers fell upon – but they would have fallen on any departure from the KJV (King James' Version). The NEB New Testament appeared in 1961 and the whole Bible in 1970.[1] It was an age of new translations: the American Revised Standard Version of 1952, which adhered as far as practicable to the traditional language of the KJV, tended to win for precisely that reason. One thinks now that to put the thought-patterns and religious impulses of 2,000 years and more ago into the language not so much of today as the day before yesterday (which is what the NEB did) is to ask for trouble – is indeed to be ridiculous if you go on to import 'inclusive' language into the text of the principal document of an exclusive culture. This is to mistranslate. Even so, the NEB was a good, because very carefully considered, scholarly translation – if you are basically interested in the literal meaning – and was made even better in the REB (Revised English Bible) of 1989. I went on representing the Press at the steering committee meetings chaired by Archbishop, later Lord, Coggan until I retired.

These experiences could be put to further editorial use. I conceived the idea of a *Cambridge History of the Bible* and presented it to the Literary Books Committee. They referred it to a small sub-committee, of David Knowles and Norman Sykes, Professor of Ecclesiastical History and, like Knowles, important author, and I seem to remember we took advice from

---

[1] I commissioned from Reynolds Stone the very beautiful emblem, a hexagonally framed cross with olives and grapes intertwined, used on the title-page and the jacket.

C.S. Lewis and C.F.D. Moule, also authors. The idea was recommended to the full Syndicate, editors appointed, and the three volumes appeared in 1963, 1969 and 1970 (superb jackets and bindings by Madeleine Dinkel). Volume III, on *The Reformation to the Present Day*, came out first, and contained my chapter on 'The Printed Bible' (68 pages, 48 plates). I take pride in it (and summarised it for an article in the *Oxford Companion to the Bible*, 1993; also an article on the English Bible Privilege). The *History* itself is to be replaced after 50 years of solid usefulness.

One of my memories of the NEB Literary Committee was a moment when Mynors turned to Godfrey Driver (Oxford Hebraist, volatile leader of the Old Testament Panel, and source of several oddities in the Old Testament as translated) and said 'What does it say in THE BOOK?' Driver pulled a little blue book out of his pocket and consulted it. It was a volume of the old *Cambridge Bible for Schools and Colleges*, edited by his father, S.R. Driver – Genesis or Exodus, I think. Some volumes of the old series, started in 1877, were still in print and in use in the 1950s, after some 70 or 80 years, but it needed replacing. By 1960 I was Education Secretary, and a commentary at that level crossed the boundary between upper school and training college. There were still examinations in religious studies, taken by a good number of candidates. So it was in my territory.

I set out to replace the old series, and it seemed sensible also to support the new translation by using the NEB as the text commented on. I found three series editors: a grammar school headmaster who taught Divinity, an Old Testament Professor at King's College London and a New Testament scholar in Nottingham. We made a good team. We devised a carefully-thought-out format: the books were to be continuous and seamless, with an introduction leading straight into the text-and-commentary, also without a break; so these two were not traditionally arranged with text at the top of the page and the commentary like footnotes in smaller type, but alternating in the same type-size, so that the whole book read like a unity. One of my textbook devices, used elsewhere, was to take out of series-volumes those parts or topics which would normally be repeated verbatim in each, and to turn them, expanded, into a whole introductory volume. So we had a collaborative Introduction to the Study of the Old and another to the New Testament, with contributions from specialist scholars, and also volumes of illustrations. These could be used independently, and also headed the two sections of the whole series.

We had a detailed prospectus and specimen set up, and circulated it to volume editors for guidance. We found contributors and got the Syndicate to give them contracts. We had an editorial meeting twice a year, most often in Nottingham, so I had to drive up in my car, with the files and a typed agenda. There we identified the contributors, recommended them to the Syndicate, reviewed progress – and in due course sales figures – dunned late-performers, planned publication. It was wonderfully efficient, and this ideal team actually enjoyed doing it so well. The Cambridge Bible Commentary had over fifty volumes in all, published in batches from 1963 to 1972. They sold well, notably Moule on Mark, which reprinted several times in large numbers. We started off publishing a net-price edition in cloth with jacket for the shops, and a 'C' terms edition (non-net, for schools) in printed linson covers; but this changed to normal cloth-and-paperback publication.

It was a model series, run by model editors, did very well in its time and is now being replaced. It depended, however, for long-term success, on the fate of the NEB itself, which has been replaced by the Revised Version and is not the most-used modern text. Though some volumes are still in print, it became a disadvantage that the now-defunct text is incorporated. But the original strategy was right. If you publish a new version of the Bible, you must support it with instrumental uses, or it will not be seriously studied. And the volumes were easy to use – a good read, even.

To go back to the beginning of this chapter: it now seems to me that Kingsford wanted there to be an officer who was gathering historical material relevant to the history and operations of the Press.[2] I am reminded that in 1955 I produced at his instigation *A Brief History of the Cambridge University Press*, a little paperback booklet in the inaugural lecture format, with thirty-two pages, a couple of plates and a handsome cover using the University emblem. It could be given to authors, visitors, members of staff of the University – anyone interested. It was reprinted every few years, and as time went by Goldschmidt's *The First Cambridge Press*, S.C. Roberts's *The Development of Cambridge Publishing* and Morison's *Tally of Types* had appeared and could be used as further sources. But the principal source was inevitably Sydney Roberts's history, a quatercentenary celebration of the itinerant printer Siberch in 1921, with all its gaps and slidings over complex questions.

My work on the Bible and my reading inevitably led me to the whole question of the Bible Privilege, a typical English story of a historical

---

[2] In the 1930s a predecessor, George Barnes, then junior Assistant Secretary, compiled the first list of books printed at Cambridge in the early years – an important initiative for the Press's history. He went to the BBC, produced W.B. Yeats's broadcast talks, became Director of the Spoken Word, founded the Third Programme, and became Vice-Chancellor of a new university and a knight.

anomaly based on the resolution of ancient conflicts of interest. There was a general view among the officers of the Privileged Presses (Cambridge, Oxford, and Eyre and Spottiswoode, the Queen's Printer) that this was a very satisfactory arrangement, because it was venerable, if odd, and typically English, and it kept out all and sundry other publishers (except Collins, as Scottish); and of course we used it now, didn't we, to preserve the sacred text from corruption; moreover Crown Copyright, being permanent, would see everyone else off for ever.

The historical truth was that an alleged seeming-perpetual copyright – really based on an analogy with the Book of Common Prayer, which was prescribed by Act of Parliament in 1662 – was vested in the title of the Queen's Printer, who had the monopoly (a bad word even in the 1950s). The only exemptions were the two university presses, whose charters were used to justify their intrusion into the monopoly – a poor self-justifying argument in itself, which had been accepted for centuries. It had suited all three thereafter to keep everyone else out.

My feeling was that the university presses would be wise to say that they found themselves in the position other publishers naturally wanted to be in. We were printing and publishing this seemingly eternal best-seller, and could well understand that others were sore that they could not enter the trade. What is more, we sold Bibles in the USA, where there was no Privilege, and its absence showed it was not needed. It was the Queen's Printer who held the monopoly, and the historical record showed that only Cambridge and Oxford had made any attempt to correct and maintain the text, which had been hastily printed and was corrupted from the start.

In 1961 this became suddenly an issue. The impending publication of the NEB struck Eyre and Spottiswoode as a threat. The two university presses co-published the NEB, whose development they had financed over many years, as a normal copyright. If the new version replaced the KJV to any extent, the monopoly would lose value. Eyre and Spottiswoode conceived a desperate plan to claim that the new version fell under the old Privilege. They printed a pirated paperback of John's Gospel as a challenge, and the Presses took them to court for breach of copyright. My part in this was in the background – to write an exposition of my understanding of the history, and to advise Kingsford and David, in the old phrase, to clear our minds of cant about the Privilege itself. It was an anomaly, a bit of historical baggage, and we now had additional reason to dissociate ourselves from the position of Eyre and Spottiswoode. This was well received by Kingsford and David, who had to take on the prosecution of the case. It didn't go down well – so far as it was perceived at all – with the old codgers in the Bible department in Bentley House, who had always liked the idea of being 'privileged' – as if it gave them some kind of historical costume, like Chelsea Pensioners.

We won the case: the NEB was accepted as a normal copyright, with the normal term. But the event was a sign of the times. The Bible had been the Press's mainstay in the nineteenth century: Cambridge had been a Bible printer and publisher which also published a few learned books. Comfortable reliance on the Bible and Prayerbook had inhibited the growth of publishing, so that Macmillan took off in Cambridge and made rings round us for years. It was hard trying to catch up in the early twentieth century. I spent many years hearing people say, when I told them I worked at the Press, 'Oh, you make all your money from the Bible, don't you?' And still, in my early days, you could go to Bentley House and note that there was a Bible department which still felt it was the mainstay, with travellers who made Bible sales before they turned to the other side and sold a few books. Our only real book-salesman was Hugh Rowe, who went to the Oxford and Cambridge accounts (a nice, cultivated man who felt himself to be a bit different – and was).

And to revert to that first visit to the USA in 1956, I went to a sales conference in New York attended by travellers who sold only the Bible, and some who did it on commission. They were not salaried, but made a comfortable living travelling the Bible Belt. Bibles were an even higher proportion of the turnover in the USA – had more or less floated the Branch in its early years. But that was about to change.

My role as historian ended with *A History of Cambridge University Press* which I found myself writing very rapidly indeed for the real quatercentenary in 1984. It was written and published in less than eighteen months. I had learned much meanwhile and so had some of the story in my head. I did also just have time to go to the archive in the University Library and get some essential detail on developments in the nineteenth century. So my shot at the story is certainly an advance on S.C. Roberts's. Most important, we had by then gone through the radical transformation conducted by Geofrey Cass. A very significant element of that process was that it was based on a historical and constitutional analysis. To his great credit, Geoffrey had plunged into the history, enough to seize on essential characteristics, so that his changes were realisations of the historical or constitutional essence of the Press. I knew enough to know he was right about this, and this was one reason why I supported him. My history does incorporate a good deal of his analysis, which he made available for the purpose, so the book serves as quite an important statement of what one might call the theology of the Press, as well as a narrative of the main events. However, writing it showed me how many gaps there were in what I knew, gaps I did not have time to fill, and so I got the Syndicate to commission a full history in three big volumes from David McKitterick.

CHAPTER 6

The English list at the Press – 1

I came to the Press in 1951 not just with a degree in English and French Literature, but with a set of presuppositions, indeed prejudices. I was a Leavisite, though he had never taught me, and at only 23 I was not much inclined to see other points of view. In a way and for a time it was my virtue, since it set me doing things intensively, once I got the chance.

I have said that the only real editor at the Press at the time was Frank Kendon, who was a puzzle to me. It was impossible to dislike him because he was so evidently a good and very modest man. It was also impossible to patronise him, because he had a number of talents, which he used to good but not widely recognised effect. But he was something which I had been taught to look down on – an old-style 'man of letters' of the 1930s and even earlier – and this in spite of his having a degree in English from Cambridge. He was one of the first generation produced by the English Tripos – with, for example, his friend J.B. Priestley – but for me in my time, and for people who thought like me, he represented the gone world of before the 1939–45 War – even the 1914–18 War – and he was of the generation that resisted the Eliot-and-Leavis movement. This was the literary England once represented by old Jack Squire (Sir John Squire, the Editor of *The London Mercury*, standing up for 'real poetry' which was mostly about the countryside. I caricature him, of course, and Frank).

In what follows, the men of letters get some definition and some credit. For I failed to realise then that they were all we had at one time; they performed well in their way, and it was not their fault that time passed and they looked discredited, even if they can be blamed for not understanding what was now going on. But it made them look passé – indeed in the way – especially in the 1930s to young professional academics in the new subject English Literature. They now look interesting and sympathetic again, given that the academics who succeeded them were self-promoting, given to feuding, mostly mediocre, and have themselves passed into history. I can say that now, having written these chapters, which have made me think again, and see my own place in a story which has continued to unfold.

I can illustrate the point by quoting E.M.W. Tillyard, Master of Jesus in my time at that college, authority on Milton, and by his own estimation one of the pioneer-founders of the English Tripos (and also what Leavis called a Ward-Boss, that is, a Mafioso-like intriguer and influence-peddler). In his account of the early history of English at Cambridge, Tillyard wrote this about one of the men of letters who had a place in the Press's English list – who figured there in a way which puzzled me, so that I was inclined to dismiss him and others like him. So was Tillyard, who says:

The young men... crowded to hear J.W. Mackail give the Leslie Stephen Lecture on him [Pope] in the May Term of 1919. Exquisitely turned out in black jacket and striped trousers, terribly distinguished with his fine features, glossy grey hair, and soft yet somehow treacly eyes, Mackail looked a kind of High Priest of aestheticism. And the delivery and the content of the lecture itself matched the exquisiteness of his appearance. Mackail was lucid and ordered and apparently final, and yet there was a treacliness in his manner that matched his eyes with singular fidelity. He told us that we must not look on Pope as a satirist only. He gained his popularity from his more lyrical and romantic poems: the *Pastorals*, the *Elegy on an Unfortunate Lady*, *Eloisa and Abelard*, and the *Rape of the Lock*, and from his translation of the *Iliad* [...] It was an excellent lecture, for it held its audience and set them reading Pope in a different way and with a new zest; more important than whether he was correct in what he said. (*The Muse Unchained* (1958), 94–5)

But he *was* correct – and very sensible too. This leaves us with the disdain and the treacle-simile in which an inferior person tries to put on superiority. I am ashamed, now, to have accepted this attitude. I did so because Leavis did something like it; but he did it with some point, since he wanted to make his specific historical revaluation of the whole course of English literature since Shakespeare, an account not accepted then either by the old littérateurs or the new academics. Neither group could grasp that Eliot and Pound and Lawrence required literary history to be rewritten, and as he was rewriting it.

The strange element in this ancient battle (I now see) is that the men of letters were really being attacked because they were not academics trained in the new discipline, and were in the way. Yet some of the people hostile to them and wanting to discredit them were not trained in the new discipline either – or not fully, since the English Tripos did not have two Parts until late in the 1920s, and a number of the new academics had been, like Tillyard, Classics-trained. One has to keep this transition in mind, and be wary of the combativeness of the groups. It was not until the generation of Empson that there were Cambridge people writing books in English studies who were wholly trained in the subject, and thinking along the new lines.

It was because of this historical background that when I joined the Press I found myself contemplating an English list which was at least partly made by old-style men of letters. And like every other part of Cambridge publishing, it was a long-established list, going back to the beginning of the century – even the last years of the nineteenth – when English was a part of the Modern Language Tripos, so far as it existed at all at Cambridge. Given that books used to remain in print for so long, there they all were, still. On the other hand, my own bookshelves, then and still, present me with most of the canonical texts of the then-new criticism. I can list them:

> I.A. Richards: *Principles of Literary Criticism*, Routledge 1924 (I bought the Ninth Impression 1947)
> I.A. Richards: *Practical Criticism*, Routledge 1929 (Seventh Impression 1949)
> William Empson: *Seven Types of Ambiguity*, Chatto 1930 (Second Edition 1947)
> William Empson: *Some Versions of Pastoral*, Chatto 1935
> T.S. Eliot: *Selected Essays*, Faber 1932 (Reprinted 1949)
> F.R. Leavis: *New Bearings in English Poetry*, Chatto 1932 (bought 1946)
> F.R. Leavis and Denys Thompson: *Culture and Environment*, Chatto 1933 (Fourth Impression 1942, bought 1946)
> F.R. Leavis: *Revaluation*, Chatto 1936 (Second Impression 1949)
> F.R. Leavis: *The Great Tradition*, Chatto 1948
> Q.D. Leavis: *Fiction and the Reading Public*, Chatto 1932 (Second Impression 1939, bought 1945)
> Basil Willey: *The Seventeenth Century Background*, Chatto 1934

One thing emerges from that list: the absolute dominance of Chatto and Windus – more exactly of Ian Parsons, who had been at Winchester with Empson and Dick David, read English at Cambridge, edited the *Cambridge Review*, went to Chatto in 1928 as a typographer, became an editor and built up the list which everyone in English studies wanted to join (including me: I did in 1975).[1] He published Tillyard as well as Leavis,

---

[1] I gave some broadcast talks on BBC Third Programme in 1971 and 1972. The literary agent David Higham Associates got in touch with me and recommended that I turn them into a book, and it was published by Chatto and Windus as *The Literature of Fidelity* in 1975.

which was perfectly sensible publishing, and newcomers like Richard Hoggart and Raymond Williams naturally sent their books to him. The jackets of Chatto's books on English studies used to print on the back cover and the inside back flap the titles of the whole English list, and by the 1970s it gave well over 100 titles, all familiar books in the profession. For years I felt I was scrabbling for the crumbs which fell from Ian's table. Nobody at the Press felt criticised by his success. It was like the Macmillan take-off all over again. (That is to say – in the mid to late nineteenth century the Macmillan brothers ran the bookshop where the Press bookshop now stands. They talked to their academic customers, made friends and then authors of them, published them and established a brilliant list under the nose of the Press, especially in economics, before leaving for London.)

To come back to Frank Kendon, he was also a poet, but of the kind which Eliot and his successors were supposed to have made obsolete – so they had, really, and it was a grief to Frank that he was written off. But among his talents was an editorial gift which made him able to see the potential in a book which the author, not a professional writer, couldn't realise alone, and Frank would not only rewrite but then *produce* – and that word covers a lot of expertise. It was a time when the Press published books of great charm and beauty as a matter of corporate pride, and Frank could enlist the talents of illustrators and the printers. I have said something about him above; he comes in again here because he was, when I joined the Press, the man who looked after books in English studies – such as they were. That phrase sounds condescending, and I did condescend at the time, or rather I failed to see the point. I now think that in some respects it was an extraordinary list, even if much of it was inevitably of a time before mine – another age, which now looks more interesting than I thought then.

Behind Frank was the figure of S. C. Roberts, referred to familiarly as 'SC', who had retired from the Secretaryship in 1948, not so long before I came, in order to become Master of Pembroke and Sir Sidney Roberts. I had been aware of him when I was an undergraduate because he then used to pop across the road from the Secretary's Building to Mill Lane to give a course of lectures on eighteenth-century literature for the English Faculty, and I had been to one or two – but gave them up because they were cheerfully simple-minded, so that I could link him with the Jack Squires. Until 1922 he had been an Assistant Secretary, as I was now, and had handled the English list, which he had taken over from his predecessor, A.R. Waller. He had even written a little book or two himself (very pretty); and as Secretary he had published many things I now admire. If you read his autobiographical book *Adventures with Authors* (1966: I found myself seeing it through the production process) about his time at the Press, you realise that even as Secretary he was in one practical sense an editor: all the books arrived on his desk first, and when he fancied a book he read it himself. If he told the Syndics he rather liked it, and it was not a scholarly book on which they would need a referee's report, they would say 'All right then'. It was a bit of fun. There was also the 'bag-opener' argument I referred to earlier: this was a book which the travellers could bring out and show the booksellers first, for they could all understand what it was about and could read it themselves with enjoyment – not like *A Treatise on Bessel Functions*.

Two other relevant people, who had been Assistant Secretaries in the 1920s and 1930s under Roberts and had stayed on (unlike George Barnes, who went to the BBC, where he founded the Third Programme) were Billy Kingsford, his successor as Secretary, who had appointed me – he had read English – and Dick David, eventually Kingsford's successor, but from 1948 to 1963 Manager of the London Office at Bentley House. He read Classics and English under George Rylands, had written a prize essay on Shakespeare's poetry which was published by the Press, later wrote a regular review of the year's productions for *Shakespeare Survey* and was a respected figure in the Shakespeare world (he edited a volume in the Arden Shakespeare). It is not clear to me now that either Kingsford or David had had any influence on choosing the English books: that was Roberts's role until it became Kendon's. On the other hand they were the men who made Bentley House: Kingsford built it and was the first Manager, David developed it into a centre of international trade while pursuing his interests in botany (where he also had status) and Shakespeare.

Which is perhaps a good place to start, since Shakespeare has been a pillar of the English list since the days of Verity's texts. And that takes us all the way back to the 1890s and the Secretaryship of R. T. Wright. Verity started with Milton and progressed to Shakespeare – and with the critic A.C. Bradley at the higher level was mainly responsible for the writing in schools and universities of essays on the plays which went in for 'character studies'. It went on till my time and beyond. In school one 'did' Macbeth by saying that he was brave and active once he made decisions, but was hesitant until spurred on by his awful wife; his defect was that he had a too-active imagination, or conscience; his sin was ambition (and so one satisfied the ghost of Aristotle: the *hamartia*, you know). Hamlet carried the indecisive thing disastrously further: perhaps he should have read *Macbeth*, or of course *Hamlet*, which would have taught him to do nothing at all, if he had read it the right way. His problem was not indecision but final disastrous action.[2]

I had been taught to look down on all that by Leavis pointing in the direction of Wilson Knight, and by L.C. Knights, and here I was, in the Verity headquarters. The texts had finally ceased to sell (I think they went on in the colonies), but they had had an extraordinary life. *Paradise Lost* had first been done book by book (introduction, text, notes) but in 1910 had been assembled into one volume. This was reprinted in two volumes: I, *Text*, and II, *Notes*, in 1929. My copy of the text is a reprint of 1934: I expect there were later reprints. I am sure I used the Shakespeare in school in the 1930s and 1940s.

However long Verity went on being used in schools, at the university level the new figure for Shakespeare was John Dover Wilson, Editor of the New Shakespeare – significant title. It could not be called The Cambridge Shakespeare: that title had been pre-empted by Macmillan in the 1860s, in a nine-volume scholarly edition which then spawned the Globe one-volume edition, printed at the Press. In this as in so much else, Macmillan in the nineteenth century by sheer intelligence and enterprise shot ahead of other publishers, notably Cambridge. I might mention here that their excellent series English Men of Letters gave that term the good name which it began to lose in the 1930s. In my day the equivalent of Alexander Macmillan was Ian Parsons of Chatto: he was the person I had to try to catch up with.

The New Shakespeare had been started with Q (see below) as co-editor, on the understanding, I suppose, that Dover Wilson would do the textual work and Q would write introductions. Everyone underestimated the time it would take, because it had been assumed that nothing very radical needed to be done about the text, and a quick introduction and a few notes were no problem. The first volumes came out in 1921, but Q soon dropped out. Dover carried on at first by himself, and the series was not completed until 1966, by which time co-editors had had to be drafted in for the later volumes. The series as it were grew up as it went along, and became the main competitor of the Arden at the higher level. It was then time to start again, and now we could use the word Cambridge in the title.

---

[2] I don't parody the Verity–Bradley line too much. An early Cambridge book, *Hamlet: A Study in Critical Method* (1931) by an Australian academic, A.J.A. Waldock, while making the 'modern' point that Bradley discussed characters as if they were real people, still goes on at length about indecision. Waldock later wrote *Paradise Lost and its Critics*, which Leavis thought the best book he had read about Milton.

Shakespeare was the main plank of the English list. Dover Wilson, like several important scholarly figures early in that century, started in education. If you couldn't get a fellowship or chair at Oxford or Cambridge, one option was to go into a branch of education like the inspectorate, write to establish your name and wait.[3] Dover's *Life in Shakespeare's England* came out in 1911, and work with A.W. Pollard established him as a textual scholar: he wrote a volume in the Shakespeare Problems Series initiated by Pollard's *Shakespeare's Fight with the Pirates* in 1920. But he also had a gift for semi-popular exposition and wrote for the Press *The Essential Shakespeare* (1932), *What Happens in Hamlet* (1935) and *The Fortunes of Falstaff* (1943). These sold well and reprinted, and became natural paperback candidates in the 1960s. They also established Dover as something between a don and a man of letters: he moved in both worlds. He became formally part of the 'English' world by becoming Professor at Edinburgh at the age of 46.

A Companion to Shakespeare Studies, edited at first by Harley Granville-Barker and G. B. Harrison (1934; reprinted many times; second edition 1971; third 1986; fourth 2001) was the natural product of several relationships, which would include Roberts's friendships and David's (he had known and been influenced by Harley Granville-Barker, who started as an actor, and became a producer and playwright. He was one kind of man of letters. His writing was based in the theatre, not the academy). *Shakespeare Survey*, a yearbook, edited at first by Allardyce Nicoll, started in 1947 and is still appearing. (It set the pattern for *Anglo-Saxon England*, which I set up in the 1970s.) Nicoll was also the author of the massive *History of English Drama* (volume I: 1923, volume VI: 1959, supplementary volume: 1973). Unlike Dover and Granville-Barker, he was a real academic, but could also turn his hand to popularisation. I got him to do *The Elizabethans* (1957), an attractive anthology of extracts and pictures, and his *World of Harlequin* (1963) on the old *Commedia dell' Arte* manages to be both scholarly and interesting – as well as a superb piece of book-production (Peter Burbidge's work: four-colour jacket with woodcuts by Keeling, who also designed the binding).

This kind of standing in Shakespeare and drama studies attracted independent scholars, so that, for instance, Caroline Spurgeon's *Shakespeare's Imagery and What it Tells us* appeared in 1935 (what it told *her*, really). In the same year Dick David's *The Janus of Poets* appeared – one of

---

[3] D.H. Lawrence observed this phenomenon: Rupert Birkin in *Women in Love* has moved straight from Oxford to the inspectorate.

the prize essays which sometimes turned into a steady seller. Muriel Bradbrook's *Elizabethan Stage Conditions* (1931) was followed by her *Themes and Conventions of Elizabethan Tragedy* (1935) and *The School of Night* (1936). *Themes and Conventions* became the first in her series of standard treatments which acquired textbook status over the years. She was at first a pupil and colleague of the Leavises, so I approved of her. ('Maggot!' he once muttered to me after she had switched allegiance: the implication being that she had been hatched within his living body.)

I have ignored, because I ignored it at the time as already outmoded,[4] the influence of the old *Cambridge History of English Literature* (CHEL), edited by Sir A.W. Ward, Master of Peterhouse, Chairman of the Syndicate (and also Editor of the *Cambridge Modern History*), his co-editor being A.R. Waller, Secretary to the Syndics. CHEL was in 14 volumes, 1907–16: slow to start, but several times reprinted and reissued. Ward was born in 1837; Waller had been a London publisher and occasional man of letters with, therefore, valuable connections: he came to the Press as Assistant Secretary in 1902, and became Secretary in 1911. The dates tell us something, and principally remind us that there was almost no academic teaching profession in English at that time – certainly none at Oxford and Cambridge – so if you wanted to do a history of English Literature, your contributors would be Classicists or Historians if they were academics, or, if they were not, would be men of letters, publishers, teachers in public schools, inspectors of education, scholars with private means and so on. To the later generation of professional 'English' academics, they would look like amateurs or interlopers, Tillyard would sneer at them and I would be puzzled.

But the aftermath of the *History* and this general author-constituency explains some apparently random Cambridge publishing in English in the 1920s and 1930s and even later. Looking at the books, I used to feel baffled. Who *was* Harold Child, author of *A Poor Player* (1939) and *Essays and Reflections* (1948: and so just before my time)? He was a gentleman-journalist with a public-school and Oxford education who had fled the legal profession, first to be a penniless travelling actor in several unsuccessful troupes, and then managing to live by his pen, writing theatre-notices, book-reviews and short stories. He graduated to *The Times* as theatre critic, then wrote for the newly established TLS, wrote a number of chapters in CHEL, was a friend of Waller and Roberts, and an

---

[4] Also being replaced from 1958 by the Pelican Guide, which inhibited competition for some time. See Chapter 7.

attractive representative of the men of letters. He provided the stage-histories in some early New Shakespeare volumes, and wrote a chapter in the first *Companion to Shakespeare*; so did J.W. Mackail (see above; now remembered also as the first biographer of Morris).[5]

Child's later little books were published because he had become a friend: SC said it would be a nice thing to do, and the Syndics nodded. There is a moment in SC's *Adventures with Authors* where he says quite candidly that A.C. Benson, Master of Magdalene, had written in saying that he had not been very well lately and would like to write something as a way of convalescing: any ideas? And SC had said 'How about a selection from Ruskin?' and it was duly published the following year. Benson was a member of a notable man-of-letters family (one of whom, according to the *Dictionary of National Biography*, was 'uncontrollably prolific'). The notable or notorious Squire was also published by the Press: *The Cambridge Book of Lesser Poets* (1927) was tipped by SC, but flopped. Actually, it is full of interesting minor figures.

All this rather corrupt amateurism (from my jaundiced point of view later) meant a pleasant life for people like Waller and Roberts, because it linked Cambridge with the literary life in London, so that one could go up to Town and give someone lunch in his or your club, or go to the dinners given by exclusive little groups with odd names, and generally speaking be in the swim. Cambridge had a tendency to be rather puritanically cut off from all that, so it was an excursion.

The most significant figure in the early period is surely Q himself. Sir Arthur Quiller-Couch, man or rather knight of letters, became King Edward Professor of English Literature in 1912, before there was a department, and, having life-tenure, died in office in 1944, the year before I came up to Cambridge. He wrote cheerful fiction; his more academic books were published by the Press and did very well indeed. They are almost forgotten now, but the volumes of *Studies in Literature*, *On The Art of Reading*, *On The Art of Writing* went out into the world in numbers that the true academic can now only envy. *On the Art of Writing* (1916) contains the un-recast scripts of his first course of lectures given in 1913–14, and one can sense in his occasional asides that this was taken as an

---

[5] One could compile a fairly representative list of contributing men of letters by looking at the contents-pages of CHEL; but also at a series of handsome volumes called *The Eighteen-Seventies* and *The Eighteen-Eighties* (I think there was a predecessor or successor) which Cambridge published in 1929 and 1930. They were by 'members of the Royal Society of Literature' and were edited by Harley Granville-Barker and Walter de la Mare. T. S. Eliot wrote a chapter on Pater in the second.

event in the University, with the Vice-Chancellor and interested outsiders attending, to discover what English studies might amount to.

Once again, the thing to remember about Q in this context is that when he entered upon the professorship there was still no English Tripos. Lectures on English were part of Modern Languages, and were given by people trained as Classicists and Historians. The Tripos itself was founded in an undeveloped form in 1917 during the First War, and both staff and students came back from the War to make it or to take it. At first it had only one Part and was meant to be taken in conjunction with another subject. Part II was not added until 1926, and it was not until then that there followed the growth of a real faculty. As for the 1914–18 War itself, at the Press Roberts, Carrington and his predecessor Gordon Carey, and in the English Faculty Leavis, Bennett, Willey, Tillyard and Lucas had served, and all but Carrington were in some sense wounded. And as for English studies, curiously, Roberts and Carey felt free to do a little part-time lecturing for the new faculty. Roberts had read Classics and History, Carey read Classics. Leavis and Bennett started in History, Tillyard was a Classicist, and so was Lucas. Mansfield Forbes, Carey's nephew, the strange child-like genius who is credited by most observers as the real inventor of Cambridge English, got Firsts in History, at 22 became a Fellow of Clare like his uncle Gordon Carey, was felt by Hector Chadwick (also a Fellow of Clare, which was the power-centre at the time) and by G. G. Coulton to be a suitable person to lecture in Anglo-Saxon, and went on from there.

And those two deserve a mention. Coulton was himself a maverick, never really fitted in to the Cambridge college pattern. A Victorian young man, he had taken orders and then lost his faith and left the ministry, taught in several schools, and came back to Cambridge in 1919 as Lecturer in English, with a noted anti-clerical bias as hammer of the monks, and a highly political figure. He was really a medieval historian, was prolific and published by the Press.

Chadwick was one of the people behind his return. Indeed he stands behind the whole story of Cambridge English as consummate fixer: he wanted to secure a Tripos in which Anglo-Saxon was not a compulsory option, so that Anglo-Saxon studies at Cambridge would become a serious subject in its own right and not a service-department handling unwilling and bored students of English. Chadwick was co-author, with his wife, of the monumental three-volume *The Growth of Literature*, published by the Press 1931–40. This treated the world's literatures as a social-anthropological phenomenon in which literary forms corresponded to the historical stage and dominant nature of the parent society. Anglo-Saxon and early Norse literature was not in any important way the parent of English: it was the spoken and written heroic art of a widespread Northern society of which Britain was only a district. The Chadwicks' approach profoundly influenced one whole strain in the Leavises' work – not that I could see this at the time. And Hector Chadwick had been a very cunning old politician (one used to hear people imitating his confiding Yorkshire accent). He and Coulton secured several crucial early appointments in English studies for their candidates. I found myself producing a book for Mrs Chadwick in the 1960s: she was a gracious lady from the previous age.

I feel fairly certain that it was Q who introduced George Sampson to the Press. Sampson was one of the more impressive men of letters. Born in 1873, he was 'delicate' and did not go to school, but read enormously. With no degree, he went into elementary school teaching (like Lawrence and his peer-group), became a headmaster and inspector, and found himself in 1919 on the committee appointed by the Board of Education to report on English in schools. Other members were Q himself, Sir Henry Newbolt (one begins to feel differently about him, too), C.H. Firth, F.S. Boas, J.H. Fowler, Caroline Spurgeon and Miss H.M. Davies. Its Report and Sampson's *English for the English* appeared in 1921. That is a remarkable and influential little book, still all too relevant. Sampson also produced for the Press the *Concise CHEL*, long delayed by his illness, and so an important wartime morale-booster in 1941, often reprinted and still in print in its third edition of 1970 (on Boris Ford's advice, I got a Scrutineer, R.C. Churchill, to revise and extend it). When one reads Sampson's chapter on 'A Boy and his Books' in his *Seven Essays* published by the Press in 1947 (like Child's essays, I suspect this was part of SC's last bounty before retiring in 1948), one realises that for him the task of 'doing' the whole of English literature in one volume of 1,100 pages would come naturally, because he had really read more of it than any of us with our degrees, and he did it with a mind which was as keen as it was open. He wrote well, naturally. He also edited for the Press very substantial selections and anthologies which can be seen as natural offshoots of the *History*.

As for Q, he found himself presiding after 1918 over the smaller war that ensued in Cambridge between old-style men of letters and new-style English academics, and the campaigns for and against Eliot's importance and influence were the open part of that half-concealed conflict. The men of letters had one leader in F.L. Lucas, still lecturing in my time, and still, from my point of view, getting in the way. He was a Classicist, had published with the Press his *Seneca and Elizabethan Tragedy* (1922), which established a sort of qualification in English: it was more about Seneca than the other element in the title. He was at King's, a friend of Lytton Strachey and the Bloomsberries, and he was dead against Eliot as poet and intellectual influence: and therefore against Leavis (Eliot's article on Seneca does not mention Lucas).[6] Just before my time Lucas published at the Press *Ten Victorian Poets* (1948), based on broadcast talks.

So Q was in the fortunate or unfortunate position of having been himself a man of letters who now had to steer the ship with a crew fighting each other. One ironic element of the battle was that the old-style men of letters, who, not having university salaries, had had to do journalism to make ends meet, but also enjoyed writing for common readers, believed there was such an audience and wanted to be read by it. Looking at the profession today, one thinks that must be a good thing. One opponent, Leavis, hated their kind of journalism and their failure to see what he saw. But he was just as combative, and also very much wanted to be read, over the heads of those he thought were mere academics or mere littérateurs. He became, without meaning to, one of the great journalists in our literature – with Addison, Johnson, Arnold and of course Eliot (whose journalism has not been collected).

This sort of oddity takes me back to Frank Kendon, for on one kind of book meant to be read widely we were in complete agreement. Frank had edited some of the books in the Sturt tradition, and of course Leavis had commended Sturt, thus starting an important debate which has been trivialised by being mistaken for nostalgia. Really it is about the cultural effects of long-term social change, especially in the old agrarian setting (still not quite dead, as it happens), though this is not immediately obvious from the first books, which recorded symptoms observed by humble participants, and could be taken as merely anecdotal.

Actually the Cambridge tradition began with Cecil Torr, prosperous, learned and witty landowner of Wreyland in Devon, who had written very engaging books of observations which he called *Small Talk at*

---

[6] His most celebrated book was on Tragedy, and everyone read it, including me, for the Tragedy Paper in Part II. It gave the standard classical stuff about Aristotle and so on, and led to the prolongation of unprofitable ideas. *The Decline and Fall of the Romantic Ideal* was also popular, and came from the Press. It is worth mentioning that, in a volume of *University Studies: Cambridge 1933* edited by Harold Wright for Nicholson and Watson, Lucas wrote the chapter on English. It is almost entirely devoted to an attack on Q.D. Leavis's *Fiction and the Reading Public*, which had just appeared.

Wreyland. The first set was being privately printed at Cambridge in 1918, and in the way such things happened, the Printer J.B. Peace read it, liked it and said to Roberts 'Why not publish it?' Roberts liked it, told the Syndics, and of course they said yes. When it was published, the world was baffled, partly because the books were uncategorisable, partly because Cambridge was not expected to publish such things; but those who read them liked them too, and they became a little fashion. The Second and Third Series followed in 1921 and 1923, and the books were so popular that a concise selection was printed in one handy octavo in 1926.

It is one of the great bedside books: it has no chapter- or other breaks but just follows one engaging topic after another until the last page arrives too soon. It was also reprinted – I suspect slightly shortened – in the little red series The Cambridge Miscellany. (Publishers used to have these cheap, one-price reprint series for their best-selling books. Perhaps the most famous was Cape's The Traveller's Library, with its pretty blue binding. They were the predecessors of paperbacks. The Cambridge Miscellany was bound in red, and very neat, and the interiors were an advertisement for the Printing House. Included were Sturt's *A Small Boy in the Sixties*, Edmund Blunden's Clark Lectures on Charles Lamb, Granville-Barker's *The Study of Drama*, Saintsbury on Shakespeare (from CHEL), Gunning's *Reminiscences of Cambridge*, SC's *An 18th Century Gentleman*, The Four Gospels in Gill's Perpetua type, with a Morisonian title-page, and others.)

It seems that Sturt, already a well-known author under his pen-name George Bourne, noticed Torr's first publication and sent in *The Wheelwright's Shop*, first published in 1923 in the same large format as Torr. Though Sturt had a public, this was in some ways an odd book, since it went into detail about the building of farm-waggons, by way of making important and more general points about the decline and death of the traditional local crafts which preceded the production-lines of modern industries. Sturt was an educated man (trained as a teacher) and a thinker, but found himself inheriting and having to run a dying business. There were actual diagrams (by 'Miss Robins and Miss West') showing parts of waggons and tools. Roberts, much to his credit, took it on, and it was followed by *A Small Boy in the Sixties* (1927), which had an introduction by Arnold Bennett.

Frank Kendon came to the Press in the 1930s. He had been preceded by his *The Small Years*, a poetic account of his childhood, accepted by the Syndics on SC's recommendation in 1929, and published with a foreword by Walter de la Mare. He had been working in London on the editorial staff of *John O'London's Weekly*, a low- to middlebrow paper of the sort Leavis scorned for getting in the way (and which we might now be glad to have, as better than what has replaced it).

Man-of-letters country life could be parodied as beer, pipe-smoke and cricket on the green, in rhyming verse, preferably triolets. If you think of Edward Thomas (tipped, actually, by Leavis) you realise it could be subtle and profound. Frank was closer to Thomas than the Squirearchy. Not at all jolly, he was a contemplative and quietist, and his affinities were with Thomas, Walter de la Mare and Blunden rather than Squire or W.H. Davies. He had come from the country, in Kent – actually from the very distinguished school at Goudhurst which his father had founded. Working in Cambridge, he cycled laboriously in from Harston. His very quiet, almost forgotten memorial is a series of books which I mention here under 'English' because they are in some un-obvious sense 'English' – not the academic study of formal literature, but truly what is now called cultural studies. One day a cultural historian will notice them. They go back through Torr and Sturt to C.F.G. Masterman's *The Condition of England*, and through him to Jefferies, Ruskin, Morris, Dickens, Cobbett, Blake, Defoe. One could say it has been continued by Leavis, Williams, E.P. Thompson and contemporaries like Gervais and Collini – but the last five are academics, though of a distinctive type, and one can see in this succession too the transition from men of letters, or, if you like, 'real' writers.

Frank's authors were typified by Walter Rose, author of *The Village Carpenter* (1937) and *Good Neighbours* (1942). More substantially, there were *Country Relics* (1939) by H.J. Massingham, illustrated by Thomas Hennell, and Hennell's own *Change in the Farm* (1936). These are both breathtakingly beautiful books, set in Bell, Frank's favourite typeface, delicately laid-out, on 'antique' paper, and the illustrations are remarkable. Hennell was a real artist, and a real writer (he spent some years in what was then called a lunatic asylum, and died violently in the Far East as a War Artist). If you compare the simple diagrams in Sturt with the drawings in Hennell you see that things have moved into another dimension: this is a form of art. Rose's books appeared in wartime, and the change in materials and style of printing is obvious, but even here one can see Frank's hand.

Given that he was a poet, given that poetry in the last century had become progressively more difficult to publish, it was natural that Frank persuaded the Syndics to publish some poetry. This was very traditional, and seems minor stuff; there were some London names, but it was mostly by Cambridge people, their wives and daughters.[7] Lucas wrote poetry, and the Press published at least one volume. He and others edited anthologies – Q's *Oxford Book* must have sold hundreds of thousands, and tempted others to imitate it in some element. In 1916 Kenneth Grahame had edited *The Cambridge Book of Poetry for Children*; Frank revived it in 1932 in a new edition with illustrations by Gwen Raverat – tiny woodcuts of great charm. This led to *Mountains and Molehills* by Frances Cornford in 1934: here the Raverat woodcuts are larger and really brilliant. Their fierce blackness and sharpness is matched by the use of Goudy Modern type – a masterpiece, as bookmaking. Agnes Miller Parker did the frontispiece for *These Also* (poems about animals, to be treated respectfully as fellow-creatures) in 1949. One senses Frank's benevolent supervision.

But during the 1939–45 War, this became something else. He was intensely pacifist and was horrified by it all. It comes out in the foreword to *Fear No More: A Book of Poems for the Present Time by Living English Poets* (1940), with a jacket showing a hand holding a leaf (olive?), repeated on the title page.[8] All the poets had consented to be anonymous – an innocent and fatal error, since readers don't know what to think if they don't have a name. The introduction must be by Frank, and has an extraordinary intensity:

Man facing himself was the title proposed for this book while it was growing; the phrase describes both War and Poetry, two ways of tackling a very old problem now grown so acute as to be almost new... Not one of us is released from the duty of contemplation. This war must be *thought* to a finish: it concerns thinkers as no other war ever did ... Poets, when they are writing, are their own antidote to herd-mindedness: they stake all upon the personal man, the conscious man, the man facing himself. In doing so, they show how to fight the battles of mankind.

Another anthology, *Landmarks* (1943), gives poems about places in England, and caters for the intense feeling about the country created by the War and its upheavals and the enforced exile of service-people. The

---

[7] I found myself seeing one volume through the press in the 1950s, when Frank began to decline. This was by Fredegond Shove, whose first name told you she was F.W. Maitland's daughter; the second that she was married to a minor Apostle with a walk-on part in Bloomsbury memoirs. I had to announce it in the Seasonal list, of which I was in my early years compiler and editor. I found one short poem I could quote complete, and then felt myself thinking 'But this is really *good*.' She had written a little book on Christina Rossetti in 1931.

[8] There is a similar leaf on the hand-lettered cover of *The Alien Wood: Twenty Elegies* by James Turner (1945). It is a paper-bound booklet printed throughout in Blado italic on very thin wartime paper. I am sure Frank lettered the cover, in two sizes and weights of his own cursive.

editors, G. Rostrevor Hamilton and John Arlott, later famous as a radio voice with a country accent and a devotion to cricket, were types of the man of letters. Rostrevor Hamilton had published with the Press in 1937 *Poetry and Contemplation*, a combative book in which he took on Richards's *Principles of Literary Criticism* – to some effect, though it made him (and the Press) look 'conservative' at the time.

J.B. Priestley had read English at Cambridge after the First War, and knew Frank from that time. He edited a selection from *Tom Moore's Diary* for the Press in 1925, before becoming famous as a novelist. The gossipy interest in minor romantics was a touchstone of 'man-of-letterism': their god was Charles Lamb. Of course, Lamb is a sympathetic and interesting figure: it was his misfortune to write the *Essays of Elia*, picked on as model in twentieth-century higher-journalism by those with nothing to say but a desire to say it urbanely. The Eliatic became the obverse of the Eliotic in the 1930s and after; often the point of reference was the *Times* Fourth Leader, turned to by readers as the day's bit of elegant nonsense. Essay-writing about nothing in particular was a school exercise in my time, so one looked for models.

My copy of Priestley's Moore selection still has its jacket, advertising *Cambridge and Charles Lamb*, edited by George Wherry, 5 shillings net, with papers by, among others, Sir Edmund Gosse and Mr E.V. Lucas, and quoting reviews by Mr Alfred Noyes in *The Sunday Times* and Mr Robert Lynd in the *Daily News*. Mr Noyes found it 'a delightful little wayside shrine to the memory of "Saint Charles"... [Gosse] draws a vivid picture in his own inimitable manner of the first Charles Lamb dinner, which was organised by Swinburne.' Mr Lynd thought 'Charles Lamb himself seems to be a guest at the dinners... No Elian could read Mr Wherry's paper... without reviving many often-tasted delights.' You see what I mean.

This taste actually produced a series of Clark Lectures on Lamb and his group by Edmund Blunden in 1932, published by the Press the next year – another exquisite book, incidentally. The lectures went into the Miscellany, so they must have been well received. Blunden was a respected figure (Leavis thought him a genuine talent and an interesting case – interesting enough to give him several pages in *New Bearings*, though the upshot was to diminish him). The lectures are, I suppose inevitably, painfully mannered in places. They must have been forgotten by my time, but they were the sort of thing which gave off a general atmosphere of dilettantism, amateurism and old-fogeydom at a time when interesting and important things were happening – as it were in opposition. I suppose it is a neat conclusion that Tillyard, Leavis's main opponent, and prepared to scoff at Mackail, edited a selection from Lamb for the Press.

A feature of the Press's English publishing that one begins to register in the 1930s is that women academics began to make their mark – not much noticed, partly because it was a slow start, and they were less combative than the men (except for Queenie Leavis, that is). I have mentioned Muriel Bradbrook. A little book on Gerard Manley Hopkins appeared in 1933. It was by Elsie Elizabeth Phare – she had been a star as an undergraduate, but the title-page felt it had to add '(Mrs Austin Duncan-Jones)'.[9] (This reminds me that the Press's only work of fiction, ever, a historical romance based on genuine original sources, called *A Cardinal of the Medici* (1937), was by Mrs Hicks-Beach, who, so far as the title-page was concerned, was called just that: she had no first name or even an initial. She explained to SC that there was another Susan Hicks-Beach with whom she simply could not afford to be associated. Discriminating people would know who Mrs Hicks-Beach was. A remarkable scholar was Sybil Rosenfeld, who produced *Strolling Players and Drama in the Provinces* in 1939, *The Theatre of the London Fairs* in my time, in 1960, and *Georgian Scene Painters and Scene Painting* in 1981. Muriel Bradbrook collaborated with M.G. Lloyd Thomas to produce *Andrew Marvell* in 1940. Enid Welsford was another author, though her *The Fool* went to Faber.

For some reason these ladies were tiny: Joan Bennett, who comes next, was minute but had a remarkable voice. I remember a lecture where, invisible behind the speaker's rostrum, she boomed out:

> I wonder by my troth what thou and I
> Did till we loved … ?

Startled, I thought that we probably had to find each other first.

She was a serious author, and the Press published her *Four* [later *Five*] *Metaphysical Poets* in 1934. It was reprinted and went into a third edition and paperback in my time (1964). It was followed by *Virginia Woolf* in 1945 (reprinted, also paperbacked in 1964), *George Eliot* in 1948, *Sir Thomas Browne* in 1962. She was, one could say, the Press's principal living author in English studies at the time – though it seemed to me a bad time. In my first years I had to sponsor books by 'respectable' (i.e. non-Leavisite) academics in English: now-forgotten Clark Lectures by

---

[9] She got a starred First in Part II in 1929, together with Ronald Bottrall the poet, Humphrey Jennings the film-maker and T.H. White of *The Sword in the Stone*.

Geoffrey Tillotson and James Sutherland – and even by notabilities such as Joyce Cary and Louis Macneice. I couldn't get interested.

I had to be interested when C.S. Lewis came on the Cambridge scene. His inaugural lecture as Professor of Medieval and Renaissance Literature, *De descriptione temporum*, caused a great stir, and it was felt that the conservative wing of English was going to get a lift in the headquarters of the opposition. He was a friend of the Bennetts, and I think they had persuaded him to apply for the new chair. Stanley Bennett was now Chairman of the Syndicate, and when he proposed that the Press should publish the new book by this famous author, they could only say yes. This was *Studies in Words* (1960), rapidly followed by *An Experiment in Criticism* (1961) and *The Discarded Image* (1964). Rather childishly, I refused to sponsor the first two, asking Tony Becher to take them on. But when Tony left, I had to take over – which was the professional thing to do, and the thing Ian Parsons would have done – and I had a perfectly reasonable relationship with Lewis. He was a bit of a bully, but I gave him no occasion, and just did the job. The books are still in print, together with the posthumous collection. *Studies in Words* and *The Discarded Image* now strike me as good books.

Back to the Bennetts, who are important in the story, partly because they illustrate the point that in the history of an institution personal relationships play a role that the historian doesn't always grasp, for there may be no surviving evidence. I have pointed out that Stanley was now Chairman, while Joan was an important author. I add that one of their daughters, Elizabeth, was married to Colin Eccleshare, Assistant Manager at Bentley House. I had a sort of relationship with the family too, since at college I had known an extraordinary undergraduate, David Udy, also taught by A.P. Rossiter, who took a fatherly interest in all his pupils. Before the war, David had thought he would be an Anglican monk, and went off to a monastery. When war broke out, he thought no, he wouldn't be a monk, he would be a commando, and off he went. He was seriously wounded, had a visible hole in the head or mark of Cain, and it affected his mental balance. He couldn't take the Tripos, had to have an *aegrotat*, but he could act – very well. He also fell in love with Kay Bennett, and she with him, and they were to be seen walking about the college with their arms round each other: touching sight, for she was good-looking, and had long blonde hair in a coiled plait (Gretchen-like), and he looked romantic. It was a difficult marriage, which broke up in the end, but for a time Kay taught English at the school where my wife Fay was teaching Spanish and French, and some baby-sitting and taking children to school went on, with A.P. being a sort of universal godfather until he killed himself in a motor-cycle accident, leaving a second wife and small child as part of this group.

So I had this kind of fringe-relationship with the Bennett family, and of course Stanley had been a member of the committee which had appointed me, came into the Press often enough at teatime and got on well with us all. He was a genial figure, impossible to dislike, and one saw him cycling about Cambridge, despite his disability, in a faded blue mac and a very old Homburg hat. His monument is *English Books and Readers*, three volumes covering the period 1475–1640; but like his teacher Coulton he also did semi-popular books on medieval England, which made natural paperbacks.

My only trouble with all this was my doctrinal affiliation. This too was not a simple matter, for the Bennetts had been friends of the Leavises until there had been some for ever unexplained row, since when they had not spoken to each other. Like Leavis, Stanley had served in the First War – had in fact lost part of a leg. Like Leavis, he was not part of the public-school world – had been one of those remarkable elementary school-teachers, without a degree; but after the War had got his degree in history 'by research' supervised by Coulton and approved by Chadwick, who steered him towards lecturing in Medieval Literature for the English Tripos (he did a lecture course on the medieval background, which I part-attended; pretty routine stuff). He and Leavis had met at Emmanuel after the War, became friends, supervised for the college, but were, I suppose, both hoping for a fellowship there. Stanley got it, and some unpleasantness in the sequence of events led Leavis to emigrate to Downing. I suspect that it was at least partly due to Queenie, who was explosive, indeed atomic, and had these terminal fallings-out. I never heard Stanley say anything unpleasant about Leavis, and he was always kind to me, though he knew which way I inclined. I think Joan hated the Leavises.

I have indicated the background to the Press's reissue of *Scrutiny*, treated in Chapter 12. I add here that though I was not greatly stirred by the books we published in English, there was in the 1960s a steady stream of respectable monographs by authors who went on to make a name. I had an increasing responsibility for them, insofar as I got them refereed and passed by the Syndicate, and also became editorially involved. One author who became notorious was Brian Vickers, whose *Francis Bacon and Renaissance Prose* we published in 1968, five years after that reissue. Vickers was the unfortunate young scholar who was elected to follow Leavis as English Fellow at Downing. Leavis wanted one of his own people to follow him, naturally enough, but made a bad choice, unacceptable to the college. The row became public and Vickers found himself in an intolerable position. He behaved with dignity, which meant that he kept quiet and left, and made a reputation for himself by his publications. I am reminded of this by having read the typescript of one of his recent books. In it he mentions as 'an important book' D.L. Frost's *The School of Shakespeare*, which I sponsored, also in 1968. Frost's first name was David, and he came up to John's in the same year as the other David Frost, who on the first day of the first term came into his room and said 'You are going to get a lot of post addressed to me.' This was the Frost who famously 'rose without trace', becoming a face and voice on television and for that reason a nationally recognised personality beknighted without any obvious achievement. I am struck by the fact that after thirty-plus years the book is seen as important.

There was also our Forth-Bridge-painting-job equivalent, the *Cambridge Bibliography of English Literature*. The first edition happened to come out in 1940 – notionally an expression of national self-confidence, actually a coincidence, or the result of normal long production times. This had to be revised as the subject developed rapidly, and I had a part in administering the new edition, dealing with George Watson and the elusive Ian Willison. It is a sobering thought that this was, over the years, probably our most important contribution to English studies, though looking after it was a bit like mowing the lawn. You had to keep doing it, but at least it was always there.

The *Scrutiny* reprint of 1963 marks a natural epoch. I suggest in Chapter 7 that just before then the influence of Boris Ford and the work of David Holbrook had already moved me and the Press in the general direction pointed to by Leavis. It so happened that I had become Education Secretary and found myself working at the school-level, where there was a dissemination or extension function to perform; and overseas travel put me in contact with ex-pupils of Leavis's. When I became Chief Editor in 1965 I was officially responsible again for the university level – but in all subjects. In fact I had never lost interest in or contact with university English while doing the school job but then, as later, was doing so many other things that I could never concentrate on it. But that was the beauty of the job as much as it was the difficulty.

CHAPTER 7

Education Secretaries

Charles Carrington left the Press in the mid 1950s, and Oscar Watson took his place as Education Secretary for two or three years, until 1958. I don't think Oscar much enjoyed the job, but accepted it as promotion. For instance it brought with it – or it did in his case, though not in mine later – a Press car: a grey Austin Cambridge. This was the only staff vehicle in the Cambridge publishing office, though the two senior Printers had them. When I came to the Press Kingsford ran a discreet Rover, but it was his own. When later he acquired a Bentley the joke went round that he had put the Bentley into Bentley House: the rumour was that the Press had part-financed it. My guess is that Crutchley had pointed out that people who ran an important printing house now had cars as part of their remuneration, that his case was accepted, and so the Secretary had to have one too; but it was not meant to be the thin end of any wedge. One forgets now that, in the period before Margaret Thatcher, punitive taxation of earned income made executives look for benefits in kind rather than increases in salary, and the benefit long outlived the situation. It wasn't clear to me that Charles Carrington had a Press car: I think he occasionally hired one. The job theoretically involved driving about visiting schools and exhibitions, and in other ways acquiring authors, so Oscar's car made a kind of sense. The rest of us were not commissioning editors; we remained in our offices and waited for MSS to arrive by post – as they mainly did. Alternatively we took the train to London and interviewed prospective authors in the Library at Bentley House. The travellers – as they were then called – did have cars, because it was their job to travel, but it was not yet an executive perk. Not until several years into Geoffrey Cass's time did I have a Press car.

   The schoolbook list was quite distinctive. The books were still printed by letterpress, like everything else we did, and sold in large numbers (multiples of 10,000, usually printed from stereotyped plates). A book adopted by a school was sold in one or more class-sets of thirty-plus at a time, at a non-net price (D terms), through educational suppliers or direct from the Press.

Figure 8. Oscar Watson throwing a pot in his cottage farm near the Loire

A course in a subject could occupy up to four fairly substantial volumes, crown or demy octavo: in theory, one volume per year. This elided the distinction that public schools started at age 13-plus while grammar schools started at 11-plus. The actual format of most schoolbooks was simple and inelastic, based on 'real' books: it was also assumed that the users owned them – had even purchased them, though they might later be sold on.

We had a team of half-a-dozen schoolbook travellers who went into common-rooms to show the books or manned exhibits at conferences. The Education Secretary might accompany them and hope to meet authors that way – and indeed I did in my time (1960 onward) go up to Edinburgh regularly in June to attend the annual conference of the Educational Institute of Scotland, where the Press had a stand – but I went on doing it partly because I never confined myself to schoolbooks and it gave me the chance to do a bit of visiting at the University as well, and other places on the way. I used my own car, and sometimes gave a lift to another editor, so we kept each other company, and had a nice mixture of business and sightseeing.

The Press in the 1950s still only published schoolbooks at secondary level, and principally to public and grammar schools – so the top 15 to 20 per cent at most of the school population. The books themselves were written as a private spare-time venture by individual teachers with a gift, or a special line in their subject, and successful books were adopted in other schools, prompted by reviews, word of mouth, recommendations by the travellers who gave out specimen copies in common-rooms, or in the end just by tradition, since successful books had a long life and one could find teachers using the books they had learned from.

The archetypal Cambridge schoolbook author was the venerable A.W. Siddons, former Head of Mathematics at Harrow. I actually met him in 1952 at the party held to celebrate his fiftieth anniversary as Press author. In 1902 he and his then senior partner Charles Godfrey had been invited by the Syndics to write a geometry textbook. It represented a revolution in mathematical education, replacing the traditional teaching of Euclid in rigidly formal logical order. Both Godfrey and Siddons had read mathematics at Cambridge at a crucial time, and were high among the Wranglers (First Class in the Tripos), then took up teaching at Winchester and Harrow. The teaching of Mathematics had hardly altered since the eighteenth century – even at the University it was still seriously behind the continent and had to make efforts to catch up – and reform was being proposed by the new Mathematical Association. *Elementary Geometry* was published in 1903, and in one format sold 20,000 copies in two years, being followed in 1912 by *A Shorter Geometry*, and by *Elementary Algebra*, and in 1913 by the Press's all-time best-seller, the *Four-Figure Tables*, which went on reprinting in the hundreds of thousands and would have gone on for ever if electronic calculators had not been invented.

Siddons later collaborated on other books with a succession of younger men: Hughes, Daltry, Snell, Lockwood and Morgan. In my time the last three were active, and I handled books for them. It was a very successful and respected tradition, with a serious ambition to keep itself 'modern' in terms of method, and gave the Press standing in mathematics at the school level. On the other hand it was all very much in what is now thought of as the private sector.

Another less 'private' source of authors was the examining bodies themselves. So A.E.E. McKenzie, Secretary of the Oxford and Cambridge (O&C) Examinations Board down in Station Road, wrote science schoolbooks and as author was passed from Charles to Oscar to me: it is easy to understand that his name and much more his position brought many purchasers (the O&C mainly examined public schools). In my own time later, A.V. Hardy of the Cambridge Board wrote good geography textbooks, to cover the pioneering syllabus he was developing – so it was more enterprising than corrupt.

A notable development which went back to Carrington's time was the growth of Commonwealth or colonial history, evolving into a study which went back beyond and transcended the imperial period. There was for instance an early history of Australia, and one of Canada. (Charles's brother was Anglican Archbishop of Quebec. I had handled his history of the Early Christian Church.) Importantly, the Cambridge Local Examinations Syndicate administered public examinations in schools in British-administered territories in Africa, Asia and the Caribbean: very large numbers of candidates took them as the principal key to their future careers. (At one point I examined in English for the Cambridge Board. When I travelled in Africa and Asia, and it was understood that I was an examiner, people more or less fell on their knees.)

Very early it was seen to be anomalous to ask African and Asian students to study English or European history in school, so that a principal factor in the development of African and Asian history as an academic interest was in order to teach the subject in schools and then to examine it – so it had to be researched and written, in the face of those in traditional history who said it didn't exist, had no literature, no standards and so on. I think one can say that the Press was and is the leading publisher of African history as distinct from the history of colonial administration – the old type of Empire-history which of course we published as well. From 1955 on, the new kind started to appear as small books, mainly for African schools, on the main regions – especially West and East Africa. The authors, S.V. Lumb (a woman), J.D. Fage, Marsh and Kingsnorth, Oliver and Atmore are still a sort of litany in my mind. (Tony Atmore is also a linking figure, since he married the daughter of Sybil Marshall. Sybil had been the teacher in the village school in Kingston, and the wedding reception was held in my garden. She also became an author, so one thing led to another.)[1]

---

[1] Sybil came to prominence as the one-woman teacher in the twenty-odd-pupils village school in Kingston, where I lived and still do. She was specially good at getting the children to write lively pieces and to paint, and became the person that visiting foreign educationists were brought to see. The school was closed, and she went to New Hall as a mature student. Her *Experiment in Education* (1963) came to the Press because of Boris's interest, but I had to produce it, and had pleasure in making it a very desirable book. I got a subsidy for the coloured plates, and used the childrens' work (including a portrait of Sybil) for the jacket and a printed linson binding. It did well, became a sort of textbook as well as popular reading and paperbacked. She went on to lecture in education at Sussex and wrote for the Press *Fenland Chronicle*, which used the reminiscences of her parents in dialect and fitted into the Sturt tradition. She made educational TV programmes. Finally she became a popular novelist, writing for Penguin popular novels which sold very well – just the sort of thing QDL and Denys Thompson had analysed.

Tony is still getting royalties from Oliver and Atmore's *Africa since 1800*, which goes on selling in revised editions. Roland Oliver became the first Professor of African History at SOAS (School of Oriental and African Studies), London; John Fage became Professor and Director of the Centre of West African Studies at Birmingham, having started as Lecturer and then Professor in Ghana; and they were general editors of the big *Cambridge History of Africa* and of the *Journal of African History*. Tony Atmore came to England to do a second degree at SOAS after a first degree at Cape Town and to work as an Education Officer (already an Inspector in his 20s) in the former Nyasaland. In the mid 1960s Oliver chose him to collaborate on the book about Africa since 1800 – the whole continent. The book's subsequent history is interesting – it went on to sell much more widely outside Africa, especially in the USA.

I must return to the African interest, which was important for me personally, and for a time to the Press's development, but I mention it here as already visible in the 1950s, a kind of mounting wave. Commonwealth or 'Empire' sales of some schoolbooks grew and grew after the War, so that the little market of English public-school and grammar-school publishing was opening out into this much bigger world. Books had to be written for it, and other publishers had spotted the trend, and also went for the market.

But then, some of the best products of public and grammar schools, after university, went out into that world, to administer or teach. I mention Philip Harris below. I also remember, for instance, that one of Siddons's later collaborators came to his own retirement in England, and opted to go to Africa for several years of very successful and useful teaching – a sort of belated 'gap'. Charles Carrington's own intellectual interest was 'The British Overseas', so he was happy to initiate all this. In the footsteps of the first colonisers came the administrators, doctors and teachers: and in *their* footsteps their African and Indian ex-pupils as administrators, doctors, teachers and writers in the English language.

This had started in Charles's time and was developing in Oscar's, something still done in Cambridge with one hand and from time to time, so to speak, but noticeable. And the Press now had a representative in West Africa, visiting schools and the universities then being set up. But Oscar was unhappy, and left in 1957 or 1958. I was offered his job at the time, but was so interested in what I was doing and the books I was handling – still felt I was learning that job, and getting a late education from parts of it – that I said no.

I pause for a moment to consider the old Assistant Secretary's role again. What was satisfying me at the time was mostly that I was dealing with interesting books, sometimes important ones, even if my role was still the old 'seeing through the press' routine – though it was also true that I was beginning to make what I hoped were helpful editorial interventions. It is a sobering thought for someone who later spent many years creating or commissioning hundreds, I suppose thousands, of books, that those which came in simply because some author had wanted to write them, had done so over years and then looked for a publisher who would recognise their worth – these were actually the best books, and the best publisher was the one who identified them. The Press was good at this: I thought I was good at it. It required a gift: you had to see the quality and interest, find the right referee and sometimes give the authors good advice.

It was also the case that there were then in most subjects academic authors who could write for an intelligent public not confined to their peers, and that intelligent public, of just sufficient size, was looking for such books; the weekly periodical literature was still interested in reviewing such books; 'academic' and 'general' publishing shaded into each other; and the number of books published had not spiralled out of sight – all these things went together. True, academic authors still write popularising books – often after having presented a TV programme. The books do well enough – for what is now a very brief life. My impression is that the popularising academic books of the 1950s were not deliberately aimed at a large down-market audience; rather, they overflowed from a smaller academic one, had more substance and deserved the longer life they got. It was the age of BBC Radio's Third Programme, of *Scrutiny* just ending its twenty-year life, of the great days of Penguin Books, of extramural lecturing followed by important books by Richard Hoggart and Raymond Williams at the Workers Educational Association ... Am I saying it was a Golden Age? Well, it was for me, and for many others.

The essence of my job was that I played an increasing part in getting these books read and accepted, was learning to present the case for them at the Syndicate table, felt an increasing ability to read them in the office and sometimes make a helpful suggestion, fed them into the unparallelled service of the University Printing House, did my part of that process, and saw at the other end a book which was a pleasure to handle and read as well as a serious intellectual enterprise: something to take pride in. I think for instance of Bolgar's *The Classical Heritage and its Beneficiaries* – a superb book. When he saw his early copy Bolgar wrote to me that the

Press 'had found it brick and left it marble'. It was one of our 6-by-9-inch medium octavos, and we had developed a sophisticated system for placing notes at the end (complex subediting job), so that it looked as readable as it was. My recollection is that we printed 2,000 copies at 45 shillings, reprinted it and later paperbacked. (And talk about the classical heritage: Bolgar's initials on the title-page were R.R. He told me they were really C.C.R.R. and the first two stood for Caius Coriolanus.)

I have already mentioned some titles: I add here Herbert Butterfield's *Man on his Past* (1955), Owen Chadwick's *From Bossuet to Newman* (1957), Steven Runciman's *Sicilian Vespers* (1958) and *The White Rajahs* (1960)[2] and Patrick Wilkinson's *Ovid Recalled* (1955). Kingsford and I both read and liked M.K. Ashby's life of her father, *Joseph Ashby of Tysoe* (1961), a classic addition to the Sturt tradition.[3] I cared about French and German literature, and standards in both were rising. Some very good books came in: for instance, Eric Blackall on *The Rise of German as a Literary Language* (1959), Walter Bruford's *Culture and Society in Classical Weimar* (1962), Siegbert Prawer on *Heine as Satirist* (1961), Robert Gibson's *Modern French Poets on Poetry* (1961) and Eudo Mason on *Rilke, Europe and the English-Speaking World* (1961) – mentioned later, in Chapter 14.

I also found myself exploring the possibilities of large-format books with illustrations, notably Beresford and St Joseph's *Medieval England* (1958), using aerial photography reproduced by half-tone, and where text and illustration were integrated in a continuous flow (difficult in those days: litho was undeveloped and half-tone required glossy paper). Steers's *Coastline of England and Wales* (1960) did the other thing, using photogravure for the plates and letterpress for the text; I did a very good jacket for it. Michael Farr's *Design in British Industry* (1955), sponsored by Pevsner, was important for me because it codified 'contemporary' design ideology and showed it in industrial rather than craft use: Farr, the prisoner of his 'contemporary' or Bauhaus taste, was a bit sniffy about what the Press did for him. It's a fine book.

It will be noticed that I say nothing here about books in English studies, which was what I cared most about, for the good reason that

---

[2] Runciman's *A History of the Crusades*, in three volumes, had come out earlier, handled by Oscar. For readers in the 1950s its overall cultural effect was considerable; long before Edward Said one learned to step out of one's Western insularity or Christian presuppositions, and accept that the Crusades were a barbarian invasion of a superior Eastern civilisation.

[3] It is characteristic of this class of books that one finds them cited much later. In 2001 I bought Jonathan Rose's *The Intellectual Life of the English Working Class* and found Ashby extensively quoted and commented on.

we published nothing much of real interest – to me at any rate – until John Styan appeared. I do remember Foakes and Rickert's edition of *Henslowe's Diary* (1961) – an important document and an interesting typographical challenge, and I mention elsewhere Brian Vickers and David Frost. But for the moment, handling books in all subjects except, now that Anthony Parker was there, the sciences, I was having a rewarding time, dealing with interesting people in other subjects where the Press's publications were highly regarded – rightly. There for instance in my office was R.H. Tawney, bringing in his life of Lionel Cranfield. I remember him as almost self-parodying absent-minded professor, very sweet. In another lighting-up performance like that with Frank Kendon, I watched him light an over-stuffed pipe, with tobacco hanging out of it. He talked as he waved the match over this charge, and he breathed out as well as in. The result was a firework display, with bits of burning tobacco flying everywhere, and Tawney still talking, still puffing, still lighting the charge and vigorously slapping himself all over to put out the sparks.

I remember also Hugh Trevor-Roper's Economic History Review Supplement on *The Gentry*, David Chambers's on industry in the River Trent area (wasn't he the brother of Jessie Chambers, Lawrence's first love? Oh, yes…), or John Pocock as diffident author of *The Ancient Constitution and the Feudal Law*, Gilbert Ryle's *Dilemmas* – it was an interesting life for a young man, much more interesting than boring schoolbooks, or so it seemed. So the Educational Secretary's post was advertised, and Boris Ford got it. One of his first moves was to say 'No, not Educational – Education', and the title changed.

Boris was already quite celebrated, since the first volumes of his *Pelican Guide to English Literature* had appeared in 1955, and it was completed in its first edition in 1958, though he went on revising it in his time at the Press – indeed his secretary rather sharply remarked, to him then as well as to me later, that it was his first priority and his Press authors had to take second place. Boris had a Russian mother, hence the name; had been a boy chorister at King's College School (he remained genuinely musical); and had read English at Downing. This made me see him as an ally, given that I felt mildly perplexed and on my own in my first years at the Press when I looked at the English list. So Boris seemed like the proverbial breath of fresh air, something new coming into our little circle from the outside world. Actually he was a brief, cold, dry wind.

I got on well with him, if only because I was younger, naive and respectful, sympathetic to his general point of view. He had been taught by Leavis: it was not clear to me then that Leavis viewed him somewhat askance, as (I now suppose) damagingly on the make, and using his Downing connection as intellectual capital. This was true; on the other hand, why shouldn't he? He used it to good effect: one has to say that the *Pelican Guide* was not only useful to hundreds of thousands, it filled the gap that the old *Cambridge History* had long left unfilled by something more modern, it was well planned and imaginatively done by real enthusiasts, and it deserved its success. People in my situation, or my elders, were shown what *they* ought to have done. Leavis too, perhaps, but then he thought he had done it in *Scrutiny* and his own books, in a way which was not facile (I suppose he thought the *Guide* was facile).

Boris's career had been extraordinary in that since 1945 he had remained in and then run the Bureau of Current Affairs (five years: he had first joined it in the War, when it was the Army Bureau), then the Secretariat of the United Nations (two years) and Schools Broadcasting at the BBC (no time at all). He was at the Press from 1958 to 1960, when he left to be Professor of Education at Sheffield, and in 1963 Professor at Sussex (Professors of Education then had ample time to write books). It is now clear to me that his main aim in these posts was to have a salary while he edited the *Pelican Guide* and later *Universities Quarterly*, and generally made his name. A number of employers had reason to think they had been used. However, sharp and self-promoting as he was, he was not inactive, was able to get a certain amount done, or at least started, because he could call at once on the contacts he brought with him, and he got himself treated with respect as ideas-man, networker and organiser.

When he left, he characteristically loaded his car with everything he felt free to take away from the office – and not just the books. Tony Becher, outraged, ran down the stairs after him and into the yard, waving a box of Press matches and shouting 'Here, Boris! You've forgotten these!'

It's hindsight which makes me critical of Boris, though also I fell out with him in my last years at the Press – but meanwhile I kept in contact, even published two substantial articles in *Universities Quarterly*. At the time I was at ease with him, thought him an intellectual ally and was impressed by his activity. He may have been sharp, but he was not lazy, and I always respected people who seemed to know what they were doing and got things done. When he went I was offered the job again, and this time I said yes. It was now in my mind that I could perfectly well go on handling some of the good books that I liked handling (someone had to do it) and do the other job at the same time. There was bound to be some interaction between the levels. It was all editing, a concept I was nurturing, and I wanted to be a real editor. Indeed something may have rubbed off from Boris; he was an initiator, an editor who made contacts and commissioned large enterprises: he had started some things which I was quite eager to carry on, especially in English, where it was becoming clear that what was done at the school level did have some relationship with the tertiary level.

There had remained some publishing in school English of the conventional sort, for instance the work of A.F. Scott, a forgotten author who sold well in his time and even gave himself airs: there was a secondary course, an anthology or two, a book for teachers. One important initiative of mine owed nothing to Boris. The *Selected Tales from Chaucer* sprang from a request from Marie Overton of the Local Exams Syndicate: they wanted to be able to prescribe for O and A Level editions of the most-studied tales of Chaucer, edited on new-Cambridge lines – with critical introductions and notes which were recognisably modern, i.e. not like Verity.

There were three examiners willing to do the job, and I knew them all: Maurice Hussey, Tony Spearing and James Winny. (It may be worth saying that Maurice was a pupil of Leavis's, and made the index for the *Scrutiny* reprint; the other two, like Jeremy, Prynne, Tony Tanner, Philip Brockbank and I were pupils of A.P. Rossiter's.) We got together and formed a plan. I introduced the rule I followed with the Bible Commentary and other series: we refused to publish in every volume the dry, reduced, standard informational pieces which were normally repeated unchanged in each (Chaucer's life, the social background – that sort of thing). We took these out, amplified them and published them in an introductory volume which was worth reading and would sell in one copy for each class-set of the prescribed text; there was also a large-format book of illustrations. This meant that each text could have a substantial critical introduction, a really useful one, as well as notes. Thirteen volumes of text, plus the introductory volumes, came out in the mid 1960s and were a great success. Some are still in print, and for thirty years or more the editors made a handsome income from them. As time went by they got used at university level. The success led me to do the same thing for Milton, edited by John Broadbent. This did less well, but well enough. The two series proved my point about the traffic between the levels, and indeed by the time they were published I was no longer Education Secretary, but Chief Editor, though still with an interest in schools and an inclination to spread myself over all subjects.

I ask myself if I have slipped this in somewhat defensively here, so that I don't look as if I merely inherited Boris's initiatives in English. But I did inherit them, of course, though I had to do a great deal to get them off the ground. And in retrospect, I see both him and me as servants of a sort of *Zeitgeist*. Both products of Cambridge English, and Leavis in particular, we were among the people who took the pure university-taught doctrine and turned it from the subject of a specialised honours degree course into something more widely influential at a lower level or even to the general public, so that it affected the life and education of people who never heard the name F.R. Leavis.

The other immediately relevant name I need to bring in is that of Denys Thompson, former English Master at Gresham's and later Head of King's School, Bruton, who had been one of the original colleagues of Leavis, an editor of *Scrutiny*, and co-author with Leavis of *Culture and Environment*, published by Chatto in 1932. This is now (I suppose) a forgotten book, but historically very important: it was the first textbook, for sixth-formers, on what is now called cultural and media studies, but it took the very sensible line that what people really needed then (and I think now) is not a bland survey, still less a sort of prospectus for future employees in the media, but an unglamourised account of what is really going on: a sort of health warning – what are these people trying to do to you, and are you willing to be manipulated? You aren't just buying a product, but are being inducted into a way of spending and living; you aren't being asked to think about it – just the reverse – but start now. It led on to general questions of what is now called life-style (should you be content with this?), but made what some thought the final tactical error of talking about the 'organic community' which preceded modern commercial and industrial society, and that has enabled enemies ever since to accuse Leavis and his group of nostalgia. If Denys simplified, so do his critics, and I come back to the organic society below. At certain moments I felt I had had a glimpse of one: I was passing as it was passing.

Actually, it was Denys who wrote *Culture and Environment*, and it was he who was strong and a bit simplifying on the organic community, but Leavis accepted the material and the treatment as coming from a skilled teacher at the relevant level, and did little more than lend his name. *Culture and Environment* reads oddly now because of its fervently evangelistic tone: there is something Victorian about it, but instead of the demon drink what it warns against is the demon present-day media-culture and all the people who manipulate you, form your tastes, deal in mindless gossip about gossamer celebrities, tell you what to think (if you can call it thinking), make money out of it, and keep you idle, stupid and bored, so that you don't know what to do with all the leisure you now have, and go on with the addictions. (I fall into the mode of discourse.)

Denys then wrote *Reading and Discrimination* (Chatto, 1934), another pioneering book, of practical criticism exercises for sixth forms, so he was already at that very early date engaged in getting the message across at school level and providing classroom material. Most importantly, from 1939 or 1940 he edited the quarterly *The Use of English* (also published by Chatto), which was subscribed and contributed to by the best people in the profession, reviewed books directed to teaching as well as the most relevant general books, and actually nurtured the sense of a like-minded, forward-looking group – mostly, almost entirely, in public and grammar schools. I subscribed and wrote articles and reviewed for it. Denys, as father-figure, blessed the initiatives of Boris and David Holbrook and Sybil Marshall – mine too in due course.

I suppose I first met him in the 1960s at meetings of the group who were setting up the new NATE (National Association of Teachers of English) – a characteristic assembly of the high-minded and the self-promoting who saw a role for themselves as the officers and the politicians of a growing movement which was turning from a minority into a mainstream. Denys, as saintly father-figure, was asked to address them. His books read as stern and headmasterly, minor prophet-like, and made him seem forbidding. In person he was slight, mild and winning; he stood in front of the group he was addressing, gripping his left wrist with his right hand (as if he was trying to unscrew his fist, Sybil Marshall said). My place in these gatherings was as the publisher's editor who had to be there because he was trying to catch whatever crumbs fell from the table of Ian Parsons of Chatto, though given an enormous leg-up by Boris, who had brought to the Press David Holbrook and Sybil Marshall. And by 1963 we had also reissued *Scrutiny*. So we were beginning to look like the coming power.

I should also mention here as one of the important figures of this movement another forgotten star, Douglas Brown. He was the Edward King of my generation at Cambridge – brilliant man of infinite promise, dying young – on the assumption that Donald Davie, who mourned him, was our Milton. Douglas had been at the Perse School for Boys, an ancient private school in Cambridge. He had been taught by the legendary Caldwell Cook, who had also taught Leavis and instituted the teaching of English through drama at the 'Mummery', as it was called, at the Perse, and Douglas inherited and carried on the tradition. He came back from being a medical orderly (like Leavis, he had conscientious objections but served in this way) to read English just after the War, and I used to catch glimpses of him as an undergraduate. I seem to remember that

Rossiter taught him too. He got starred Firsts, and went back to teach at the Perse because he felt it was a duty: I think he even insisted on teaching for a while at a secondary modern school. He had a very characteristic manner: once or twice I had the shock of meeting pupils of his who had adopted his dress (grey tweed jacket, open-necked dark shirt, sandals) and above all his manner and voice: gentle but *very intense.* One was tempted to look down and watch the shaft of the message entering one's breast. Douglas too was asked to address meetings of the new association, and it was interesting to see what happened. He had an extraordinary way of capturing his audience, like what we now call a cult-leader. What he was saying was very compelling, about our *duty*. A friend said he now knew what it must have been like to have been one of the faithful at Nuremberg, addressed by Hitler. And at the NATE meeting I watched a cynical man with a hearing-aid making a note. It said 'Thoroughly insincere'. Douglas managed to write one or two small books and finally consented to go into university teaching, at York. Then he died.

David Holbrook, like Boris, had read English at Downing. He was a year or two younger, came up first in 1941, but completed his degree after active service in the War. Like Boris, he could be seen as one of Leavis's shock troopers going out into the wide world and spreading the doctrine. Like Boris, he was seen by Leavis as a thoroughly equivocal influence, part harmful. There was an odd element in David's character at that early time: as if he had to make up time (lost in the War?), he was desperate to be recognised, especially as an author. In any letter from him there was enclosed a regularly revised printed leaflet which listed the growing number of books by David Holbrook, including the schoolbooks. There must have been twenty or thirty titles by the end. He was always writing letters to newspapers and was finally written off by them as a self-advertising bore. His remarks about Leavis, private and public, were ungenerous, as if he had to disavow any influence, even call it harmful. Leavis at first responded with the occasional aside about 'a certain self-publicist' and finally wrote David one of his excommunicatory letters, saying 'Let me tell you what is the matter with you. You are jealous, of me.' This was the truth. To his credit, perhaps, David kept the letter, and showed it to some people (not me). Perhaps he felt it showed up Leavis.

On the other hand, I have to say that David was and is an engaging person. There was an innocence in all that, a naivety, which was part of his openness, his never-quite-grown-up charm. He did also have great energy, and a lot of real talents. I still read his poems with pleasure, because his best self is in them. They are simple, direct, modest and true, full of good feeling, and reach something near impersonality. His house is full of pictures he painted himself, and though one can see they are by an amateur they are a pleasure to look at, show his own pleasure in landscape, in the outside world, and his ability to see and respond. His novels are clearly autobiographical, but one of them, *Flesh Wounds*, has an account of the Normandy landing on D-Day and the days of fighting after, including his wounding, which is the best piece of reporting of that war that I know.

My part in the story is as editor of his work on the teaching of English in English secondary schools, and this work is historically important. I should say that though we are on good terms again, I fell out with David too, over later developments in his work, when he was no longer addressing the secondary school but was taking on the world. He was bitten by the psychoanalytical bug (the alternative, since the 1930s, to Marxism or Christianity for people who paradoxically wanted both a determinism and a salvation). David's work with children, often deprived and with difficulties, led him to the writings of Winnicott and Bowlby and others. These were thoughtful men with insights of a kind, but the insights could be turned, and were, into clichés, and David began to write material, including would-be literary criticism, in which writers' 'problems' were 'explained' as damaging their work, and the term 'schizoid' was freely used. It became quite a crusade: it didn't do to be schizoid, but most other people were. This was not just derivative and unconvincing, it was also a daft kind of campaigning, and I didn't buy it. Specifically I turned down some long argumentative books of his, virtually on my own initiative, at least once without a report, and he was understandably aggrieved. We wrote each other long letters. He did get some of the books published elsewhere, though not all, because he was causing others to write him off too, but to him I must have seemed a person standing in the way of the truth.

This was depressing because at the outset I had had great faith in him and what he was doing. Boris knew him and his work, and brought him to the Press, but left before the books appeared, so it was my role to develop this, at first, star author. There were three significant books: two on the teaching of English in secondary schools, *English for Maturity* in 1961, and *English for the Rejected* in 1964. *The Exploring Word* in 1967 was directed towards English teachers in training. The largest plank in this reformist platform of the 1960s was the Leavisite, or if you prefer the Arnoldian, contention that good literature, the best literature, should be taught in all schools just because it was the best that had been thought and said by talented people representing, over time, English culture to English readers. Literature is the consciousness of the nation, representing itself to itself. It was wrong to fob children off with cheap popular rubbish on the ground that only a minority could rise to the best, which would be wasted on the others.

The point about David's work was that it started not in the grammar or public school, where the other innovators were, but in what was then called the secondary modern. He had taught there, successfully. He was addressing first of all the fact that at that time the 11-plus exam separated off the 25 per cent (at most) of talented children from the 75 per cent (at least) of those graded less intelligent. He reported at the beginning of *English for Maturity* the Principal in a pleasant modern school-building saying 'Of course, we get the duds here.' The novel aspect of David's campaign was that Leavisite and other Cambridge-educated graduates in English had until then, like Denys Thompson himself, gone willingly into public and grammar schools and taught at near-university standard in the sixth forms. It had benefited me: I dare say I got something above present-day university standard. Their pupils duly went on to Cambridge and other good universities, and the cycle continued. This was a minority culture, but not doing what it ought to do – disseminate itself. What David was saying was that the other children, the majority, might not be taught in exactly the same way, but they must be given at least an exposure to the same standards: their powers of expression could be notably improved, and their self-worth too.

English for the Rejected pushed related buttons, but harder. The 'rejected' were after all the majority of the age-group. The title was found shocking, as it was meant to be, and I had done the jacket using a child's pen-portrait of an accusing or suffering face superimposed on a background of childish, barely readable handwriting. This was meant to assist the shock.

The books made a stir, sold well, reprinted in paperback. They were adopted as a sort of textbook for teachers in training. The obvious question 'What do we use for classroom material?' was met by David's anthologising gift. The books which he produced were printed in first impressions of 20,000, with rapid reprints. There was a verse anthology: *Iron, Honey, Gold*, first in two and then in four volumes; a short-stories anthology: *People and Diamonds*, in two volumes; a drama anthology: *Thieves and Angels*. All these gave selections of real literature, well chosen for interest and difficulty. *English for the Rejected* was accompanied by a course: *I've Got to Use Words*. A later book, *Children's Writing* (1967), gave teachers in training examples of the sort of thing children could be got to write.

I don't know whether it was my idea or David's or Kingsford's to persuade King's to elect David to a fellowship for two years, with the Press paying the stipend of £2,000 p.a. and treating this or a portion of it as an advance on royalties. This enabled him to write full-time, producing the books. And 'Fellow of King's College, Cambridge' on the title-page did the books no harm. It was a good idea: indeed other publishers now routinely paid large advances which enabled writers to settle down to their writing; perhaps we got it from some news item. I repeated the experiment (without the fellowship) once, with a good English teacher whom I found in Uganda, but it was not a great success that time.

The success of the Holbrook books, the stir they made, brought in books by like-minded people: for instance *Understanding the Mass Media* by Nicholas Tucker (1966), which took Denys Thompson's work into the new era of TV and pop music. Tucker had taught in comprehensive schools, went on to lecture at York and had a productive career. There was also the work of D.C. Measham: *Fourteen: Autobiography of an Age-Group* (1965) used work he had got by asking his pupils to write about themselves and their lives, and, each child, to make it fill a whole exercise-book. W.R. Page found himself faced with a group of London teenage girls on day-release courses in his college, and got them writing for their own magazine, which gave him the title for his book: *Introducing 'The Younger Woman'.* This gave insights into contemporary teenage attitudes. In 1969 Denys Thompson edited a collection of studies by like-minded younger teachers called *Directions in the Teaching of English*; in 1972 there was *English through Drama* by one of his contributors, Christopher Parry, of the Perse and the Mummery, and the principal Douglas Brown lookalike, or soundalike.

But by now we were in another era, and I was no longer primarily responsible for the schoolbook list. I have not thought about or looked at these old books for years, for the flow of new initiatives first wipes out memory of the old, retirement follows and one naturally reflects more about what later seems more glamorous. But now that I look at them again, I see them as a coherent and serious attempt by imaginative and energetic people to address one main plank in English education. The painful feeling that it did not make the difference it should have made is due to the thought that the comprehensive movement overtook us all. It was partly motivated by the sense of shame about the 'rejection' which David had highlighted, but it produced a revolution in organisation which overwhelmed the need to think harder about how to teach the streams which had once been separated and were now forced to converge, but still consisted of children with widely varying abilities.

One odd result of comprehensive education showed how little anyone had foreseen all its effects. I spent a lot of time and effort on *The Cambridge Hymnal* (1967), one of David's crusading ideas. Most hymns are awful, words and music alike. He wanted to produce a hymnal, primarily for use in schools, in which a much smaller number of hymns were admitted: they had to be good verse set to good music. His music editor, Elizabeth Poston, was a like-minded composer with good contacts and the incidental advantage of living in Rook's Nest, near Stevenage, the house Forster had mythicised in *Howards End*. It was nice to drive out and visit her there. We wrote, of course, to Britten and Tippett, who were of course too busy but wished us well. We even wrote to Stravinsky, suggesting he might like to set words by Eliot. I remember no answer, though it was noticeable some years later that he had set *The Dove Descending*, but had made it so atonal that no school choir could grasp it, still less perform it. Narrow escape. But we did commission new settings from minor composers. I spent Saturday morning after Saturday morning working out the copyright situation for each hymn, and I suspect we established some copyrights which have been infringed ever since, notably Elizabeth's setting of *Jesus Christ the Apple Tree*. I then had to discover how to produce a book consisting primarily of musical setting. The *Hymnal* was received quite well, but was not a success for the unforeseen reason that in a comprehensive school of over, say, 400 pupils there is no space in which an assembly of all the pupils can be held, that in a 'multicultural' community the Christians may not be or be treated as a majority, that the teachers have no faith and are no longer willing to put on a show, so will not conduct a service… and so on. Time had run out for the morning assembly with hymn and prayer which had been standard in my time and David's.

There was another large and important movement showing itself on the horizon, with a relationship to the English-for-the-English movement worth thinking about. This was English for non-native speakers, at first distinguishing between English as a Foreign Language (EFL) and English as a Second Language (EL2), before becoming generalised as English Language Teaching (ELT). The early terms showed that some distinctions were recognised. For Europeans, English was 'foreign'; for many Africans and Asians English was the language of instruction in secondary schools and universities, the language of government and the lingua franca between different local languages. The impending end of Empire had suddenly made people think: there were large populations – in India, for instance – where English was widely used, but where nobody was now taught by a native speaker, or even by someone once taught by a native speaker. There was no doubt that the language would go on being used, but given one or two generations of what the English could think of as degeneration, would it mutate as the Romance languages had done from the original Latin, so that people in different countries could no longer understand each other?

The British Council had set up teacher-training agencies in the major countries, and they had done pioneering work. This was also the crusading or imperialist age of linguistics, and the applied linguists and phonetics specialists were involved as well. The French had a comparable situation in Francophone territories, and had turned their attention to the problem. I met interesting French educationists at the conferences.

I began to go to this other set of conferences, meeting a quite different mind-set. One issue which linked the two Englishes was the question of grammar, now becoming the question of structure. The bugbear in both camps was traditional, formal, Latin-based grammar-teaching. The obvious objection was now at last being made: Latin grammar did not actually apply to English, but had been used because no alternative had been worked out for the vernacular. This produced an irrational hostility to the notion of grammar-teaching, and the root-and-branch rejection of the old model produced the situation in which you can now address a class of adults wanting to learn a language, use the word 'verb', and have someone put their hand up and say 'What is a verb?' (Yes, really.)

There is a huge gap here, and I can present myself, as C.S. Lewis did in his Cambridge inaugural lecture *De descriptione temporum*, as an interesting survival of a bygone age. When I was 8 or 10 I was taught French by Miss Gertrude Crawford, born I should think in about 1880. We learned from Siepmann's French course, with illustrations showing Frenchmen in *chapeaux feutres*, with Imperial beards and spats, standing in front of new-fangled autobuses in the *Place de l'Opéra*. In my exercise book I had four pages carefully folded into columns in which I had set out, for regular verbs in *-er*, in *-ir*, in *-oir*, in *-re*, the complete conjugation in all the persons and all the tenses: the whole verb-paradigm in all four declensions. This meant that when as an undergraduate I went to the old Cosmo (later the Arts) Cinema in Cambridge, I got the joke when Fernandel, as nicely spoken (well, rather mincing) French clerk, was taken aback when the girl he had asked out for the evening turned up with a friend. He said '*J'eusse préféré que vous vinssiez seule.*' Two imperfect subjunctives! How we laughed! Along with Lewis Harmer and the *Académie française*.

The doctrine now was that you learned a second language as you learned your native one, by hearing and repeating and so acquiring structures without recognising them, or at any rate without analysing them. The logical implication was that if you wanted to learn German, the best thing you could do would be to be born at the age of 0 years 0 months to a middle-class German couple speaking Hochdeutsch and spend your early years with them. If that was not feasible, the offered alternative was ruthless repetition of 'structures' in the language lab; so the labs sprang up (the tape-recorder was still expensive and cumbersome, using reels still, and needing a technician to maintain it, but becoming standard equipment). Teaching-material was needed, of the kind which could be repeated into the machine, until the process became fully audio-visual and reduced the need for separate publications. Then some balance returned, calling for courses using books, together with some moderation of the dogmas.

At any rate this English-teaching was becoming big international business, with Oxford and Longman leading the field – Longman in particular, who had had a far-sighted editor, I think even before the War. It was primarily an export market and favoured publishers who had overseas offices, especially in India and Africa. This leads me to my next chapter. I simply say here that I made efforts to build up an ELT list, with not a great deal of success – except that it counted to be in there trying, and noticed as interested. Not surprisingly, my main success was in an area where Cambridge had the classic text – Daniel Jones on the pronunciation of English, published in 1909 and then still in print and much used. Jones had built up the first university department of phonetics at University College London, which had a world-reputation, and I found there J.D. O'Connor, who wrote *Better English Pronunciation*, which was a success and is still in print. Related and also still in print was the brilliant *English Pronunciation Illustrated* by John Trim and Peter Kneebone in which Kneebone's comic drawings gave Trim's comic examples a weird life. (Vowel-discrimination: The zoologist wonders about bugs: the botanist wanders about bogs. Funny enough, but see the drawing. It was John Dreyfus who put me in touch with him.)

These real successes were like overflows from what I was doing in formal linguistics, mentioned later (Chapter 10). Otherwise the authors of my ELT ventures were people who had been teaching in the Middle East or India, especially with the British Council, and the results were modest, and the books long forgotten. What I can say for them is that they just managed to maintain a presence, so that when Adrian Du Plessis took over the enterprise in his extraordinarily systematic way, there was something to depart from. It has been my fate or my virtue that I started a great many things which others took up, systematised and did much better.

The point about the phonetics books is that I was by now (1965) following up tips given me by my serious connection in linguistics. And indeed most enterprising publishing is that: finding good advisers and following what they say. It brings me to my (my?) major success in schoolbooks, the Schools Mathematics Project (SMP), where I can deflate myself by saying that all I did was to take a tip from the Mathematics Syndic, Frank Smithies, who at a certain meeting said that there was a man called Thwaites who had got in touch with him, and he seemed to be running an interesting scheme down in Southampton... Frank Smithies never said a silly thing, and was listened to. Was this at a Syndicate meeting, or a Schoolbooks Committee? I think it was a Friday, and to my credit I did ring Bryan Thwaites at once, and was on the train to Southampton that weekend – I think: anyway, I lost no time.

At Southampton I met Thwaites, impressive and charming man, and the principal members of his team. I am taken back to the beginning of this chapter. Charles Godfrey had taught at Winchester: so had Thwaites, before he went to a chair at Southampton, and the core of his team were public-school masters. It's a thought: in the private sector, as we call it now, people had the energy and the intelligence to attempt something new. On the other hand, they knew that what they were doing had to be viable in state schools as well, and so were drawing in like-minded teachers in boys' and girls' grammar schools, where the material could be tried out over the wider age-range. Pergamon Press, Thwaites told me, were interested in the scheme and wanted to publish it, but Pergamon was run by Robert Maxwell, and he was already known to be unscrupulous.

I went back to Cambridge and at the next meeting got the Press to commit itself in principle to the whole scheme. This was a larger commitment than we knew, in part because we engaged ourselves to produce very rapidly the trial material which had to be taught in the eight participating schools for a year at least before it was published the following year in revised form – and to maintain this rhythm indefinitely. Apart from the cost, it was a large administrative job to keep getting the material out in time. We did: the first book (*Book T* for Transitional) was published in 1964, and looked handsome, with illustrations by Cecil Keeling and David Gentleman. Actually, we overdid it, and had to become more workaday and less extravagant.

The Project took off in a wonderful way and rapidly became a substantial seller as well as a commitment. I remember Dick David saying to me once, rather wistfully, 'Do you think it might bring in £100,000 a year?' I thought a moment and said yes. It began to matter, because in the 1960s the Press was getting into difficulties, and forecasting turnover and cash-flow became urgent. Actually the SMP made a steady million or more a year for a fair number of years, when a million was worth several millions now; and when Geoffrey Cass arrived he quickly saw that it was a major cash-delivering asset and had to be maintained and the SMP Foundation, as it became, kept happy. It is still running. I don't think anyone has ever counted how many titles have appeared: it must be hundreds.

As a postscript I mention another scheme, run by the Association of Teachers of Mathematics. These were good teachers in the state sector, and I remember going to another writing weekend which they ran. It produced a very helpful book simply called *Some Lessons in Mathematics*, which did very well; and the relationship helped us to say that we were not entirely in the pocket of the SMP. This became quite important, but was a good problem to have.

The characteristic of educational publishing in this period was that it moved from the small private ventures of the past into a new era of large curriculum-renewal schemes. These brought together under a coordinating body sizeable groups of writers who produced the draft-texts which were pondered at conferences, underwent trials in selected schools, were revised and then published. These were major ventures and had to be sponsored and financed by official or charitable bodies. The Nuffield Foundation was one of these sponsors, and Tony Becher was organising some of the schemes. Through my contact with him I secured the Cambridge Classics Project for the Press – more or less my farewell performance as Education Secretary.

In terms of format, the two to four demy octavo volumes, which might or might not once have had some illustrations (line-blocks or half-tones in black and white), were being succeeded by the fleet of small pamphlet volumes in larger formats, usually quarto, favouring illustration in colour. The core texts, which had once been a whole year's work, might now be divided into three, each a term's work; and they could be taken in any order. They were supported by little topic books, each dealing at comfortable length with a subject mentioned in the main texts. The whole set could be thought of as like a pack of cards, which could be shuffled and re-dealt. Lithography was taking the place of letterpress, and colour-printing was becoming the norm. Texts became less prosy. I am thinking here of a world-history course, the *Cambridge Introduction to the History of Mankind*, which I produced, edited by Trevor Cairns. It had something like sixty little volumes. The format lent itself also to the history of art. It was the transition to the formats of today.

Similarly, one might say that the SMP was a key to the future and showed why my little ventures in ELT could not succeed: there now had to be an organisation or at least a group producing educational material as a joint venture with continuity, testing material before publication and revising it later. The day of the single good teacher producing a course on the lines of 'how I do it myself' had passed.

CHAPTER 8

Africa and stations East

A significant proportion of my time and energy as Education Secretary was taken up by African schoolbooks. My main ally, and the hero of this chapter, was Philip Harris. He was four or five years older than I was, so had been through the War, saw active service in the infantry, had been under shellfire and was left very slightly deaf by it. After the War he had read History at St Catharine's, done the Colonial Office postgraduate course and gone into the Service in West Africa. He had started as Assistant District Commissioner, but as the 1950s wore on and Independence became something to plan for, moved into preparatory functions. He taught local government at tertiary level, indeed he wrote a book on *Local Government in Southern Nigeria*, published by the Press in 1952. He had been Private Secretary to Chief Awolowo, who at Independence became Prime Minister of the Western Region, and then he moved to be the Press's West African representative in Ibadan. (Until then the Press had had representatives working on commission, and acting for more than one publisher.)

Trade had become so substantial that a full-time sole representative was needed, and the Press built Philip a house and office in Ibadan – Cambridge House. He had a wife and four daughters, all four born in Nigeria. Philip was tall and handsome in a very English way, with a fresh pink face and wavy fair hair. He was easy to get on with, and though in theory I was his senior in rank at the Press, I looked up to him as someone older, who knew the territory and the people and was absolutely clear about the job.

We were now publishing for West African schools on a serious scale, and had it in mind that with the foundation and development of tertiary education, especially the new universities, there would be a market at the higher level for all Cambridge books. Local schoolbook publishing was meant to support the main business in the region.

Heinemann, Longman, Nelson and of course Oxford were in there already, and were much bigger than we were. Heinemann was publishing

Figure 9. Philip Harris as a young man

its African Writers Series. Achebe had published *Things Fall Apart* in 1958, and it went into the series, of which he was founding editor, in 1962; by the mid 1970s there were some 150 titles in it. Oxford published Wole Soyinka's *A Dance of the Forests*, though in fact it was first offered to us and we declined it. I remember glancing at the manuscript in the old Syndicate Room, and being both dazzled and baffled by something so far outside my experience. Our trouble was that, having published Frank Kendon's poets and Christopher Fry's first play, we had decided that we would no longer dabble in the odd work of literature when it took our fancy. So we said no: as a matter of policy we now didn't publish fiction, poetry or drama. Oxford on the other hand had a poetry list.

The significance of that little episode is that Philip was in touch with all the coming people, got in first and was offered the first work of the future Nobel Laureate. As it turned out, Soyinka later spent a year in Cambridge, and I got to know him a little, and he gave us his *Myth, Literature and the African World* – currently in paperback.

With *A Dance*, I could, if I had thought of it and stretched a point, have used the device under which we did actually publish African fiction – in the form of 'readers' for African schools. Readers were little, limp-bound books, bought in class sets and handed round the class to encourage private reading of texts which were long enough to count as a book but not so long as to be discouraging. For English schools I produced readers in French on the related argument. In Africa it was a question of getting the children to read fairly substantial texts in the second language, perhaps in schooltime, given that many homes had no light to read by after sundown; and it quickly became clear that a text with an African setting, especially by an African author, had an authenticity and a potential interest which an English set text could not.

I was especially against taking a classic text, abridging it, reducing the vocabulary and simplifying the structures, since this removed most of the features which made the work worth reading. A lot of that went on, and was justified by the language-teaching theory which I was engaging with in ELT. Its ancestors were C.K. Ogden and I. A. Richards, who had in Basic English reduced the vocabulary to 850 words and the grammar to a few structures, and found they could still write what they wanted to write. My own reaction was to wonder what happened when students met their 851st word? Delight, I hoped. And what happened when they opened Shakespeare? Ah, *but*, the argument went, Shakespeare was very English, at best European – total cultural difference, you know – all that English history, all those references to classical mythology – really only for inheritors of the tradition. And then, the language: all that imagery, and the archaic forms... I parody only a little: there was a serious argument about cultural differences and how far they were bridgeable. Had African and Asian readers ever seen a daffodil, or experienced the Northern seasons: what would they make of Wordsworth and Keats and Tennyson?

I am glad to say that I had all this blown up for me, and in an exemplary way, mostly by African schoolchildren when I went there in 1961. I can't remember now when I first read *Things Fall Apart*: now that

I read it again I realise that, as if effortlessly, it demolishes the reverse argument. Here, in his 'second' language, my language, a writer of genius conveys to English readers – to any readers – in one quite short book and by what used to be called the 'direct' method, the core values, the ways of thought and speech, the habits and customs of his historic culture, showing it entire – an actual organic community, the remembered society of Achebe's parents and grandparents, still largely available to him, and captured in the book just at the moment when the Western world moved in and convulsed it. You don't need to have been to Nigeria, or to know anything about it, and yet this completely different set of ways of being in the world and among one's own people comes across as clear, natural and worthy of respect. It can be done, by a writer of genius, and after the event it looks simple. It's what writers are for.

Our little readers were by Nigerian, Ghanaian and Sierra Leonean authors: some titles (*Kossoh Town Boy*) and some authors (Cyprian Ekwensi, Wellesley Cole) stick in my memory. They had illustrations by African artists. They served the purpose well, and I can imagine them being looked at appreciatively by a historian.

I think our first book at the tertiary level by an African author was a geography of Ghana by E.A. Boateng. At first he used the 'E' – for Ernest; but as time went by he used the 'A' – for Amano, and one understood why. I met him when I went to Ghana, and he asked me to dinner with his family. Some years later I asked him how things were going in Ghana. 'Alas, poor country', he said, 'Almost afraid to know itself.'

At the secondary level we were publishing a fair amount, across the curriculum. I got my revenge on Lewis Harmer, the Professor of French, by publishing a French course for Anglophone African schools. This was a rational thing to do: there were ex-French colonies – or about to be ex-French – neighbouring the about-to-be ex-English ones, and, without an African language in common, they needed to communicate. The author happened to be an experienced and competent English woman teacher. The concept was more than Harmer could tolerate, since he could hardly bear to have even the French interfering with their language, and when the project came to the Syndicate he started to argue against it. I talked him down. I went on later to produce editions of the classical African texts in French – Camara Laye's *L'Enfant noir* and Birago Diop's *Contes choisis*, and Abiola Irele's edition of poems by Senghor. There was also a pioneering book on African literature in French by Joyce Hutchinson. These were instances of schoolbook publishing and regional-market publishing transforming into something of general cultural importance.

The whole African publishing programme began to take off in 1960, the year of Nigerian independence. Until then we had been publishing in a modest way for secondary schools and were way behind the other major publishers. But now Philip was able to use his connections to present a programme of general books marking the event and making our presence visible.

So we published in 1960 personal statements by the three regional political leaders: an autobiography by Awolowo, another by the Northern Muslim leader Ahmadu Bello, and a collection of leading articles and speeches by Nnamdi Azikiwe. Zik was a charismatic figure, later to become President of the Federation. He was in London at one point, and I called on him in his hotel to talk about the book. He was very tall and handsome, dressed in flowing traditional style, confident and charming. I was very careful to call him Sir. He had edited a very independent-minded newspaper in colonial days, no doubt deplored by the colonial administrators being given a hard time by him; and a good part of the book reproduced his leaders. These were in a characteristic high-stepping rhetorical and figurative style, which had gone down well with the original audience, who read him, loved him and cheered him on, but I didn't want stuffy English readers to mock it as some colonial bounder getting above himself and making free with the language ('So unlike *The Times*'). So I did a very delicate editorial job on his book and Awo's (Bello's was very sober, and I suspect it had been written for him, or rewritten).

There was an interesting cultural issue here: the first book by a West African writer which made a stir in England was *The Palm-Wine Drinkard* (1952), by Amos Tutuola. It was written in a sort of baroque style which could allow superior people to mock it as infantile or barbaric or pretentious. I think it revealed something essential – vigorous or playful, even from Dr Johnson's slightly doubtful point of view – 'metaphysical' in West African writing. Soyinka's *Dance* had a related streak in it.

Well, our books came out together on time, and made the right kind of impression.

The other book which has remained in my mind is *Art in Nigeria, 1960*, by Ulli Beier, published in collaboration with the Nigerian Ministry of Home Affairs, designed by Beier's friend the artist and photographer Mick Pilcher and printed by Lund Humphries (very Bauhaus). It introduced to a general and Western public modern artists like Ben Enwonwu, standing between the traditional culture and the modern international styles, but it also represented the vernacular arts as still vital, even including local sign-painters. Beier went on to produce other books for the Press, including collections of African writing for schools, but most notably *African Mud Sculpture* in 1963 and *The Return of the Gods: The Sacred Art of Susanne Wenger* in 1973. (When I presented the last to the Syndicate, the Chairman said 'Is this about some *silly tribe*?' 'No, sir', I said.)

These were important books for me, not just because one had the pleasant shock of recognising the vitality and quality of the art-works, but because they led into the culture, which at first seemed startlingly different, and then, thanks to Ulli, became comprehensible and provoked thoughts about old European vernacular styles and popular cultures. I try to sketch this below. At this point it is sensible to say something about Beier, who was one of the most extraordinary men I have ever met.

He told me some of his story, and I picked up a certain amount from others. He was German-Jewish, born in Berlin in I guess the late 1920s. His family got out and went to Israel, or rather Palestine, as it was under British administration. After the War he wanted to come to England, but had difficulty under the immigration regulations, and spent some time working in a circus as a bareback rider.[1] He came to England as a student, and found himself doing phonetics at University College London. With that qualification he went out to Ibadan as lecturer in the language department. There he 'went bush', as the colonialist expression then was – that is to say, he lived in the town and not in the university's reserved and very modern accommodation meant for whites, ate local food, dressed down and made friends with local people, especially intellectuals and artists. He got to know everyone who counted, who was doing interesting work. So, of course, did Philip Harris – but from his Europeanised base. Ulli gave encouragement, set up Mbari, a sort of club and intellectual meeting-place where writers and artists and musicians could get together, and where a kind of group-ethos emerged. He was a tireless intermediary, quite selfless in that he did not have wares of his own to sell, other than his spokesmanship itself. He married Susanne Wenger, an Austrian artist,

---

[1] I think I remember correctly. I tend to confuse him with another extraordinary Jewish Africanist, Simha Arom, whom I met much later. Simha also started in Israel, was a violinist, leading a symphony orchestra. In the 1967 War he was wounded in his bowing-arm, so had to take up the horn, and went on playing in the same orchestra. Emigrating to France, he became a musicologist specialising in African traditional musics. He used the development of the stereophonic recorder to tape, in performance in African locations, the independent voices in African musics which were both polyphonic and polyrhythmical, but not notated. Sandy Goehr introduced him to the Press, and we published the English translation of his foundational work.

who carried his approach even further by being accepted as the priestess (if that is the word) of a Yoruba cult, and re-created and furnished with her own work the impressive shrines in the Oshun grove, which produced a revival of the local religious practices. She and Ulli routed simple clichés about African art: that it had been entirely traditional and local (therefore good, if 'primitive'); that the introduction of Christianity had fatally damaged it and produced bad derivative art (but some of it was good); and that African artists were now condemned to follow European art at a distance, and must therefore be derivative and second-rate. The true situation was more complex: there were class and commercial factors which had been ignored, there were older external influences (from Portugal, for instance). In fact the modern African situation escaped that sort of black-and-white summary: its persistent African-ness would prevent it being merely derivative. It was the case, moreover, that the traditional arts were extraordinarily complex and vital: for instance, *African Mud Sculpture* examined the powerful and often comic images which used a medium which was bound to disintegrate, and where the whole point was the act of making – the creation itself – a very 'modernist' notion, Westerners might think.

From time to time Ulli would come to England, and I enjoyed meeting him and talking to him. Those were the days when in London you wore a dark suit, carried a rolled umbrella and a briefcase, and even wore a bowler hat. To see Ulli loping out of this sombre crowd in his colourful safari-shirt and cotton trousers, with his bare head and brown face, lifted the heart. After some years he found he had done what he could in Africa, and went off to Papua New Guinea to repeat the process. He was a hero.

The books marking Nigerian Independence made a stir both locally and in the West. 1960 was also the year in which the *Journal of African History* started publication. This was all Philip's initiative: he knew the English Africanist historians, notably Fage and Oliver, and the leading African, K. Onwuka Dike, who became Vice-Chancellor of the University of Ibadan. He also knew the administrators and, on the other hand, the intellectuals, artists and writers whom Ulli had got together. The result was that Cambridge became a leading publisher, not in terms of absolute turnover – though it became large enough to be important – but in terms of influence and prestige. It made sense that when in September 1961 I made my first real editorial visit, it was to Africa, and I did it with Philip.

It lasted nine weeks, which was a bit crazy: when I got back I came out in boils. The basic plan was that Philip would guide me around West Africa, and we would then go together to East Africa to see whether the territory, about to see Independence, offered the same scope as the West. So we travelled to Ghana, and then Nigeria, driving right up from Lagos to Ibadan to Jos to Kano, where we took off for Johannesburg (you couldn't then go straight from West to East). After a couple of days with our agents in South Africa (a dreary experience after the intoxication of Independence in the West), we flew to Entebbe for Lusaka, then travelled round Uganda, Kenya, Tanganyika and Zanzibar by car and local plane – nice old Dakotas, familiar from wartime, comfortable and safe but not pressurised. We were both deaf on landing in Zanzibar. But they could land on grass airstrips, and I remember coming down with the Mountains of the Moon and the lakes in the background in Uganda, with giraffe and elephants standing at the edge and watching patiently. We went to schools, ministries, universities and libraries to register the Press's interest, driving some thousands of miles over mostly laterite roads (that is to say, red-dirt roads, which rose up in a cloud behind us. It also penetrated into the car itself. I remember opening my case in Northern Nigeria and finding my clothes all red.) In all this Philip was the planner, guide, intermediary – and usually the driver.

At the start, from London I flew to Accra, and remember the shock of emerging from the plane to feel as if embraced, swallowed, by a great warm wet bear. One got used to that: I also enjoyed swimming on the beautiful beaches in Ghana and Tanganyika, by way of an hour or two off. I remember crossing the Niger on a ferry, also calling at Michael Cardew's pottery at Abuja and buying a tiny pot by Ladi Kwali. Once, as we were driving through the forest a goat wandered into the road in front of us. We had to hit it, or go off the road, and it went up into the air, came down and seemed to wander off.

Otherwise it was all work. We came back with some books and some large series-proposals: in particular Philip set up the *Journal of Modern African Studies* and the *Cambridge History of Africa*.

One aspect of my travelling, now and later in Asia and Australia, was to meet members of the Leavis diaspora – pupils and colleagues of his who had felt they would never get over the opposition in England, and did useful teaching in Commonwealth countries. So in Lagos I found Robin Mayhead, in Uganda Geoffrey Walton.

Robin had taught in Colombo before going to Africa. He was a gentle, very intelligent man, also a mother-dominated homosexual who had that extra reason for getting out. Both in Colombo and in Lagos, he had a 'boy' in the old colonial sense of the term as well as in Robin's sense. They cared for him, and he taught them to read and write. He came back to the

UK later, had a post in Stirling, was blackmailed by a confidence-trickster, became alcoholic and died young. Together we set up a series called British Authors, which was meant primarily for students doing an English course outside Britain, especially in the Commonwealth. As was now my habit, I got him to introduce the series itself with a general or 'way in' book, *Understanding Literature* (1965), which gently put aside the hitherto-perceived obstacles or cultural impediments, and also made the case for literary study in countries where the pressure to acquire a paper qualification simply in order to enter a profession and make a salary might provoke the question 'What is the point of doing literature?' (Almost everywhere, you might now think.)

The series went on for a good many years and became a straightforward introduction for students anywhere, since it became clear to me that the so-called cultural barrier faced by the overseas student and as pressed by educationists and language-theorists was only a special case or intensification of the problems of *all* students once tertiary education ceased to be the preserve of a small and highly prepared group. Robin himself did Keats and a good book on Walter Scott. Some of the books which started in the series are still in print: for instance, Jacques Berthoud's *Joseph Conrad*. Jacques later became Professor at York, where he joined the austere R. T. Jones ('Robert Tudor Jones', Leavis explained to me: he approved of him and taught alongside him as Visiting Professor), who did George Eliot. Jacques had been one of a group in South Africa, colleagues or pupils of a remarkable woman teacher at Natal, Christina van Heyningen – the local equivalent of Leavis. The group was far too liberal for the government, caused trouble and had to break up and emigrate: I pursued them as possible authors in Canada and Australia as well as England. I quote Jacques' letter about this group in Chapter 13.

This was a series at tertiary level, and in theory I was supposed to be hunting for schoolbooks. As I said earlier, I never confined myself; the beauty of my position was that I could get books in all areas, even the sciences at school level. I was also embarked on my Leavisite crusade: there were authors out here whom Ian Parsons of Chatto, back there in London, would not get if I got in first, and there was also the more insubstantial something I was feeling my way towards, and which I understand better now – if I am not doing what we all tend to do in retrospect, making a flattering sense of long-past fumblings.

When I started to write this I meant just to record the sort of facts which might otherwise be lost – people's names and contributions, organisational matters, forgotten books and so on. I find that remembering one sort of thing brings back other sorts: also that one is not just passing on one's own sense of how it was, but now bringing up to the surface, Proust-like, a deeper sense which was not consciously held at the time but now seems the important thing. I always knew that going to Africa was important for me, and this was partly because Philip and I, driving over great stretches of forest and bush, talked to each other about what we were doing. Similarly at night in some former government rest-house, with no-one else there, we continued to talk over our very colonial dinner and breakfast. I must go into the policies we constructed, for ourselves and for the Press, because they kept me active for the next twenty-five years. I do this later, in Chapter 10.

But that isn't all: there was a set of things which presented themselves to me, which I took in as momentary impressions, and which have remained with me. It is in writing this that I make sense of them. Of course, I may be manufacturing it, or distorting it, or blowing it up into something more significant.

It started in the schools of West Africa. Some of them were the best schools I have ever been in, and especially Achimota and Mfantsipim. These were big and relatively old boarding schools in Ghana, and one was run by Methodist missionaries, though I saw no sign of evangelising. They were highly selective, so taught the absolute cream of the age-group. I suppose they were fee-paying: I forget. The upshot is that these very intelligent young people were intensely if rather narrowly committed: one teacher told me he only had trouble when he was perceived to stray from the syllabus. My visual memory is of standing at the edge of the big compound in one of them. There were low buildings round this ample square, overhung with trees, and with a well in the middle (or have I imported a symbolism?). It was break-time, and the handsome and graceful young people lingered peacefully about the well, looking, with their big dark eyes, like so many antelope at a watering-place.

I attended some English lessons, with my doctrinal preoccupations set to click into place, and had some valuable shocks. In one school, the children, aged, I guess, about 11 or 12, and mainly from country communities, were being taught about Chaucer. I was surprised, and puristically shocked that he was being taught in modern English – forgetting that at the same age in England this would also be true, supposing that Chaucer was so much as mentioned. The teacher began to read the tale: it was one of the 'youth and eld' tales, perhaps the Miller's, suitably bowdlerised, I suppose, and the choice caused me further surprise. But the teacher had said no more than that a rich, old and ugly man had married a pretty and lively young girl and watched over her jealously, and the whole class roared with laughter. The response was immediate and genuine, more whole-hearted, quicker and sharper than a modern English audience of the same age would feel. It must have been what Chaucer wanted to provoke and then refine, and was closer to his ideal audience-reaction than anything he would now get in his own country. A pattern of active, socially endorsed attitudes had been engaged: the two cultures bent towards each other.

In another school they were doing Shakespeare, reading aloud and taking the parts. I seem to remember that it was out of doors. They were doing *The Merchant of Venice*. Here was my cultural test-case, as it had seemed. I was startled to see how well it went: in particular the boy who was Shylock did it with a wild bravado, throwing himself about, acting with his whole body, loving it. 'A part to tear a cat in' suddenly had meaning; he was doing that. None of your Method-inspired modern 'realism' – the realism of inhibited moderns; this was what it might have been like to watch the original performance in 1605. Nor was there any modern sense of racialist complications: here was a bold bad man of the sort one is openly compelled by, forced to sympathise with. I didn't at this moment ask myself 'What century am I in?' but the thought was hovering near.

It came closer in Nairobi, a place which depressed me in its heartless modernity. I was standing looking at the new high-rise buildings and the straight broad streets when, scuttling towards me, as if from under a stone, there appeared a horrifying vision: a crippled African beggar with tiny wasted legs flying up about his ears, and propelling himself along with his long arms like oars; he was on a little trolley which you only saw as he went by. 'Where have I seen that before?' I thought. 'Oh, yes, in Breughel or Bosch, the Northern sixteenth century – lots of them then.'

What is also in my mind is that I have two persistent related images which have stayed with me for many years, and if I ask what it is I remember, or rather why these images have remained, I find myself giving them a related meaning.

What they have in common is that on both occasions I was being driven somewhere, looked idly out of the car-window, saw something quite briefly and registered it, my eye being like an open shutter which let something into my mind, and then closed on it as an image.

The first time was during my military service in Austria. I had to go to the Jugoslav border and take custody of a Jugoslav deserter, who had crossed over and given himself up. I was given a revolver (no ammunition, of course) as a badge of office, and went off in one of our trucks, driven by a local. On the way we went through a village, and there on the green (as we would say in my village here) was a fine old Gasthaus, in front of it one of those strange tall maypole-like things they had, with its wreath. Under the pole was a group of musicians in their green hats, Lederhosen, white stockings and clumpy shoes. It was a wind-ensemble; they were playing something folky, a dance. I caught enough to think 'Good Lord, it's like Mozart – the great Serenade.'

My idea of Mozart, to that point, was a cliché-ridden one, all white-powdered wigs and satin breeches and ladies with beauty-spots; a minuet for me was a courtly dance. But no, I suddenly grasped it started as a country dance, and in much of his music Mozart was closer to his folk origins than, say, Vaughan Williams to his. He didn't have to try to recover anything: he had been born into it and only had to go down the street, look and listen.

So I could have said 'What century am I in?' that time too. All the more so, in that when I got that poor deserter – looking remarkably like an unsuccessful variant of the good soldier Schweyk, hung about with hand-grenades and in a uniform that looked like 1914–18 – when I got him back to Graz, I asked, somewhat innocently, what would happen to him. 'Oh, he will be interrogated and then sent back over the border', was the reply. 'And what will happen then?' 'He will be shot, probably.' I had lived through the War and was now involved in its tortuous aftermath. I took the reply calmly. What century, indeed: *our* Hundred Years' War.

So I didn't go to Africa as representative of a superior civilization: just one that is further down the road – not altogether a good road. My related second memory is this time of being driven in a pleasant modern taxi by a cheerful Ghanaian driver. I think it was back from Cape Coast to Accra in strong afternoon sunshine. Over to one side was the fishing village we were passing, green, gold and brown, under palms. It was as if turned away from the road, standing quietly in the sun, no movement visible, looking peaceful and part of a way of life that had not yet changed: houses that had been built that way for generations, the home of a settled people. What century is this? looked for a moment as if it could be answered by, What sort of question is that? In this moment all centuries were the same.

What I am struggling towards is something like an unexpected sense of community with the apparent other. I could have looked at Africa and seen all the differences: all that distance away, the tropical conditions, the landforms, the vegetation, the colour-difference, an apparently diametrical oppositeness. And this difference is fortified and compounded by saying, as one now does, this is a 'developing' world, while we are 'developed' people.

But what was coming through to me was more like a set of unexpected reminders: the line of 'development' is the line we have been on, and still are. But I won't continue that figure, because I don't want the derogatory sense of other peoples' backwardness, except in the form of reminders of where we have been ourselves. The children who laughed at Chaucer were in a specific respect culturally predisposed towards him; something we have lost. The boy who loved throwing himself into Shylock gave me a sudden glimpse of something in my people's past. The crippled beggar reminded me of images of past European poverty. My Jugoslav deserter had first given me a sort of fast-forward from Mozart's Austria to that of 1949; he had also given me a fast-backward-and-forward through the horrors of Balkan history, of European wars being fought today. My Ghanaian fishing-village offered a vision of the community life of African agrarian societies, then as now under threat, and to be replaced by some desperately accelerated race towards 'development'.

So when I re-read Achebe's *Things Fall Apart* I was made aware of the things I had seen, and I could say 'This was *their* organic community, only two generations back; I have been in contact with it, it existed there and is still not quite lost: it reminds me of ours, Ulli Beier served it.' The organic community presented by Denys Thompson might be a simplification for modern English beginners, and both good and bad for that reason, but it pointed to something real which impatient modernisers want to deny. I had seen it.

Nor is this entirely by the way: I can come back to the matters in hand by pointing out that in 1959 the Press had published Snow's Rede Lecture *The Two Cultures and the Scientific Revolution*, which sold hundreds of thousands of copies, and was received by many as wisdom. It seemed to be saying that important modernist writers were hostile to progressive views like Snow's, and (though there is no logic in this) it seemed to be because they were ignorant of science. If Snow had been saying merely that a modern education should leave everyone with useful general knowledge about the sciences which now determine a great deal of modern life, one would say that was no more than a truism. But Snow's logical leaps, or rather lapses, were that all scientists thought alike (so, thinking to define a culture, he defined a herd) and if they applied their uniform progressive thinking to the problems of the undeveloped world they would develop it more rapidly, and if we didn't do it, the Russians (who were showing the way, he thought) would, and we had to find the money, because there wasn't much time. The answer to poverty was industrialisation. Hadn't we shown it? Oh yes, one might think: try Rotherham in the 1980s and after, and ask the Asians who moved into Bolton and found that the scientific revolution, in ways which Snow failed to predict, had eliminated the industry they had migrated so infinitely far to work in.

Conversely, as if to make up, in 1963 the Press reissued *Scrutiny*, and I have to give that a separate chapter (Chapter 12).

The politics of my working with Philip were no doubt clearer to him than to me in 1961. He was employed and controlled from Bentley House, the headquarters of the world sales organisation. There was a head of overseas sales, Joan Bunting, a slightly prickly but highly competent person. Philip was not an editor, but in building up Cambridge's profile and sales in his territory, he was acting more and more like an editor, and sending to Cambridge, through me, for acceptance by the Syndicate, what looked more and more like a West African list. My visit meant that I could present proposals as partly or really mine, but he was the power, and when we went on to East Africa together we were acting to increase the Press's markets as well as its output. It seemed acceptable at first, but it detached Philip, made him seem more independent, perhaps out of control – at any rate not under the Bentley House thumb. It also associated me with him, as an editor who was interfering in sales and marketing matters. I think we began to appear like a pair of loose cannon.

At some point – I forget the date – Philip came back to England, and to Cambridge as another Education Secretary, and we became to all intents the Cambridge editorial team, covering everything but the sciences. We had worked out together a policy and a method and were deliberately setting out to expand the Press's publishing. As our title suggested, we departed from the schoolbook base, but I had never confined myself to it, and we both now started to commission books in entirely new subjects. We were viewed with alarm, especially by Colin Eccleshare, who wanted to rein us in. This takes me into the Secretaryship of Dick David, from 1963, and I give a chapter to that time (Chapter 9). Here I will simply complete the Philip Harris story.

He had left the Ibadan Office to a successor. As Independence progressed in Nigeria, things really did fall apart. The Biafran War killed Christopher Okigbo, a talented poet who had been Philip's assistant, but used the post to further the Biafran cause rather than sell Cambridge books; and as time went by it became progressively more difficult to work the market. The staff had to be Nigerianised – fair enough – but it also became impossible to get bills paid, or to take the money out of the country. The other publishers who were more deeply involved than we were faced a crisis – it almost broke Longman's – and there was a big shake-out. In Geoffrey Cass's time the operation was wound right down.

But the advantage of being a university press was that we also published in African studies at the higher level, and the books sold well outside Africa at that period. So something was rescued: and also we had built up a body of editorial experience which was transferable, and a set of interests which were generalisable or interconnected.

By that I mean, to take one instance, that when Jack Goody offered a book of studies called *Literacy in Traditional Societies* (1968) with a crucial chapter called 'The Consequences of Literacy' by himself and Ian Watt (they were friends and both Fellows of St John's), I felt a link with my own interests. Watt had written a well-known book on the beginnings of the English novel – published by Chatto, of course, in 1957 – a book which some thought dependent on Q.D. Leavis's, if only because they both grasped that the novel was the product of a particular moment in a changing society. The link was stronger because I also knew and liked, and used as referees, the Lienhardt brothers, one of whom, Godfrey, had read Part I English under Leavis and then gone on to Part II Anthropology and a post at Oxford. The Goody–Watt volume opened out in several directions: it was the virtual foundation of the Press's remarkable list in literacy studies; it also formed part of a determined effort in social anthropology and sociology. It also linked back with the African list: so for example I had a particular interest in *An African Popular Literature: A Study of Onitsha Market Pamphlets* by Emmanuel Obiechina, followed by Obiechina's *Culture, Tradition and Society in the West African Novel*. Obiechina had been a pupil of Jack's. His book, published in 1975, was the fourteenth volume in the African Studies Series. The Onitsha pamphlets were an ephemeral popular literature – the equivalent of our old chapbooks – rescued from oblivion. They also have the wild naturalness one felt in Soyinka, in Zik's editorials and the *Drinkard*.

Philip left the Press in the mid 1960s. His marriage was in difficulties; but also he was the main object of hostility from Bentley House. I was made aware of this when one day, quite unexpectedly, he and I were both called into Dick David's office and given a formal telling-off. I didn't know what it was all about: I only gathered that we had got above ourselves and it wouldn't do. We just listened, and left. I think Dick felt he had to do it to placate Colin: I go into all this later. I was puzzled and upset: there seemed no logic in it. We were the people who were turning the Press into a successful, modern academic publisher, weren't we? But Philip understood the absence of logic, and took it as a hint.

He went first of all to London, to head a new organisation called the BDC (Book Development Council), set up by the Publishers Association with help from government. It seemed an escape from antipathies at the Press, and was a job tailor-made for him. But to Philip's horror, as Colin moved up the hierarchy of the Publishers Association, he became ex officio Chairman of the BDC and was able to go on harassing Philip. He had a breakdown, left England for Australia to run Pitman's office there, married again, had a heart attack and died.

Before he left the Press he and I did one more epic tour together, of the Far East, the territory then administered for the Press by the Donald Moore agency in Singapore, with offices in Hong Kong, Manila and Tokyo. This was in autumn 1964. By this time we were not so much interested in schools, and were mainly visiting universities. I had set up the *History of China* and wanted to contact contributors. Denis Enright was Professor of English at Singapore, and introduced me to Norman Sherry, so that I came back with *Conrad's Eastern World* in my bag. We went to Kuala Lumpur, to Borneo, and, on the way to Hong Kong, to Manila – easily the most awful place I ever visited. My key recollection is of two notices at reception desks, one requiring you to hand in your gun before entering, the other telling you not to throw your cigar butts into the pond because it killed the fish.

In Singapore Donald's courteous staff, a sympathetic hunchback called Raymond Li and Goh Kee Seeah, took us out one evening, mostly to have 'steamboat' (a rice dish) at the air-terminal restaurant, but with two not very cheerful young Englishwomen, whose function, I think, may have been to provide further entertainment at the end of the evening, though we did not test the theory. By the time we reached Hong Kong it was as easy to go on Eastward as to come back the other way, so we went round the world via Honolulu and San Francisco to New York, where we attended a sales conference in a state of severe jetlag.

The visit did not have the same effect on me as Africa had had. The Nanyang (South Seas) Chinese who in all these territories occupied the administrative posts and did most of the trading were courteous and intelligent. They were second- and third-generation English-speakers, with a formidable Westernised surface, hiding, I hoped, a deep Chinese cultural allegiance. But they were in their own style colonialist: they had got there before we did and were as impenetrable as the English in their manner. As for the places I saw, they were romantic in a literary way. I had produced Runciman's *White Rajahs* in 1960, and read Alfred Russell Wallace's *Malay Archipelago*. And there in Singapore was the Raffles Hotel, still, and the waterfront was not yet fully modernised. In Jesselton in North Borneo I had the whole Conrad experience, standing on the ancient waterfront, the godowns looking just like the photographs in the books about Conrad, watching the violet light at nightfall and smelling the spices that hung in the warm air. In Kuching I saw a longhouse or two on the way to a school. But it was literary tourist stuff, really, merely picturesque. It taught me nothing.

After these editorial visits I always wrote a formal report to the Secretary, with copies to the sales officers, listing places visited, people seen, books acquired, possibilities for the future, so that it did not seem like junketing, but a natural part of an expansive publishing policy. But, as I have indicated, it was not well received, and I have to go more fully into the reasons for this. We had entered the new age post-1963, and Dick David's Secretaryship.

CHAPTER 9

Dick David as Secretary

Dick died in 1993, having retired from the Press in 1974. In 1994 there was published a memorial volume of reminiscences by his family, friends and colleagues. I wrote two chapters in it. What follows is an amplified version of the main chapter, in which I add some things which could not be published then. I am also able now to make use of Trevor Gardner's memoirs, published just after his death in 1997, which show that, as University Treasurer and Syndic, Gardner was a crucially important actor in the drama of the years 1969–72.

The Press which Dick joined in 1936 as Assistant Secretary to the Syndics was not substantially different from the Press of 1951, when I joined with the same title. He had an important role in the process which turned it from what it was into what it is. But as in all profound dramas, the hero is not only an actor, one who does things: he is also acted upon by forces which have been building up for years, discharge themselves through him and in so doing prove his true nature.

To explain what happened in the 1960s and after, I have to go back a long way in time, to the days in which people joined a firm at 15 and worked there for fifty years or more; so folk memories were long, and the pace of change was slow. I write now, well after 2000, as someone who worked with Dick from 1951 until his retirement and, with him, went through the storms of the late 1960s which followed his becoming Secretary in 1963, and which led to his resigning the Secretaryship in 1970. A painful aspect of this is that at first he and I were in conflict, and I must account for this. At the time I had little grasp of what was going on; it was something I had to find my way through – and I guess this was true of him too: I think he lost his way seriously more than once, but found it heroically in the end.

If now I have a clearer sense of the forces at work, it is because I have had more than thirty years to think about it, and also because for the quatercentenary of the Press in 1984 I found myself writing its history, and at the last years of the story thinking, 'Ah, now I see: if only we had realised then …' So a page or so of history is necessary.

The first modern phase of the Press began in the 1890s. During the nineteenth century it was primarily a large printing business in Cambridge, with a special line in Bibles and Prayerbooks. It did also print and publish a small number of learned books undertaken by the Press Syndicate in its role as scholarly publisher; but if you were the University Printer you would think of that as a minor sideline. There was in London a small office initially called the Warehouse, and the name sufficiently indicated its role: the Bibles went there for distribution, and so did the books. The important person was in Cambridge: the University Printer.

The great John Clay, appointed University Printer to rescue the business in the 1850s, also set up the London Warehouse in 1873, and in 1874 he took on the additional, unpaid role of Secretary to the Syndics – which meant that he, rather than as hitherto the Chairman, conducted the correspondence: about the printing business in the main, but also about the growing publishing programme. The most important thing about Clay's position was that he held all these roles himself, and so was in modern terms a Chief Executive. He was also a Partner in the whole business: he, or the Clay family, had invested in it, and so he looked across the table at the Syndics as their equal, not their servant, and he knew about the business in a way that they couldn't. They were academics, delegated by the University to supervise for a year or two the operations of the Press and to represent the University's interest in its conduct and its role in the learned world, but they could not, in that limited term of office, learn much about its detailed running.

That position changed: first of all when the Syndics in 1891 appointed R.T. Wright, one of their own number, to be their Secretary, and recognised this as a permanent, salaried office – a University office. In doing so, they were undoubtedly doing two other things as well: reducing the power of the other member of the Partnership, Clay, by setting up a formal counter-role through which their interest could be set against his if necessary; and declaring that the publishing business must now be seen as an identifiable concern which needed to be fostered and led, and was not to be taken as a mere tributary supplying the Printing House with a little work and the Warehouse with an initially small flow of titles which, being mostly scholarly books, were very hard to sell. The addition at much the same time of schoolbooks and edited texts meant for prescription in public examinations produced a substantial change in the rate of publication and its nature, as well as the financial results.

The Secretary was the Syndics' controlling instrument and mouthpiece. The other thing they did, unwittingly, was to store up trouble for the distant future by not fully defining the constitutional relationship between the now distinct roles of Printer and Secretary (I have pointed out that Clay too had at an earlier point acquired the title of Secretary, and this confusion was symptomatic of a messy situation).

The Press went on evolving between then and 1936, but slowly and not radically. The forces set up in 1891 were not obvious, and not felt at all by most people. Between the two dates the main developments were the end of the Partnership itself, the steady growth of the publishing business, and the consequent relative decline in importance of printing, so that post-1945 – I can't give a date, but I would place it in the late 1950s or actually in Dick's early years as Secretary – the publishing turnover became the larger. I guess that my own activity as expansionist and leader of a team of specialist editors had an effect on this: certainly it speeded it and made it decisive.

At the end of the Partnership, in 1916, the University Printer had changed his status, becoming, like the Secretary, the Syndics' appointment and hence their other principal servant. It was clear what his function was: he ran the Printing House, and did so without much interference (or control). It was still not made clear what the Secretary's functions included: he ran the publishing business, and in some general sense advised the Syndicate on the whole printing/publishing operation. Was he therefore the Printer's superior, if only in the last resort? The issue was not brought into the open. When things were going well it was not a problem.

Indeed in Roberts's time as Secretary the issue could be said to have been silently decided: Roberts claimed to have found and to all intents appointed Walter Lewis as Printer; and Lewis, though he was in intimate control of the Printing House and in some sense was setting the whole tone of the Press by making it an outstanding practitioner of the Monotype process and typographical design, had no great interest in or feeling for the other side of the business. As long as he was not interfered with in his own sphere, he largely ignored the other – except as a source of work, and of interesting design problems.

The other thing which happened during the first half of the twentieth century was the transformation of the Warehouse. Clay had managed it at first by going up to London once a fortnight and looking at the ledgers. As the business grew, he appointed a son as Manager. It became the London Office of the Press: no longer just a warehouse, but the place where the accounts of the whole publishing business were kept, the stock was held and controlled, the binding was organised, the advertising designed and placed, the travellers had their headquarters, the increasingly large overseas sales were administered. It became a power-centre, partly because it did the practical or hard-nosed parts of the whole publishing operation as it was then conceived. It was in the world in a way that Cambridge was not, for London was then inescapably the centre of the trading and communications network (which in those days meant the shipping and railway systems) – and for that matter the intellectual and political world of Britain and its Empire.

All this was summed up and made manifest in 1939 when the London Office moved to its new building, Bentley House, 200 Euston Road, London NW 1 – as it said in the imprint on the verso of all title-pages. So this, it must have seemed, was where Cambridge publishing took place. And Bentley House became, politically speaking, the seat of an empire, or at least the castle of a barony. Given that it was a good 50 miles from Cambridge, was large, more or less self-contained, employed almost as many people as the Printing House, and was exercising clear and useful functions, it became an Us, as distinct from a distant and mysterious Them in Cambridge. Very long-serving members of staff could in the 1930s or even the 1940s remember the indignity of being the Warehouse, where one was told what to do by grandees in Cambridge. Now all was changed; but there was a sort of folk-memory of oppression.

What made it all right now was the building itself, the sense of role, the fact that the London Manager was, since R.J.L. Kingsford's day, visibly an important person. It was Kingsford who got Bentley House designed and built; he carried on as London Manager during the Second War, becoming also an important President of the Publishers Association, having to organise the allocation of rationed paper and the insurance and replacement of bombed stocks for the whole English trade. When in 1948 he succeeded S.C. Roberts as Secretary and moved to Cambridge, it was possible to feel that an important pattern had been set up: the Manager would become Secretary. If London was the place where the real work was done, when you left London to head the whole enterprise you were well versed in the business and would treat Bentley House with proper respect as the sharp end.

Here was another political issue waiting to crystallise, alongside the one about the Secretary's relationship with the Printer. One basic trouble was that publishing seemed to be something done in Bentley House, while printing was done in the Printing House. What, then, was done by the third entity, always referred to as 'the Syndics'? It was possible at the low and practical level to think that 'the Syndics' provided handicaps, in the form of unsellable books (did they have any idea how unsellable they were?) and interference, compounded by a snobbish academic superiority which still looked down on the Warehouse – or so it was felt.

So much for the background. The Cambridge Office, the Secretary's Office of the Press, which Dick joined in 1936, was the tiny group of six or seven people I have already described: in botanical terms a sort of epiphyte, lodged in the complex of buildings which was the old Press, going back from the Pitt Building almost to the Cam. The Secretary's Building was the little two-storey red-brick one backing on to Mill Lane, with an aerial bridge linking it to the Pitt Building on one side; on the other was that baize door at ground level which opened on to the noisy otherworld of the bindery. Most of the ground floor was occupied by the Syndicate Room, with its hollow square of tables round which the Syndics sat, and where I was interviewed for my job.

In the upper floor, the Secretary had a large office and the Assistant Secretaries smaller ones. For a long time there were two Assistant Secretaries. One, Frank Kendon, was a fixture in Cambridge, and the nearest thing to an editor that the Press could boast. The other, the junior, was understood to be learning the job in Cambridge, and would in due course go to London. There was also the Education Secretary, who looked after schoolbooks. So there was this group of four officers and gentlemen in Cambridge, served by an equally tiny group of secretarial staff (also, at first, men). The whole entity was not just epiphytic, but parasitic in that the printing staff performed for it all sorts of functions now thought to be the publisher's affair: specifically design, costing, subediting, progress-chasing – or what there was, in those days, of those things.

The Secretary himself was (perhaps; or at a push; or in his own estimation) the head of the Press. He was also head of the publishing business and editorial director. The London Manager had some of the roles of managing director, of operations director, of finance director, of marketing director. In a family-sized firm two men on good terms can carry all that off. In a bigger firm in bad times, not: another problem in waiting – if only because those roles were neither defined nor adequately filled once the Press had started to expand in the 1960s. Meanwhile, across the courtyard the Printer was pretty well independent both of the Secretary and the Syndicate: they let him get on with his business. Again, in good times he could be allowed to get on with it.

Those *were* the good times. In the 1930s the Press was primarily known as one of the world's best printers. The new technology of Monotype single-character hot-metal relief printing had in some of its crucial design aspects been pioneered at Cambridge. It was not just that Stanley Morison, who advised both the Monotype Corporation and the Press, tried out new designs for elegant typefaces in Cambridge books. Much more, the Printing House staff discovered how to use the technology for learned and scientific printing: producing, in the way I have described, for virtually every book a tailor-made design which gave its every feature its own typographical solution. If from a superficial point of view this was 'fine printing', it was seriously fine printing. In particular, mathematical and scientific formulae were handled with extraordinary skill.

The Press was still led by the Printing House in this respect: the whole organisation was besotted with design. S. C. Roberts had started, of course, as an Assistant Secretary long before. He found he had more or less to invent book-jackets (for the Press, that is) and so became interested. It was he who got the Printer Walter Lewis and Morison appointed, and he was delighted with what that great pair did for the Press through their work at the Printing House. Kingsford, in London, designed the bindings (and very fine they were too) having first, at Cambridge, produced a series of seasonal lists, each set in the latest Monotype face: they are precious collectors' pieces now. Dick, as Assistant Secretary, played his part in this collective passion; he once told me that he had had a brief affair with Bodoni.

Dick went on to London for a year or two, then off to the Navy during the War. He saw real action – had a destroyer sunk under him in the Mediterranean – and then came back to London to be Assistant Manager under Kingsford. When Kingsford went to Cambridge as Secretary in 1948 Dick became London Manager.

Something else has to be said, or at any rate surmised, here. If it seemed natural for Kingsford to succeed Roberts, that could have been taken in two ways. The obvious one is that Kingsford was Roberts's natural successor. He had proved it by his quality and distinguished service, and by his grasp of the business as it then stood. But I have suggested that it was obvious, now, that a particular kind of succession was being established: the London Manager was the next Secretary-in-Waiting. This complicated the position of Printer vis-à-vis Secretary.

The other thing to be noted is that Roberts and Lewis retired almost at the same time. Lewis's natural successor as Printer was Brooke Crutchley. Brooke had applied to be Assistant Secretary on going down from Cambridge in the 1930s, had not been appointed then, but he had been invited to apply for the Assistant Printer's job shortly after, and

Figure 10. Bentley House

appointed. It was his impression that Roberts had said to him then that it would be possible later to move over to the publishing side; but now was his chance to be Printer, and a very good Printer he became.

I think the period 1948–63 was Dick's Golden Age. Tall, handsome, with a winning manner, he had a natural physical authority and was respected: and since he was a transparently good man, a gentleman, he was loved as well. My snapshot memory of those years is of Dick and Colin Eccleshare taking a trainload of Bentley House staff on the annual outing to some seaside place like Margate where everyone (memory says) had a wonderful time and got on well together. I do also remember dropping in from time to time on the daily session of 'morning prayers' held in Dick's office or Colin's, where senior staff started the day with a sort of briefing on current problems. It was all friendly – perhaps a little self-satisfied.

In 1951 I remember meeting this dazzling figure, the London Manager, still young, with his beautiful voice. He said 'I'm very pleased to meet you.' I had been told that you had better not say that; but if this evident aristocrat could say it, it could only be because he meant it, which was warming.

Figure 11. Dick David and Colin Eccleshare at 'morning prayers' in Bentley House

During those first years I went to Bentley House perhaps one day a week, for meetings with the staff or to see an author. It all looked happy and well-conducted, and in some senses it was indeed more in the world than Cambridge was. I was too junior to be aware of incipient problems, or to realise how flawed the whole set-up was. Like everyone else, I had known nothing else, and it seemed perfectly natural. Dick meanwhile was President of the Publishers Association at a crucial time: the wave of public feeling against price-fixing washed up against the Net Book Agreement (an industry-wide agreement that net prices would not be undercut). He had to organise the Association's defence of the Agreement in the courts, and this was successful: the Agreement stayed in force until relatively recently, and its loss is not entirely beneficial. Publishers and booksellers were united about this; all breathed again. Dick's successful term of office, with his long years on committees and strenuous travel with delegations, later earned him his CBE. The pattern had been confirmed: the London Manager became President of the Publishers Association; and this said something about the Press, about its London Office and about the kind of man who ran it – and the Publishers Association.

Kingsford retired and Dick came to Cambridge as Secretary in 1963. My impression, my speculation, is that at this point Brooke Crutchley felt he ought at least to be considered for the job. Unlike Lewis, he was a Cambridge graduate and knew the University system. He had spent the War as a senior civil servant, helping to win it; he had since proved himself as a Printer of a quite distinct sort, with a talent for management and innovation, who had made a mark in the wider world. Would he, I now wonder, have made a better Secretary than Dick? Either he was not considered, or he was turned down. Nothing of this reached our level, and I am simply speculating about some remarks Brooke later made to me and a cryptic sentence in his memoir. I am half-supported, however, by remembering two other odd remarks.

On my first day at the Press, Kingsford, welcoming me, said something to the slightly apologetic effect that he couldn't promise me *his* job. Nothing was further from my mind, since I was only 23 and had just stepped inside the door, so I was startled. He explained that Oscar Watson was only a few years older than I was, and so... In other words a certain progression was established in his mind as natural and inevitable. And later, in Dick's time, when things were really bad, and I was saying and doing things Colin Eccleshare disapproved of, he told me in an angry moment that I had only to shut up and wait: my turn was after him. Meanwhile I should pipe down. Oscar had left, of course. But that apparent certainty about succession was the thing which would have queered the pitch for Brooke, if he had wanted to cross over.

Whatever the case about Brooke, one more painful memory of mine confirms this tribal certainty about who should be Secretary after whom. I feel so bad about this affair that I have rather suppressed it in my mind ever since, and so I can't say exactly when it occurred. But it must have been in the mid 1960s, so perhaps I was already Chief Editor, and there was an editorial group I was leading. My friend and ally was Peter Burbidge, who had become Production Manager, with a larger group under him. The politics of this set of changes was that there was now a distinct Cambridge force, or rival barony, which was not as large as the London one, but was becoming increasingly influential and was taking London's place as the sharp end of the business. Bentley House simply published what *we* produced. Feelings as between the two offices sharpened, and I think Dick began to feel that he was torn between two forces.

For some such reason, or because he was urged to by Colin, or just possibly because he sensed opposition from Brooke, he put to the Syndicate a draft paper which he wanted the Syndics to recommend to the University as a quasi-Statute. It said that it was widely accepted within the Press that the London Manager should be recognised as *de facto* Secretary-Designate, so the arrangement should be made a rule. This paper went, I think, to some ad hoc committee like an appointments committee, and was going to go on to the full Syndicate and thence to the University. I had not been shown this by Dick: nobody had; and it was going to go to some meeting at which I was not going to be present, and I don't know now how I got to know about it: somebody must have tipped me off. Anyway, I did read it, and hit the roof. As I remember, I consulted colleagues, and with their support I wrote a letter to Frank Lee, then Master of Corpus and Chairman of the Syndicate. I said that the supposed general rule was not immemorial, had only been applied twice; it did not enjoy the support of the senior staff, and should not be presented to the University as if it did. I sent a copy of the letter to Dick. It was his turn to hit the roof. He called me into his office and asked me if I had consulted anyone else; I replied that it would have been absurd to write such a letter unless I was assured of wide support. I had even approached Ronald Mansbridge, who had said the plan was Dick's way of paying Danegeld to Colin.

So Dick called a meeting of senior Cambridge staff – the people whom I had spoken to – and made a dramatic entrance talking rather wildly about Pearl Harbor. As it happened, we thought he had done a Pearl Harbor on us. Nonetheless I apologised for having done what I did – and indeed I was genuinely sorry to have done it, but could have said that it was his action which had provoked a near-mutiny. And perhaps he now saw that in this inter-office feuding there were two sides, and it was not necessarily sensible to take the Bentley House view. It was a bad moment for us all. But Frank Lee killed the proposal: it went no further. Did Colin ever hear what happened? Did Brooke? I don't know.

The troubles of the later 1960s have tended to erase from the memory the substantial things which Dick did during the first few years after 1963. For one thing, the Secretary's Office and staff moved into the Pitt Building. The printers had just moved to their new building in Shaftesbury Road. This forced crucial changes: the old epiphytic relationship reflected the fact that they were just across the courtyard and one could pop over and have a word with them, and they had always done some things. Now that they weren't there, we had to do them. It was as if Nanny had left and we had to grow up and do things for ourselves.

We suddenly had to have a real production office, which would deal also with the other printers we had increasingly been using. So Peter Burbidge in his department had designers, estimators and progress-controllers. The subeditors came on to our staff, under him, and then under Chief Subeditors responsible first to him and then to me. As output grew their number grew – a problem in the making. I also remember one or two of them as characteristically innocent idealists of the 1960s pattern – and so natural idiot-troublemakers.[1] I had begun to have a team of specialist editors. So we were becoming a real editorial and production office, and to fill the Pitt Building. In what seemed no time at all the Cambridge Office changed into a political power.

And another power became felt – New York. I mentioned that in the row with Dick I had consulted Ronald Mansbridge (familiarly referred to by his initials, FRM). It was not so much that he was on my side as that he was not on Colin's. When the Branch was set up in 1950 it was made clear that it was not to grow into the Cambridge equivalent of Oxford's virtually independent overseas pro-consulships, where local publishing distracted the Branch from dealing with Oxford books from Oxford (I have met Oxford authors who were published in Oxford but not in New York, and vice versa). So there would be no editors. This was self-defeating, in that the USA was then as now the largest source of authors as well as the largest market. For a time the problem was not faced (for one thing we had no-one who was called an editor, even in Cambridge). As it happened, we did publish some best-sellers by American authors – Walt Rostow's *The Stages of Economic Growth* was a notable example. But if I remember correctly, Rostow was a friend of Ronald's, and it was all right to recommend a friend from time to time. George Gamow, the zany

---

[1] I remember a grievance-session in which one of them asked why we were publishing all this élitist academic stuff. It marked the moment at which I realised that use of the word élitist is always oxymoronic.

Russian physicist who wrote engaging popular science (still in print) was so much a friend that he married Ronald's assistant.

As long as the Branch had no editorial function, it was possible for Bentley House to say that New York was just an overseas selling office, and therefore part of the Bentley House empire. Philip Harris and I had similar problems in West Africa. At the personal level, Ronald was prepared to take orders from the Secretary, but not from the London Manager, especially Colin Eccleshare. He therefore appointed two editors, Miriam Firestone and Bob Adamson. Miriam had been taken on as Publicity Director in 1958, but in 1962 (she thinks: I suspect it was in 1963, when Dick took over) she was made an editor, and so was Bob. She had been pressing Ronald to do this, and at first he was unwilling, because he knew it was not in his remit. If he gave in, I am convinced it was because he needed to be able to tell Colin that New York was not part of his empire. Of course, it created another problem – with me.

For I was now a baron. As virtual or actual Chief Editor I found there were these editors in New York, whom I had not appointed and was not directing. Actually, Ronald might well have said to me 'Don't worry; they aren't meant to do anything much.' They were his diplomatic move against Colin. Moreover (since this is my spill-the-beans section I might as well say this here) Ronald, though he was a powerful figure in his own right and did epoch-making work as Manager of the Branch, had a curious personal characteristic: he wanted to do, or direct, everything himself. He didn't want other people taking initiatives. He therefore appointed small people who would do what they were told, and only that. For that reason he was a good Manager only for as long as the Branch was small enough to be so directed. I have to make the obvious exceptions: Jack Schulman, his right-hand, was a massively sensible and independent-minded person, on whom Ronald depended for business skills and sound judgement. And actually Miriam Firestone was lively and equally independent-minded, and became a good editor (she brought John Searle to the Press). Bob on the other hand was hopeless, though sweet. My general diagnosis is confirmed by a passage in a letter from Miriam:

One day FRM announced that we were all to spend the morning cleaning out our desks. That afternoon he called me into his office, handed me three letters concerning editorial projects, and asked me to follow up. Glancing down at them I said, 'But Ronald, these are 15 years old.' Sitting up very straight, he answered icily, 'Fifteen years is not long in the life of this Press.' In answer to the first letter I received an irate response from an author who informed me that we had published his book years ago under a different title, that it was out of print, and it was high time to reissue it (it had had a dismal sales record). In reply to the next letter, in a large, shaky, spidery handwriting, the author said he was still working on his manuscript from time to time when health permitted but wasn't sure when he would finish it. No reply at all to the third letter.

It doesn't look like a considered editorial policy. But in those days 'policy' was a word not often used, except by me. For other people there was no need for policy: we were the Press and did what we did.

So all that was slowly brewing. To go back to the move into the Pitt Building when the printers left in 1963, one little thing sticks in my memory. The old Secretary's Building had been hung with photographs of our Victorian and Edwardian predecessors: grand figures from the Syndicate like Maitland, great editors like Acton, with white flowing hair merging into white flowing beard ('Looking as if he were groomed for Cruft's', Oscar Watson had said). When we left, the question was, what to do with these? Dick positively did not want them hung in the new offices; it would show we were living in the past. They went down to the basement.

The Pitt Building had been built for the Press in the 1830s, but had never been seriously used or even much inhabited. Now we had to use it; in particular the huge Oriel Room (mainly meant, as the name implies, to have that great window and a vaulted ceiling) had been theoretically intended for Syndicate meetings, and was now so used for the first time. It was a fiasco at first: all sound shot up into the ceiling and remained there; nobody could be heard across the room. Dick called in the architects, and a system of hangings restored audibility.

More significantly, the new roles were identified and filled. Peter Burbidge became Production Manager in 1965, when I became Chief Editor, a function which Dick had expressly devolved from 1963 on, so I was acting in the role from the start, and if he wouldn't give me the appointment then, it was because he was unsure of me. So, there was going to be an editorial department, and Dick and I made the appointments. I got to know him a little more as we held the interviews. He was a good judge of people. Appointments were necessary because there was an explicit programme of expansion: the Press was consciously to seek more books, and to decide itself what sort of books they should be, and in what subjects.

Soon after coming to Cambridge, Dick sent round a memorandum to senior staff, in effect asking should we expand? The Cambridge answer was yes. Dick wanted any expansion to be controlled, and I remember

Figure 12. The Oriel Room in the Pitt Building, with a Syndicate meeting in progress

writing a contribution called 'Possibilities of Graceful Expansion' – graceful, because we didn't want to fall on our faces. As for the basic question, there wasn't really a choice, I thought, and I believe Dick wanted the answer yes. This was the time when academic publishing was booming, and general publishers had moved in. All our competitors were in the market-place, or rather calling on the universities, commissioning books, and we had to be there too. Moreover the market itself was both changing and developing. I had been, until this point, mainly responsible for schoolbooks, virtually all of which have to be commissioned, and I had learned how to do that. The skill had to be applied to other kinds of book.

This was untraditional. The unspoken ethos was that the Cambridge Press was a great publishing house, and people came to it. It then decided whether to take on this book, which existed and could be judged. You made fewer mistakes that way. The essential character of the old-style Syndicate meetings where Assistant Secretaries read out the minutes from the big blue book and pipe-smoking Secretaries talked easily to pipe-smoking Syndics was that they were discussing in a friendly way a book which had been written in a subject they were familiar with, and a referee they knew had told them what to think about it. Very occasionally they would offer a well-known person a contract to write a book – perhaps the Secretary recommended a popularisation of an existing book. But in the main it was a question of judging the already written.

There was also a reasoned case made against over-expansion. I have suggested that Kingsford had decided that the Press could publish a little more without changing its nature, and that may have been in his mind when I was appointed. But it was a matter of going up from the current 100-plus books a year, to … well, not very many more. In 1964 we published 150 books. It was pointed out that once you exceeded a certain number the senior members of staff couldn't 'know' all the books in the way in which they knew them then. There was something in this: a traditional publishing house was a small unitary entity, where everyone was concentrating on one manageable stream of new books, and the backlist which that stream had formed. If you published many more you presumably had to have more than one such imprint – like Oxford: and we were not going to go their way.

Dick made a crucial change in the way Syndicate meetings were conducted. There was now to be a formal paper presented to the Syndicate for each book considered. The Cambridge editor making the proposal would draft this, and the whole increasingly large batch of papers would be carefully gone through – indeed forensically torn at – during a long meeting of the staff on the Monday before the Syndicate meeting: a working lunch with white wine and rather nasty sandwiches on new white bread, which Dick provided.

This meeting was important because the individual editors, not, as in the past, the Secretary, were recommending to the Syndicate that these books should be accepted or declined. The whole case was made in the paper, and only the formal decision left open. The presumption was that if the case was good the recommendation would be accepted. It was my idea that the papers should take a given form, with details of projected length and cost, and estimated print-numbers at the head, followed by a description and supported by referees' reports. The whole batch would be placed in order in a folio manila folder, with the agenda for the meeting inside the front cover as an index to the whole, with the minutes of the last meeting as the first item and a key to the advisers' names as the second. (These were the days before xeroxing: the whole lot had to be duplicated on stencils and run off on Gestetner machines by groaning secretaries.)

It was this batch of papers, in draft form, which was discussed at the Monday meeting, then revised and sent out in final form on the Tuesday. The aim at the meeting was to test the case being made and to anticipate any objections. At the Monday meeting, Bentley House was represented in force. There arrived by train either Colin or his Assistant Patrick Tickell (a rather blasé ex-advertising agency man with a very upper-class manner) or both; plus the Matriarchy, as we called Colin's female support troops. These were Joan Bunting of Overseas Sales, competent and a bit sharp; Gillian Page of Journals, highly competent and quite pleasant; and Priscilla Oakeshott, who was highly political and whom I found more difficult to get on with. They were Colin's closest allies: his cabinet. Bentley House also evolved a new group called Publication Managers, who were presented as the equivalent of editors: they saw the books through the publication process at Bentley House. The notion was that we in Cambridge saw the books 'in' and they saw them 'out'.

There was a certain logic in this, but it also expressed the illogic of the two distant offices: it was a duplication forced by the Press's divisions. It was not just uneconomical: it provoked hostilities. The implicit message to us was not we are your allies, but we are watching you to see you don't get out of hand, especially at this Pre-Syndicate meeting. In fact Bentley House produced no ideas – we were doing that. They were just, in parliamentary terms, the opposition.

I now think that behind the Bentley House posturing there was a suppressed anguish about the implicit parallel with Oxford, an inferiority. In my early days, working at Bible House, I often in the lunch break wandered about the old book-trade quarter round St Paul's. There in Paternoster Square was Amen House, a fine old building in which Oxford then had its London office. And when the NEB New Testament was published I found myself collaborating with Oxford people, organising a Bible exhibition in the Chapter House of Westminster Abbey. My counterpart at Oxford University Press was the young Roger Norrington (now a famous conductor and Sir Roger). He was the son of the Oxford Secretary. I went on meeting Oxford people over the development of the NEB, and became aware of similarities and differences between the two Presses, and especially in this matter of the relationship between the home office and the London entity.

The main difference was that Oxford had three imprints. There was the Clarendon Press, really run by the Delegates in the sense that they approved every book published under that imprint: the Secretary ran that show. There was Oxford University Press, which published schoolbooks, childrens' books and other money-making enterprises. And in London there was the Publisher, a named person – Geoffrey Cumberlege or John Brown – who ran with minimal supervision and maximum éclat a whole publishing house, became a big name in the Publishers Association and expected to be knighted. Sir John Brown made more impression than the Oxford Secretary, who was an ex-don and a scholar. I am fairly sure that Bentley House was eaten up with jealousy by this comparison, wanted to make the same sort of impression as Amen House (later Ely House in Bond Street) – and therefore had both to build up Bentley House itself and to contest development in Cambridge, New York and Ibadan.

Meanwhile at the Syndicate meeting itself our new routine needed careful easing-in. The Syndics were not about to suddenly give the nod to a whole raft of new books, often in new subjects, proposed by young enthusiasts. So although we had made a careful case on paper, each book was nonetheless talked through at the meeting, to make sure we got the right decision. Geoffrey Elton had to be answered. Syndicate meetings were revolutionised. They had longer agendas, and there was more talking by more people. It was my job to stage-manage all this, to do a good deal of the talking myself, and to sweat gently throughout. I found myself, from now on, sitting on the Chairman's right and managing the whole of the editorial agenda. It also became my role to go to the Chairman's college on the Friday morning, and with him to identify any potential difficulties. What, in this long agenda, should he pause over?

It was not a small step to go on to propose that books should be commissioned, and contracts given at the stage of commissioning them. The assumption was that the editors were giving professional advice, and that the projects being presented were part of an editorial policy, which was itself stated in papers, and discussed. The Press – or my bit of it – was now being conscious about its activity, and editorial policy was the leading edge. In setting up that system, Dick was committing himself and the Press to a change of ethos, to a radical modernisation and to expansion as an inevitable consequence. It was his major innovation, though it may have seemed simply a more sensible way of doing business at the Syndicate meetings.

To people in Bentley House expansion, especially by commissioning, was a risky policy. They would be required to pay the bills and to sell the books. How could they have confidence in untried people doing new things on a large scale? The gap between Us and Them was now exposed. I have suggested that there had been an assumption in London that when Dick went to Cambridge he would represent the London view, restrain hotheads and, generally speaking, keep things going pretty well as in the past. And here he was now ... well, going over to the enemy would be stretching it, but ... and so on. I think he must have felt increasingly lonely: he wasn't sure of us in Cambridge and was losing support in London, where his old friends were. Certainly, I was dug in on my side of the argument, so was more like someone he had to restrain than a friend or an ally.

This was a tragic situation in the making. The people in Bentley House, as in Cambridge, were serious, hardworking and knew their job, but the Press was becoming factionalised, and Dick was in the middle. The arguments started as between expansionists and steady-staters, but were exacerbated by the separation of the two offices and poisoned by the historical pressures. What the situation pointed to was the need for a single organisation in one place – which could not for constitutional reasons be London. Yet it was unthinkable to the Londoners that they should leave the centre of the world – their world, that is. At the personal level, I as arch-expansionist was doing dangerous things without sufficiently consulting the people who would have to bear the consequences; and I had no intention of consulting them further because I would be told, if anything, to stop.

The strategic argument (expansion or steady state?) was conducted against a background of worsening trade conditions which could be pointed to by both sides as reason for doing what they wanted to do. In the late 1950s and early 1960s academic publishing had been as easy as falling off the proverbial log. There was at first no inflation to speak of – or at any rate, we didn't speak of it. Governments were pouring money into tertiary education, and university libraries were opening all over the world. You could sell a substantial first impression of a monograph in less than three years, reprint, or paperback. A large part of our expansion was initially in increasing the numbers printed for each book. But new subjects were opening up, and of course you had to publish in them.

As if by some great cosmic hand, the tap was turned off, in 1969 I would say, and times have been harder and harder ever since. By then, the Press was already in trouble: that was the year in which publications rose to 200, in an expansion which was continuing quite fast and deliberately: I was making it so. The dozen or so inhabitants of the old Secretary's Office had already risen to some forty in the Pitt Building: the new production office, the new editorial team, the subeditors, the secretaries and administrators. A corresponding increase of staff – perhaps not so large – had taken place at Bentley House. To make the obvious point, overheads had risen and were going on rising. Meanwhile a little inflation over a number of years was cumulatively making nonsense of backlist prices – and backlist sales were 75 per cent of turnover then. If your list is not paying for its replacement at current costs and you are also expanding, your overdraft will increase from year to year. The Cambridge–London argument could then be rephrased as 'You are spending all this money and that is getting us into trouble' as against 'You aren't raising the revenue which will pay for our necessary expansion.'

I was to some extent aware of this. I remember doing in 1970, initially for my own information, a survey of publications in English between 1960 and 1970, taking nearly sixty books published during that time-span. I gave the sales figures for each and tried to deduce some lessons. It was not just a matter of saying this book was a succcess while that was a failure, but an attempt to generalise about publishing in the particular subject, and more widely. The lesson I wanted to draw was that one could not just think book-by-book, though you had to do that. You had to know that if you published ten books, two or three would be successes, two or three would be failures, and the rest would be in between. It was important to increase the success rate, by watching and learning what went well. As important, you had to reduce the cost of failure.

This took some time to learn: it sank home in Geoffrey Cass's time. This was partly because one is aware of most phenomena *after* the event, while publishing is always about the future: so we went on doing what we had done for some time. For instance, our attitude to numbers and prices changed too late. In the early 1960s we could sell editions of 2,000 or more, easily. That meant that if the desirable price was, say, 25 shillings, and to get that price you had to print 2,500 or 3,000, that is what we did. It followed that we were always going nap on every bet and landing ourselves with maximum stock. Meanwhile, costs were rising – we were aware of that – and the market was beginning to decline – we were not yet aware of that. Failure was becoming more expensive at the time when we were overprinting quite seriously. One thing my exercise was able to document, by contrasting the insufficiently changed prices of the old books with what we now had to charge for the new ones, was that the backlist – that 75 per cent of our turnover – was indeed underpriced: we were trying to finance our expansion by relying on new book sales and did not yet see that they were falling. What was also not clear then was that even the new book prices were eroded by rapid inflation, the day after they were published.

Backlist prices were fixed at Bentley House. The previously reasonable inference had been that when you reprinted you took account of current costs. If you had not reprinted you could not justify a price-rise. This was an industry-wide assumption, and went on disastrously long. I remember standing in Heffers bookshop in the Cass era and listening to an assistant giving customers an earful about the wickedness of the Cambridge Press, who raised their prices for no reason that he could see. This was a time when inflation was already in double figures. The notion that you could ride it out by being virtuous was slow to die.

I can't present myself as having more than this grasp of the problem, but that much I had. I think Dick had some inkling too – though he did nothing about my memorandum. But part of the Press's problem was that no member of staff was really qualified to give financial guidance. Our accountants were only that – book-keepers, really. Our auditors merely certified that the accounts were honestly kept. Dick saw that there was some sort of gap, and appointed to the Cambridge Office a retired accountant of a fairly senior sort, who was, I seem to remember, part-time. I've no idea what he advised. It had no visible effect.

It was now that relations between Cambridge and Bentley House became really bad. Dick found he was isolated, with his authority questioned on all sides. Crutchley was having difficulties with his side of the business and accepted no interference from a Secretary who could not solve his own problems. There was an armed stand-off there. But Bentley House would not take any direction from Dick either. The separation of the offices was an ideal arrangement for those who wanted to go their own way with no interference. That was the age of laboriously mediated inter-office memoranda, with copies to one's allies; or personal letters trying to make a point or administer a rebuke. One could ignore these, or one could enjoy getting in a shrewd answer. The paper-war took the place of reforming action. I did my share of this: one couldn't not take part, and I had an interest to pursue. It was poisonous, took up a lot of mental energy and got in the way. We were all lost, but I can at least say for us in Cambridge that we were aware of a growing crisis, and had some ideas, while Bentley House didn't want to know. It was not as if they had a policy: they just wanted to go on as before in the hope that things would sort themselves out – for instance when the NEB was published.

The Syndicate became aware of the looming crisis, as from year to year the overdraft grew, the bank muttered and the University itself made uneasy remarks. Given the whole knot of problems, it was clear that restructuring and relocating the Press was essential to any lasting solution, but these ideas were resisted from within. Business meetings of the Syndicate became longer and tenser, and I could see Dick getting greyer and greyer in the face, until we tottered out weary and depressed at 5.45. Most members of the Syndicate didn't really think it could solve the problems; but it did its best by setting up committees and asking for reports, and so generally adding to the burden.

There are really two heroes in this story. The obvious one is Geoffrey Cass, who turned things round. But seeing a role for such a person, finding him and getting him in place required a far-sighted other person in a position to do what could not be done from inside the organisation. That person was Trevor Gardner, who became University Treasurer in 1969, so was ex officio a member of the Syndicate.

He had been Assistant Treasurer for three years, had got to know all the key people in the University and grasped how it worked. After war service in which he became a staff officer, he had been a very distinguished colonial civil servant, finally becoming Minister of Finance and of Local Government in what is today Zambia. In a way the University was a come-down as a sphere of operations, but he brought to it a width of experience, a kind of energy, a grasp of affairs and a shrewdness which we had not seen in his predecessors.

It was observable that some people disliked him. Partly it was his job to say disagreeable things in hard times, and he was a plain speaker, though always in measured terms (perhaps that made things worse). Partly it was because he was perceived as a bureaucrat by those who saw themselves as hampered by 'mere' bureaucrats, and he was not, in the terms I mentioned earlier, 'clubbable'. I think he hated all that – saw it as getting in the way. And partly it was his appearance. There was a TV children's programme at the time called *The Magic Roundabout* in which charming little animated creatures had gentle adventures. I watched it with my children, on days when I got home in time. At the end, always, a figure called Zebedee came swirling in to land on a sort of undercarriage-spring, saying 'Time for bed!' Zebedee had a round bald head like a lampbulb, a curved moustache, very black, and gimlet eyes. He was the image of the University Treasurer, who seemed to have a similar role. My impression of him over the years was of absolute integrity, more tact than he was credited with, genuine intellectual interests which he kept to himself, the gift of remaining silent at times, and the complementary gift of saying what had to be said when it mattered.

I guess he kept a journal. Since he was on 120 committees, this was almost certainly necessary. At any rate his account of his service on the Press Syndicate is very exact about dates and the sequence of events.

At his first Syndicate meeting in October 1969, the Syndicate considered the report of a committee set up to consider the problems created by the separation of the offices and the ambiguities in the relations of the principal officers. I had had some part in the investigation, since the committee had as a first step asked the senior officers to propose their own answers. As a result, in addition to the memorandum-writing, Dick and I had at least once got onto the London train, and had a long day's meeting with Colin. I don't remember that anyone else was present. What I do remember was that it was an impossible occasion: Colin would neither listen, discusss, nor even propose ideas of his own. He talked endlessly – had to be rudely interrupted – without having any proposal. It was mere stalling. Dick and I came back in despair; and I found myself sending him another letter saying that whatever happened he had to deliver us from that – meaning Colin. It was a gruesome reminder of the earlier embarrassment, but now he had to see that I (or we) had been right. I think the experience prepared Dick for what he had to do.

So in effect the officers had no proposal to make, beyond the feeling that it was now inevitable that the Press should be united on one site. But how to do that? In any case the Syndicate had two businesses to deal with: the Printing House was also in trouble, and the relationship between Secretary and Printer was another problem.

At this first meeting Gardner said that there must be a Chief Executive with authority over both businesses. The idea was rejected as too radical: it may be that the Syndicate saw itself as controlling agent or arbiter. The Printer and the London Office should remain as they were, independent. (It is surprising that they took this view about Bentley House, which had not ever, in my experience, been accepted as not under the command of the Secretary. It gave Colin carte blanche, and was stupid.) Dick was to become Publisher, and nominally in command of publishing (except for Bentley House, it would seem). Gardner himself was to take on the role of Secretary. In a way, all this seemed crazy – without solving one problem it created others. However, by making Gardner Secretary the Syndicate had, without meaning to, given him the incentive and opportunity to assume the role of financial director of the whole Press: both businesses. Given that this was his expertise, and there was nobody else in sight who could or would argue with him over this crucial – indeed deciding – set of issues, he was, given time and skill, in the best position to influence events.

His first proposal was that the Printing House and the publishing business should be supervised by two Sub-Syndicates; then that there should be a business Sub-Syndicate. He was a member ex officio of all three; but this characteristically academic way of meeting a problem came up against the unwillingness of the members to adopt drastic measures. One way forward was indicated in his next proposal – that outside members with business and financial expertise be appointed to the supervisory bodies.

The next step was to brief the senior members of the University appointed by the Financial Board to examine the accounts in 1970. They made an official comment – a warning of the way things were going – which was impossible to ignore. It was repeated the following year.

To cap it all, the Chairman, Frank Lee, was failing in health, and finally died in the spring of 1971. One has to say that this was a delivery, and crucially well-timed. The fact was that Lee had had at least one stroke while in office. He had always been friendly and kindly, but absolutely determined not to bestir himself or take things seriously. He specifically resisted the advice of Gardner, saying it was alarmist. It was the case that as Head of the Treasury, before he came to be Master of Corpus, he had had Stanley Bennett's son as brilliant young rising star – Colin Eccleshare's brother-in-law. It may have been an example of the club in operation. I had found him all too easy to get on with and thought him in decline. I told Dick so, and his reply, which I remember, was to the effect that when he thought the time had come he would 'knobkerry Frank'. Perhaps it was fortunate that he never reached for his knobkerry, for when Lee finally died, it was not Dick who found his successor, but Gardner, now Secretary. He squared the Vice-Chancellor, Owen Chadwick, and persuaded Alex Todd to take on the Chairmanship.

Now things were coming into place. Todd was a peer, Master of a college, head of a leading department and a Nobel Prize Laureate, and therefore carried authority with Syndics and academics generally. He was also a very shrewd and impatient person who stood no nonsense: people were a bit frightened of him. He was aware that he was brought in to clear up a mess.

By this time the Press was three years into a deepening crisis, and very near some perilous brink. The whole scale of the operation, and the jobs of many people, were at stake. And it was not only the publishing business that was in trouble: times were equally bad for printers, who were faced with a collapse of the market at the time when they were replacing the old technology with new techniques of computerisation which made hot-metal obsolete. Since the move of the Printing House to Shaftesbury Road the two businesses had faced each other at arm's length. The relationship was not only more distant, it was less friendly: historical chickens typically come home to roost in bad times. The old relationship between Secretary and Printer was now tested to breaking-point.

In 1970 Dick did that remarkable thing: he withdrew from the post of Secretary, and accepted that he was indeed head of the publishing business, with the new title of University Publisher. This placed him constitutionally on exactly the same level as the University Printer: so that ambiguity was now cleared up. The two divisions, as it was now appropriate to call them, were supervised by Gardner's two distinct Sub-Syndicates, each with a chairman, while the Syndicate as a whole was responsible for the Press as a whole. The title of Secretary had passed for the time being to the University Treasurer, and it was not just the title but the function (whatever that was: actually he defined it for himself). This helped Gardner in his crucial actions when a new Chairman had to be found, and then when later steps were taken. In an odd way it confirmed that the Secretary was indeed the key role – but only when it was not exercised by the head of one of the businesses, and by someone with a set of clear objectives.

For the staff of the Press, Dick's move was a bombshell. I have indicated all the hallowed assumptions associated in the publishing business with the title of Secretary, and the network of relationships which now seemed undermined. It affected actual careers, or at any rate hopes, and it threw the whole politics of the Press into confusion (not a bad thing to do, at that moment). Specifically, it destroyed the old supposition that the career-progression in the publishing business was from Assistant Secretary to London Manager to Secretary. One or two people, myself included, saw their prospects alter overnight.

On the other side of the divide, the Printer's staff also saw a possible avenue closed off to them. Who now would become head of the whole Press? Even those who had no personal ambitions might feel that the top management of the Press had been weakened. Politically minded people said that you don't undermine your own position voluntarily. If it is obscure, turn the obscurity to your advantage: occupy the ground and work the system.

Dick didn't think like that, and it was a blessing. He was above personal manoeuvring, and was looking for the right thing to do for the

Press's sake. Nonetheless he was perfectly well aware that others thought this was an abdication, therefore weak. Bearing that, and in silence, was a sign of his strength. To Todd, Gardner and the Syndicate it was a sign that they were dealing with an honourable man who would not let self-interest get in the way of a solution – and had a proven willingness to think the unthinkable, which was what was needed.

Dick and I came closer at this time, partly because we had had to sit through all those stormy meetings together, like the one at Bentley House, and were, so to speak, holding each other's hand in order to get through it all. I told Dick I had no wisdom to offer on our general problems; I was an editor. But I was not clinging to the past.

Meanwhile Gardner and Todd had devised a general plan, accepted by Brian Reddaway as Chairman of the new Business Sub-Syndicate. The old Business Sub-Syndicate had simply been a group of the more business-minded members of the Syndicate as a whole, and while it had been quite useful in Kingsford's time, it was now out of its depth, and in any case was too representative of the whole failed entity. What was now to take its place – but not immediately – was a Finance Committee independent of the Syndicate, with external members – from the world of finance and business: Sir Alan Wilson of Glaxo (also as it happened author of a classic scientific treatise, *The Theory of Metals*, and an FRS; it now occurs to me that I had done the jacket for the book) and Sir Robert Taylor of Costain's and the Standard and Chartered Bank. He had been a distinguished colonial civil servant. Until that mechanism could be put in place Todd himself became Chairman of the Business Sub-Syndicate.

Gardner brought up again his proposal that there should be a Chief Executive, brought in from outside, and this was also now agreed by Todd. Meanwhile they set up a special committee to investigate the Location and Management of the Press. It was at its direction that Dick and I had gone to London for that meeting with Colin. The committee reported in November 1971, recommending more centralisation in Cambridge, though leaving a warehouse in North London (history repeating itself). Crucially it also reported that a senior appointment be made from outside, in order to manage the relocation and plan the long-term future of the whole business.

So when, round about then (my memory is of the late summer, but this must be wrong) I came into Dick's office one morning at coffee-time with my finger in *The Times* at the gossip-column, where it said that Geoffrey Cass was leaving Allen and Unwin and looking for a new challenge, I found that Dick had the same thought. This was a man we knew and who knew us, and he had the skills we hadn't. It was the name to mention to Gardner, and Dick rang him that day.

Geoffrey had done a consultancy job at Bentley House in Dick's time there. I had met him briefly and casually – registered no more than that he was a tall, handsome, friendly young man to whom one said hello. He had gone on to do a more substantial job at Allen and Unwin, where old Sir Stanley, the real mind and energy of the firm, had found him so useful that he took him on and made him Managing Director. It was a success, but Sir Stanley died, to be succeeded by his two sons. They forced Geoffrey out, leaving him with a justified horror of such people.

In December I noticed in the Pitt Building carpark a very distinctive cherry-red Bentley, and on the stairs I passed Geoffrey Cass. 'Nice to see you', I said. I now know that he was going to see Gardner and Todd. He came to the Press within weeks.

To those who wanted to go on with the old structures, it would be a disquieting move. My support indicated to Dick that the Cambridge Office would accept change, which we would expect to be radical, though we did not foresee its full extent. Dick knew that senior people in Bentley House, old friends, would not accept it, and that he would lose them as friends. This must have been very hard.

What then happened was that Geoffrey Cass came in as Managing Director of the publishing division in January 1972; set about putting that business in order; and in September of that year became Chief Executive of the whole Press, with Printer and Publisher reporting to him. Dick had therefore facilitated a transformation in the constitutional structure which from a crude point of view demoted him.

This too – this misrepresentation – he had to accept. I remember feeling anguished and gloomy about it until he retired in 1974, wincing in particular at what I imagined to be the view of young newcomers who had not gone through the ordeal of the previous years, of facile commentators from outside, and some remaining discontented insiders. If the original action had been heroic, living with the aftermath must have been galling, but I heard no word of complaint from him. However, he must have remembered Othello's phrase: 'every puny whipster' could have looked across the room in meetings and thought 'he's a loser.' Some at Bentley House, seeing that the end was near, may have seen him as a traitor.

These people had not lived through his trials in his position; nor had they made the analysis which was forced upon him. It was easy for people to say, he had only to bring in an outsider with financial and organisational skills who would do what was necessary under his direction: he would have remained Secretary and the old regime would have been preserved. But it was the old regime that was the trouble: it was destroying itself. Dick's authority as Secretary was questionable by the Printing House so long as he was also visibly the head of the publishing business. He could neither exercise nor pass on to a successor a headship which was not accepted by half the Press. He also faced disloyalty from within. As for succeeding him in the publishing business, nobody in what were now the factions – Cambridge, London, New York – would have been acceptable to all three. He had to go on holding the publishing factions together while another man came in and as swiftly as possible moved to a position of unquestionable authority over both businesses. Only the Syndicate itself could make this happen, only Gardner and Todd could manoeuvre the Syndicate, and Dick's action in resigning the Secretaryship was an essential first step. The publishing division had then to be unified, so that geographical separation did not produce pointless antagonisms with their stultifying counter-activities and tribal loyalties.

Geoffrey Cass had numerous advantages in terms of skills, experience of remodelling organisations and financial expertise; he also had the right temperament. But above all he was not identified with any of the tensions which we, who had grown up (perhaps I mean failed to grow up) in the old dispensation unconsciously inherited from the whole previous history. The rest of us can now be forgiven; Dick can be seen as the hero he was. He saw what had to be done, and what he could do himself; did it; accepted that others could bring to bear skills that he did not have; supported them; and lived patiently with misunderstanding and loss of friends.

He had initiated the processes of editorial expansion and modernisation; and by the time he left, the Press was in an infinitely better state than he had found it in. And then, as time went by, there were those, who, the more they thought about it, the more they admired him and felt grateful to him. Did he know that? I hope so, but I fear he was too humble to take it for granted.

CHAPTER 10

Chief Editor 1965–78

The heading seemed to come naturally – it was my formal title for a time – but the implications make me ask myself if I am in danger of taking more than my share of the credit for what follows – the success story of the 1960s, 1970s and after: that part of the Press's activity which was succeeding before Geoffrey Cass arrived, and continued under him. It was a collaborative effort by a remarkable team. However, I don't want to be mock-modest either, if only because I was there at the beginning, I appointed them – with Dick David at first – trained them so far as they needed training, led them and set the example by doing a lot of it myself. I also evolved what could be called the theory. The official history of the Press in those years naturally concentrates on the major difficulties of the organisation, which nearly led to its collapse.[1] This is the positive side: what was growing within the apparent decline.

But I am limited by what I can now remember about very intense and increasingly varied activity by a fast-growing group all those years ago. Naturally, what I did myself comes rapidly to mind, and takes the foreground. But the others ... who came when, and what did they do? I have to get that clearer in my mind. I haven't remembered every name, though I can see the faces still.

To the beginning. I still have the letter, dated 15 February 1965, from Dick David. The letterhead has the Cambridge shield in the centre, as always. On the left, under Dick's name as Secretary, are Assistant Secretaries A.K. Parker MA and A.L. Kingsford MA; on the right are Education Secretaries M.H. Black MA and P.J. Harris MA, over Production Secretary P.G. Burbidge MA. Down below the shield is Assistant to the Secretaries Margaret Hampton.

---

[1] David McKitterick's final volume of his *History of Cambridge University Press* appeared in 2004, after I had written the first draft, but I did get him my notes, and he takes some account of editorial development.

It must have been a Monday, as the letter begins by saying that on Friday last the Syndics confirmed my appointment as Chief Editor on a salary of £3,250 rising to £3,750, and I was now one increment up at £3,375. Importantly, Dick added that the Syndics had now agreed that the traditional title Assistant Secretary should disappear except as a formality for the purposes of Statute B.III.6 – that is, to secure the status of University Officer and the right to an ex officio MA (as had happened in Peter Burbidge's case).

There was some detail about holiday entitlements, and a reminder that in 1961 the Syndicate had decided that the Press must go over to salary scales comparable to commercial rates rather than the previous adherence to academic scales, and now they were adjusting holiday entitlements downwards accordingly. But the crucial point was the new title, and the role it implied. No more Assistant Secretaries, and by extension no more Education or other Secretaries. Peter Burbidge must have received on the same day a letter creating him Production Manager, and Parker and Anthony Kingsford had become Editors. But Dick retained the old title of Secretary to the Syndicate, with all its ambiguities (specifically, was he senior to the University Printer?). Anyway, the letterhead would have to be changed, to give the new titles.

So now we had an editorial department, with the four relatively senior men listed on the new letterhead, to whom Dick and I had since 1964 been beginning to add a succession of juniors, male and female. We also had a production department headed by Peter, who went on combining some significant personal editorial interests with his managerial function.[2] He had designers, accounts people, progress-chasers: the beginnings of a real department.

But the subeditorial group, which he had founded and developed while he was on the Printing House staff – just three people, including him as Chief Subeditor – had been headed first by Anne Phillips, who had taken his place, and then by Judith Butcher: and she was now responsible to me as Chief Editor for her team which moved across the line and into the publishing division. It was also growing rapidly as the number of books in the Press increased. Several subeditors, having begun in that job – notably Diane Speakman and Penny Carter in 1967 and Jeremy Mynott the year after – progressed naturally to editing, having had that excellent training.

---

[2] In particular he supervised the progress and production of Joseph Needham's *Science and Civilisation in China*, became a friend of Needham's and helped found the Needham Research Institute in Herschel Road. He also looked after books with special production needs.

An important evolution here: the subeditors had, on the Printer's staff under John Dreyfus and the old Monotype regime, been closely involved in the design of the books they were responsible for and oriented towards the printer's composing department. They were now more narrowly copy-editors, with that opening into editing. But their number increased as the output of new books grew, and this became an unsustainable overhead, so that in the end the job had to become free-lance, with a staff co-ordinator.

So the Press was re-shaping itself – the old Secretary's Office was turning into something like a normal publishing house's editorial and production office. But then, it simply had to. My story began with the historic entity, the old CUP in and behind the Pitt Building in Trumpington Street – principally or visibly a very substantial hot-metal, still mostly flatbed, printing house. Or perhaps I mean audibly, since you could hear the then-modern printing-machines crashing rhythmically like mechanical waves as you walked down Silver Street – and from other directions the peppery stutter of the Monotype casters. The Secretary's Office, where something silent, invisible, more mysterious and no doubt minor called publishing took place, was in the little red-brick building behind the Pitt Building on the Mill Lane side. The printers were among the major employers in Cambridge and dominated the scene (the local name for the whole organisation was 'The Pitt Press'). In the production of the Press's books, they performed crucial functions – notably design, estimating, scrupulous press-reading. They also provided subediting and progress-control as part of their own complex operation, and the publishers must have seemed to them like handy subsidiaries, feeders who supplied a certain element of what they took in and produced. And indeed, a good many authors came to the Press, from the 1930s to the 1960s, precisely because they wanted the Printing House's standards of design, accuracy, reading and sublime presswork.

And now – since 1963 – they had left the centre of Cambridge, where they had operated since the 1580s, and gone off to their new building in Shaftesbury Road, a good mile or more away. It might just as well have been 20 miles. So there was no more popping down the corridor or across the court to talk to a designer or subeditor, or to pick up a copy of my latest dust-jacket. No more visits by John Dreyfus, taking me through the features of the latest specimen page. Nor indeed, as I now remember, once in a blue moon to find myself doing something very odd, like going over into the composing room where on the 'stone' – actually a level metal bench – in seemingly endless long galleys was the type-metal of a big book which had by some extreme oversight been set up before it was discovered

Figure 13. The new Printing House building, opened in 1963

that the author had written it as a single several-hundred-pages-long chapter (organic unity for you!) and I was required to carve it while it was still hot, skimming through the galleys and duly marking it up into Parts, Chapters and subsections.

But something else had been going on – for me at any rate. If I was now going to be Chief Editor, it was because I had – on the way and in fits and starts – learned to be a real editor: having first watched Frank Kendon doing some of the classic editorial functions very well, being virtually co-author of his beloved country-life books. Then there was Boris Ford, well-known contact-man with his own good ideas. Following him as Education Secretary, I had been commissioning, setting up and beginning to see through some very large editorial schemes which took years to complete: fifty-plus volumes of Bible Commentary, fifteen or so Chaucer texts, the same again for Milton, thirty-plus of the little History of Mankind series, an endless procession of the SMP and so on. But above all it was travelling in Africa with Philip Harris in 1961: serious editorial visiting in universities and education ministries as well as schools, looking for books and authors – and not just schoolbooks, for we had projects for journals of African studies and a *Cambridge History of Africa*: talking seriously with him as we drove or flew those thousands of miles, and discussing what we were doing. In effect we were beginning to work out an editorial policy which could eventually be formulated, stated on paper and implemented by the editorial group which had to be created to fulfil it. And there was the second tour, of Asia in 1964, when we went round the world, to finish in New York for a sales conference.

Policy: I don't think the word had been much used, if ever, and certainly not in conjunction with the word 'editorial'. We were the Cambridge University Press, weren't we, and we did what we did. Just look at the books. That had been the implicit line. It was not a stupid attitude, since the books did indeed seem better than words to make any case that might need to be made. It was a remarkable list, built up over the best part of a century – say 1890 to 1960 – by our just being there, being offered manuscripts and proposals, taking advice where necessary and saying yes to the good ones. It did all build up and hang together. Many of the authors taken on that way were (some still are) household names – in the university household at least. One can partly account for this by saying that in those years, despite two disastrous wars, the English and Scottish universities found a modern role and had a period of excellence, and their teachers, researchers, scholars were able to write, at considered speed, works of lasting quality – just for the sake of it, really. Even leading scientists then wrote books – what we called the 'big blue books' in which the printers displayed their skill at setting mathematics or chemical formulae. The list was strong in the old-established subjects: the books had what must now seem an unbelievably long life. It was not silly just to point to them and say 'That's what we do.'

On the other hand, it *was* stupid to do that and not think 'What is happening out there? Are things changing?' One can list some changes quite easily. By the 1950s university populations were already increasing rapidly – from a very small base, after all – both throughout the developed world and in the ex-colonial territories then becoming independent. More academic books were being written, and many more copies of each title sold: so-called 'commercial' publishers had realised there was now a growing and valuable university market and went into it, especially in the humanities, where the books did not present special setting-problems. They didn't wait in their offices for authors to come knocking at the door, as we mostly did: they were knocking at the authors' doors and offering contracts. New universities were being founded, especially in the USA – but in England too there were some interesting new foundations. And they were not just offering the old subjects in which we were mostly strong, they were offering new ones or new combinations, so that suddenly fresh categories were needed in catalogues and entirely new lists needed to be built up. New markets were opening in Asia, Latin America, Africa. And the USA was no longer a useful extra: it was becoming the major single market, the major source of talent as well, and it was absurd not to seek authors there. Who was going to get to these targets first, or if not first, most intelligently?

Under our old system a certain number of books had been commissioned. This was obviously true of the collaborative histories, where someone had to have the concept, appoint editors and give them the power to commission chapters. It was true of the relatively small number of series, where series-editors wrote in from time to time to say that so-and-so should have a contract to write such-and-such. These were monograph series at the advanced level, and someone – well before my time – had set them up. The old Literary and Scientific Books Committees met two or three times a year and entertained ideas for books of a more general nature, ideas then pursued by the Secretary. Boris Ford had set up and I had exploited the Schoolbooks Committee, where he and then I followed up the ideas. And from the 1920s the Secretary, dining in college or at his club, was open to tips that so-and-so was writing an interesting book … He could write a speculative letter and see if it produced an offer.

So yes, schoolbooks were nearly all commissioned, and at the other levels there was some opportunistic commissioning, but what there was had not been done by the old Assistant Secretaries acting purely on their own initiative. I think I was the first one to propose a Cambridge History – of the Bible, and soon of Islam – to the Literary Books Committee, and it took a major effort of self-confidence to come forward and do what only Syndics or their grand old advisers like Lord Acton had done in the past. And of course 'history' had meant Ancient, Medieval and Modern, with the addition of Economic – Europe seemed the automatic centre, though if you looked again you would notice India and the Empire – seen of course as colonial.

But overwhelmingly – with that important exception of the schoolbooks – the annual output consisted of books which had been written and submitted by the author, could be sent to referees as completed projects and the reports put before the Syndicate. You made few errors that way, and they were mostly errors of categorisation: the book did better or worse than expected. And the 'fields' that we cultivated were traditional to the verge of hoariness.

I am tempted to think of myself as the person who did most to change all that. And indeed, I did – at first – do more than anyone else, which is why I need to step back and see that I was pursuing more systematically some moves that others had started. I have mentioned the names of the people who had put ideas into my head. I am fairly sure that Kingsford was gently moving in this direction, which was partly why he appointed me, encouraged me and set me off in certain directions. He was the archetypal quiet man, who got on and just did things, and has tended to be overlooked. For instance, it was under him that Assistant Secretaries were encouraged to present some proposals, with the advice they had taken, to the Syndicate, and speak for them, where before only the Secretary and Education Secretary had done that. It began to imply the power to take modest initiatives, a changing role. When I became Education Secretary he supported me in large ambitious projects and worked skilful measures like David Holbrook's fellowship at King's.

I am even more sure that Dick David meant to expand and change things when he came in as Secretary in 1963, and here he was, making the innovations implied in the letter to me. In a previous chapter I mentioned how, on his arrival in Cambridge, he had asked us to write papers on the need for expansion, and that I had written one called 'Possibilities of graceful expansion' – or something like that – 'graceful' because we didn't want to fall on our faces. I was identified as expansionist, and mistrusted by steady-staters at Bentley House, but Dick was backing me.

Crucial to the new regime was what was perhaps his most significant change, also mentioned in that earlier chapter. Business was now to be presented at Syndicate meetings as a set of papers: a typed and duplicated document for every proposal, in a standard format, drafted and signed by an editor, and ending with that editor's formal recommendation to publish (or in certain cases, not). Instead of just turning up on Fridays – as they had for three-quarters of a century – to find before them on the table a simple printed agenda, with the Secretary talking them through the business, Syndics now found themselves receiving on the Tuesday before the meeting a quite fat set of papers in a manila folder. Inside the front cover was a numbered agenda which was like a table of contents for the whole collection. Referees' names, not identified in the papers, were given in a separate key.

We, the editors, had gone through the draft papers in that long editorial meeting at lunch-time on the Monday, with the sponsoring editor making a brief presentation, while the rest tried to foresee the places where a discussion might centre, and so to make the papers as clear and convincing as possible.

I mentioned these meetings too in the previous chapter, in particular the slightly jaundiced attendance of a Bentley House contingent. I add here something which strikes me now as the most significant element. The obvious point of those meetings was originally to test our own presentation of particular bits of business, and to foresee objections that might be raised by the Syndics. Were we making a good case for this book? That was meant to get us through the meeting on the Friday without looking foolish for not having seen some obvious objection.

But in the long term the meetings were the regular occasions on which we were also first formulating and then executing an editorial policy. First of all in the less general sense: here we were, presenting the business we had ourselves brought to this point. But it became clear as we went on (clear to us too) that this was a long-term process in which the present proposal had to be seen as part of the whole output, and part of a plan for a particular sector of the list. The more we did it, the more we realised what we were doing. We did indeed have other meetings at which we talked about policy, considered as something where we were standing back and looking at things in general and over the longer term, and individual editors did for such meetings produce papers for their subjects; but the Pre-Syndicate meetings were the seventeen times a year at which the essential process was carried on. And I think this is still true as I write, so Dick had set in motion a crucial historic process, and I had taken it and used it as a way of getting done what I aimed to do.[3]

But Dick and I differed in an essential matter here. In the working relationship with the Syndicate Dick thought the analogy was with the Secretary as Premier treating the Syndicate as Cabinet. No, I thought to myself, that's too like the old days, with SCR (Sydney Roberts), and Billy Kingsford at the time I joined the Press in 1951. It was like that then: but I remember saying later to Bernard Williams, then a Syndic, that it was the editors, and the officers generally, who had now turned themselves into the Cabinet; the Syndicate was like a Parliament which was being asked to pass our draft legislation. He saw the point, since he had been married to a Cabinet Minister – 'Are they going to vote you down?' he said. They hardly ever did; but that must have been because the measures were mostly perceived as well-considered.

That different conception of Dick's shows how old attitudes could linger into the new circumstances which he helped to create. It became important when things began to go badly in the late 1960s, and Dick turned to the Syndics not just for support but for an executive competence they didn't have. They eventually accepted his stepping-down as Premier, and in came a new administration which was much more clearly like a cabinet with a considered programme. Well, the analogy can be over-pressed. What was certain was that the relationship between old-style Secretary and old-style Syndicate changed for ever, even if Dick, who was initiating crucial changes, did not see all that he was doing. Who does?

The other thing which happened as if incidentally was that my voice became the one heard most consistently at Syndicate meetings. This was not obviously a new departure, because as Education Secretary I had been presenting large projects which I was commissioning and had had to talk the Syndics into accepting them – sometimes talking quite hard. In theory

---

[3] Jeremy Mynott writes:

> I remember the shift from an emphasis on presentation to a discussion of policy – should we be doing this, on what basis? That made the meetings more adversarial in some ways, and it was often harder to persuade one's colleagues about a new venture (especially Anthony Parker!) than it was the Syndics. Later the pre-Syndicate meetings had to be devolved by Group, because of the volume, and we then invented the 'Agenda Committee' to oversee the whole process. A further innovation (mine, I think) was a separate 'Green Paper' to give more detailed attention to any project needing an investment of more than £100,000. I suppose that was the final stage in the move towards Cabinet government, with the Syndics acting more like Trustees.
>
> Worth saying that the meetings always had the other important function of being training sessions for young editors – I certainly absorbed values and criteria for assessment as well as practical publishing lore; and when I was running them deliberately attended to that function.

the new way of presenting papers reduced the need for words to a few general or introductory leads into the discussion, and as the editorial team grew the newcomers took on this role. But I was now like the conductor of this opera, presenting the whole performance, and had to step in from time to time; and I was still doing a large proportion of the commissioning. A routine which became an institution is that on the Friday morning of the Syndicate meeting I went to the Chairman's office and took him through the agenda, in a brief replication of the Monday meeting. We then ran the editorial part – the major part – of the Syndicate meeting together, with me sitting on his right.

Back to those new appointments. In the 1960s, especially at first, there were quite a few, partly because some people did not stay for long, and so Dick and I found ourselves – usually in Bentley House – interviewing candidates fairly often: the advantage being that we got good at it. I can remember some of the people who came and went: for instance Charlie Higham, a Cambridge archaeologist trained in new techniques, and I think our first Ph.D.: he went back into university teaching, moved to the Pacific, and became a professor and a useful author. He was versed in the then latest ways of recording and managing data, and I remember him getting the Commitments List onto punched cards – then the 'in' device – and running purposeful skewers through the punch-holes. As author he started by writing two 'topic books' in my big school history series for secondary schools. There was Anne Mather, good young marine biologist, who came at the same time, but also went back into research.

Longer-lasting was Frances Welch – tall, thin, stylish and self-assured, who took on economics, where we badly needed to revive our list and reduce our dependence on the Cambridge Department of Applied Economics and the London National Institute of Economic and Social Research. She was followed by Jo Bradley and Cathy Cunningham, who was a civil servant and went back into something administrative. Frances stayed longer and had an effect, charmed the economists so well that she married one and left. She was a bit cool, actually, and watching her taught me the valuable lesson that in an office in which there were now both young men and young women it was the relationships between the women which you had to watch as much as the obvious one. They could be very sharp to each other, or rather behind the other's back. And they tended to be much more willing to work with a man than with another woman.

Then the stars began to appear, and to stay. Alan Winter was appointed Editor in the biological sciences in 1968. He had a Ph.D., had taught in universities in the USA and England, knew the subjects and the people, had an outgoing personality and began immediately to have an impact. Anthony Parker had been quietly looking after all the sciences, and to some effect. Initially Alan's appointment signified development of the life-sciences in particular, but Anthony lost heart in the early 1970s, and Alan took over the whole group. Quite rapidly, he developed into the leader of a team of effective scientific editors. Mathematics, for instance, a very Cambridge subject, needed to be consciously developed, and I remember Charles Lang, who did well, but went off to found a software firm. Simon Mitton took on what used to be called astronomy, another Cambridge specialism, and he revolutionised the list.

Patricia Skinner had come even earlier, in April 1966, and even more rapidly became a key figure in the Press's editorial development, since she took over what had been a virtual vacuum before the brief tenancy of Frances Welch, and she now had a wider brief, also rapidly developing a group of junior editors. She had the advantage of knowing people in particular circles, and so identifying who was good and promising, and who was doing what. This was an important element in the overall strategy: just to enter an entirely new field as a complete ignoramus (my approach to linguistics) meant depending entirely on good advice and good luck.

It was as important to look at seemingly traditional subjects and see where they were now going – what elements were developing in important new ways. Indeed Charles Higham had started to do this with archaeology, which was becoming more technology-oriented. Classics was moving away from the old Housman-style textual obsession – indeed the literary study was moving towards the approaches pioneered in Cambridge English, and the philosophical and historical aspects were equally influenced by the neighbouring subjects. Modern Languages, or rather the study of European literatures, were moving in that direction too, and here I felt I knew what to do and who to approach. History and politics, anthropology and social studies were being renewed by the Cambridge school – Patricia's friends and contacts. In English, dramatic texts moved from being something to be read like poetry into something to be grasped as presented by actors and received by audiences. It seems a banality to say it was a time of change and renewal, but it really was. Above all it was a time when what had been separate areas of study were looking over the fences and appropriating useful approaches from each other.

An odd aspect of it for me is that as old-style Assistant Secretary I had handled Peter Laslett's edition of Locke's *Two Treatises,* John Pocock's *Ancient Constitution and the Feudal Law,* Ventris and Chadwick on

Mycenean Greek, Grahame Clark's *World Prehistory* and John Styan's *Dramatic Experience*, Gilbert Ryle's *Dilemmas*... Did I grasp the implications? Hardly at all, at the time. But it was now a positive advantage to have had at least a toe in so many subjects, if I was to direct a group of editors doing it all systematically, from knowledge and understanding.

For it was also the time when new disciplines were being created and had to be entered, and this was in itself a new experience – for the Press as well as for me and the new editors. It meant taking a deep breath, partly because it was often against the opposition of conservative-minded Syndics like Geoffrey Elton. The most obvious novelties were area-studies – which combined historical with other approaches – and social studies and linguistics. Philip Harris and I had grasped in a general way that we needed to get into, for instance, sociology, which for me then was no more than a word; and we took some initiatives, but in a way that had to be undone, or some of it had, since we hadn't always gone to the right people. I had had the advantage of serving in the Intelligence Corps in Austria with David Lockwood (I still have a photograph of him which I had captioned 'Hangover in the Stadtpark'), and when he co-authored with John Goldthorpe the series on *The Affluent Worker* I got it, and it was a success. But otherwise we made some false starts – as one does if not well-informed and directed. Patricia knew what to do and where to go – had in a sense married into a network of first-rate contacts. She knew how the topic was really a bunch of approaches, some of them more profitable intellectually than others, and who was doing the best work.

We – the editors and production staff – were all still in the Pitt Building. I reckon that in 1966 there were now about forty people, including six of us editors, as compared with the dozen or so in 1951. Dick and I had the two big offices on the first floor on the right of the tower as you face the building from Trumpington Street. I was at the Silver Street end. The advantage of having so much space was that you could have a small meeting in the room – and also that I could have opposite me, on the other side of a big partner's desk, a young editor or quite often two in training. I could pass things over the desk and say 'What do we do about that?' or 'Read this and tell me what you think' – good ways of getting into the swing.

To a large extent because there was nobody else to do it and I saw it had to be done, I did enter some subjects myself, and with more success than sociology. The most obvious one was linguistics. I had had to take some account of it, or rather of applied linguistics, as Education Secretary, in my not very successful attempts to enter ELT. By the early to mid 1960s there was a kind of linguistic imperialism, with Chomsky's more dogmatic followers wanting to colonise neighbouring subjects, and I took a sour view of the effect on literary studies. People in the humanities also tended to snort when linguistics was presented as a 'science'. But it was one, in the German sense of *Wissenschaft*, and one had to agree that the formal study of language as a general phenomenon was bound to be a serious intellectual enterprise, and it had entered an important phase.

In Cambridge it had been known as 'Comparative Philology', and the Professors I had been aware of simply knew a lot of languages. There had been Professor Jopson, for instance: nice little old man who knew twenty or more. He was a characteristic old-style don, and when my son Peter was born looking like just such a little old man, it seemed appropriate to nick-name him Joppy, until he grew younger, so to speak. But the other Joppy was succeeded by Sidney Allen – key figure and in intelligence terms star informant – who was originally a Classicist, then a Phonetician: he wrote and we published *Vox Latina* and *Vox Graeca*. He came to Cambridge from London, the long-established centre of linguistics in England, where much had been going on under the pioneers J.R. Firth and R.H. Robins. He was influential in that he knew what was happening and who was doing it, was doing some of it himself and wanted to move things on. Though never Professor of Linguistics in Cambridge, he was the power. He had also supervised the research of a young man formerly at Christ's called John Lyons, who had gone on to SOAS and then went up to Edinburgh to help found, as Professor of General Linguistics, one of the new departments – lodged initially alongside English Language. Sidney advised me regularly, and really most of the credit for our publishing goes to him – except that I had the sense to ask him for advice, followed it up very energetically and systematised it into a publishing programme.

I think it must have been in 1965 – it might even have been 1964 – that I drove up to Edinburgh, having announced to Abercrombie, the Professor of English, that I was prospecting for authors, since we wanted to enter linguistics, and could I take the whole department, or at any rate those who were interested, out to lunch, and where was a good place? Well, it was not quite as crude as that, but very nearly, and the good place was a French restaurant in the Grassmarket. About a dozen people did come, including John Lyons, so there was quite a bill for the meal. But as one result we published Lyons's *Introduction to Theoretical Linguistics* in 1968, in cloth and paperback, and it took off like anything: it sold over

100,000 in the end. That initiative also led in due course to a journal and a series of monographs: Cambridge Studies in Linguistics. The first journal led to a second and a third, and the series too had its offspring. It was a matter of getting to know, and to appoint to the journals' and the series' editorial boards, the heads of the still small number of departments – influential people who were producing pupils who went as staff to the other departments starting to open up.

I look at the bibliography of the first edition of John's book, and see there are already references to articles in the *Journal of Linguistics* volumes I, 1966 and II, 1967. I had founded it by bringing together, again on Sidney Allen's advice, senior members of the still new Linguistics Association of Great Britain, who wanted a journal – as we also did. We wanted a monograph series as well, and members of the group provided the editorial board of the Cambridge Studies, which we also owned: it has produced over 100 titles, and offshoots such as textbook series. The board were those heads of the main British departments, especially in Reading, headed by Frank Palmer (also a best-selling author), which gave us access to the upcoming talents – including, for instance, David Crystal, who later became a star outshining all others. If I look at the bibliography of Lyons's later book *Language and Linguistics* (1981), the number of titles in it which come from Cambridge is, I guess, already equal to or larger than that of any other English publisher.

When I made an editorial visit to the USA in 1967, I called on Chomsky and colleagues of his at MIT – not so much to woo them for the Press as to make sure they registered what we were now doing. And an increasingly important element of the Cambridge programme was provided by US authors and editors, especially in Applied Linguistics and Sociolinguistics, which took the subject closer to social studies. Dell Hymes became a friend, and edited one of the American-centred journals.

By this time we were pursuing journals as a matter of policy. I need here to glance back to the 1950s, and to explain that at that time we did publish a certain number of journals, but most were published on commission for a learned society. That is to say that the University Printing House printed them, was satisfactorily rewarded for the printing and counted on journal work as assured. The Press published the product, passing on to the society the printing cost plus a commission of 12.5 per cent and passing on the receipts from sales less a commission, also 12.5 per cent. The commercial result was virtually negative, in that the commission hardly covered our overhead, and as book-publishers we regularly found our own product held up by the priority given to journals in the Printing House. That produced a negative attitude to journals as an obstacle.[4]

As the 1950s progressed, it became clear that journals were selling in increasing numbers, and new journals were being founded. Our own journal *Fluid Mechanics*, invented by a Syndic, George Batchelor, did increasingly well – and Batchelor, who was a bit of an entrepreneur as well as a first-rate scientist, also sponsored and edited a related monograph series, which also did well. A lesson there, about publishing in a subject. It also began to be understood that if you actually owned and financed the journal yourself, you had a blue-chip investment, and it couldn't be taken away. We took on the new *Journal of New Testament Studies*, for instance, and owned it from the start. The inverse lesson had been learned when the *Economic History Review* (as I think it was then titled) left us: the society had realised that the journal went mostly to their own members – and they supplied the list – and to libraries on another list which we supplied: they didn't need us and could save the commission. We could not afford to lose journals like that, but could not prevent it if we did not own them.

I haven't counted the number of journals I started or took over. There were some also which I tried to get – the *China Quarterly*, for instance – which refused to be taken over in my time but came later. I should mention that whenever we did start a new journal, there was some potential for inter-office tension, since Bentley House was supposed to be running journals, and here we were in Cambridge, inventing new ones or taking over others. Fortunately the responsible person in Bentley House, Gillian Page, was sensible and helpful, and we got into a start-up routine of having meetings with the editors and her, and working out who did what and when. She did also attend the Syndicate meetings at which the decision was made. We were passing over the responsibility to her, and she did her job well and was respected by the journal editors.

To jump forward almost a decade – when I was well established in the Editorial Director's role – it struck me that I was now in a position to found a list in any academic subject I chose, and if I entered linguistics because I thought I ought to, I could start a music list because I was an

---

[4] Commission publishing has not disappeared, especially for scientific journals. I can imagine it becoming significant again. Here it needs to be remembered as part of the history. As a young Assistant Secretary I found myself seeing through the Press a number of books published this way. For individual authors (e.g. the difficult Chiote Philip Argenti or the urbane bibliophile Geoffrey Keynes) it was a higher form of vanity publishing. But some important series – e.g. Sraffa's edition of Ricardo, published for the Royal Economic Society – gave the form a serious status.

enthusiastic musical amateur and it would be a pleasure; so I did it. Music had become important at Cambridge, and it was producing ex-students who were both star performers and influential scholarly figures in the Early Music movement. I had once, in my first years at the Press, bumped into Thurston Dart – pioneer in that movement and himself one of the star performers – on the platform at Cambridge station, and he had asked me if we 'did' music. 'No we don't', I had replied, and ever after deplored having to say it. If I had gone back to the office that day and asked why we didn't, the answer would have been that we just didn't, with an extenuating clause about the difficulty of printing music scores – in the old days this was a specialist engraving process done by a very few printers. Now I could reverse that, and did.

As so often, there were little beginnings one could build on. In schoolbooks Boris had accepted a songbook for secondary schools by an enterprising young teacher, Geoffrey Brace. It was published in my time, and I took more volumes from him and others. They sold extremely well. David Holbrook edited the *Cambridge Hymnal* with Elizabeth Poston (a serious production exercise, using a music-printer, and hours of work on copyrights), and she introduced me to Douglas Robinson, Chorus Master at Covent Garden, who did a selection of opera choruses (and got me to some fascinating rehearsals and the first night of *Moses und Aron*, which was his own triumph).

And there was a growing general interest – a market opening up. Joseph Kerman's *Opera as Drama* had appeared in the 1950s, had been paperbacked and everyone was reading it. Opera was the current thing: not just as an evening-dress event for toffs or the source of favourite arias and choruses for the rest of us, but as a historical dramatic form, raising questions about the relationship with other forms, and between poetic drama and music.[5] Dick David was a more than competent musician – he played the cello, sang in the Bach Choir and had set himself to see as many operas as he could – and he and Peter Burbidge and I had regular evenings in which we played records to each other. Like them, I was building up a collection of what were then called 'long-playing records' – LPs for short. Indeed Peter carried his enthusiasm to the point where he and a friend edited for Faber in 1979 a *Companion to Wagner*, in which he, Dick, Michael Tanner and I wrote chapters.

So I felt cheerfully free to set about getting us a music list, and decided that it could reflect my own interests and tastes, since they were so much

---

[5] In Austria in 1948–50 I had gone to the opera in Graz and Vienna, and discovered that it was the normal evening entertainment for cultivated people, a natural part of urban social life.

the flavour of the time. Opera, and especially Wagner, but also the Early Music tradition in which opera had developed, were to be the main centres. They linked with our drama list, and the new movements in music analysis related to what I had been doing in literature.

I had learned also that though it paid to start with a bit of a bang, on the other hand it took years to develop your own rumble of approaching thunder. To do this quickly in those days you could look around and see some good classic texts which could be taken over and revived (not something my predecessors would have approved: they thought that all Cambridge books must be first publications). So, for instance, I had done a good book on Wallace Stevens's poetry by Lucy Beckett, who became a friend. I discovered that she was married to John Warrack, professional clarinettist, then music critic for the *Telegraph* and reviewer in the *Gramophone*, and his standard life of Weber had appeared briefly from a general publisher and gone out of print. So we undertook a second edition, and it became part of our first wave of music books, which also included a reissue of Ernest Newman's four-volume standard biography of Wagner.

The other thing you could do was to translate important works (another kind of publication we didn't use to do), and I commissioned translations of Westernhagen's more recent studies of Wagner. Looking round the German scene also led to the influential and productive critic Dahlhaus, regularly translated by the excellent Mary Whittall – whose husband Arnold also wrote good books on opera and on modern music, especially British composers. So the network began to build up. By a stroke of luck an unpublished series of lectures on the *Rise of Romantic Opera* by Edward Dent, Professor at Cambridge in the 1920s, translator of the librettos of Mozart's operas, and wonderfully lively author, was discovered and edited by Winton Dean: it hit both the scholarly and the popular note. For the longer term I started a series of monographs edited by John Stevens and Peter le Huray – the nicest pair of editors I ever had the pleasure of dealing with – and it produced really good scholarly books (also starting with a revival, of John's *Music and Poetry in the Early Tudor Court*). I couldn't coax the journal *Early Music* away from Oxford, but started a yearbook, which still appears.

All this began in 1975, with 1976 seeing a substantial output. I found I needed help to keep it going: Clare Davies-Jones stood in for a year or so, and then Rosemary Dooley came. She was professionally qualified in music – the normal succession in this process was that I started something as an amateur and then receded into the background when a professional took over, though I could not lose interest.

One of the initiatives which most concerned me was the series of Opera Handbooks, which I set up because I wanted to do something rather like what I was trying to do in European literatures, especially my Major European Authors series. I devised this plan, printed as the General Preface to the series:

This is a series of studies of individual operas, written for the serious opera-goer or record-collector as well as the student or scholar. Each volume has three main concerns. The first is historical: to describe the genesis of the work, its sources or its relation to literary prototypes, the collaboration between librettist and composer, and the first performance and subsequent stage-history. This history is itself a record of changing attitudes towards the work, and an index of general changes of taste. The second is analytical and it is grounded in a very full synopsis which considers the opera as a structure of musical and dramatic effects. In most volumes there is also a musical analysis of a section of the score, showing how the music serves or makes the drama. The analysis, like the history, naturally raises questions of interpretation, and the third concern of each volume is to show how critical writing about an opera, like production and performance, can direct or distort appreciation of its structural elements. Some conflict of interpretation is an inevitable part of this account: editors of the handbooks reflect this – by citing classic statements, by commissioning new essays, by taking up their own critical position . . .

The first volume appeared in 1981, *Parsifal*, edited by Lucy Beckett – in some ways the best volume in the series, from my point of view, because it stuck so closely to the prescribed form and was readable by amateurs or people in other fields. As the series progressed, it was taken over – I suppose inevitably – by period specialists and analytically minded musicologists, and the quantity of musical notation grew, and put off the amateurs like me. It became more like a monograph series, to its disadvantage.

In 1983–4 I found myself simultaneously writing and publishing the quatercentenary *History of the Press*, also another book of my own, and drastically rewriting the Opera Handbook on *Der Rosenkavalier*, which we had mistakenly commissioned from the wrong sort of journalist. Most musical journalists in those days were both critically sophisticated and well-informed, and wrote excellent books, but this one was a mistaken choice. Given that the libretto by Hofmannsthal is a serious work of literature and – to my mind – better than the music, it was easy to make the treatment much more sophisticated, and I rather enjoyed being like the prompter, hidden in the front of the stage under that little dome. Quite a lot of what got heard was me.

Figure 14. The quatercentenary celebrations, 1984: me holding a copy of the just-published *History*

Linguistics, music and the new social studies were new departures. Linguistics in particular could be developed in a sort of abstract way, systematic and neat, while music lent itself to free improvisation. Some of the other new developments were built on odd little foundations already existing in Cambridge and being gingerly developed – Latin American studies and Asian studies, for example.

Figure 15. Geoffrey Cass, my wife Fay and myself at a quatercentenary evening event

Latin American studies started for me and the Press with the publication of John Street's dissertation *Artigas and the Emancipation of Uruguay*, which I handled in the old days as Assistant Secretary. It was rather cosy, as Jack's wife had taught mine Spanish at school, before we all came to Cambridge, so he was a sort of friend. The University founded a Centre of Latin American Studies, and Jack was Director. We began to talk about a series of monographs. I remember being in his office one morning, discussing this, and his secretary brought me a cup of coffee. She brought him a glass of sherry – Spanish, of course. However, she also brought him at his request a second glass, and it was not a surprise to discover that Jack had disappeared some time later in order to be treated, and was no longer Director. It was part of a tragedy: his wife died early of cancer and his life collapsed. But in 1967 we started a series of monographs, Cambridge Latin American Studies, edited by David Joslin (Professor of Economic History, and a friend of mine – who also died sadly young) and for a time John Street. In 1969 we started the journal, edited by Joslin and Blakemore, of the London centre.

Meanwhile I was doing something about Spanish-American literature. The very good, nice, helpful and much regretted successor of

Edward Wilson as Cambridge Professor of Spanish, R.O. Jones, had done for me a selection from Gongora, one of my and Wilson's enthusiasms, in 1966. He came from London, and tipped me that Jean Franco, then at King's College London, was the best person to do an introductory book for students. I visited her, got a scheme from her, put it to the Syndicate, and in 1969 we published her *Introduction to Spanish-American Literature* in cloth and paperback. It did very well, and is still in print. Another good contact was Gordon Brotherston, a colleague of hers when she went on to the new department of the new University at Essex; he started with a book on the Spaniard Machado (1966), but like others turned to Spanish-American literature. His books on the novel and poetry came out in the 1970s, and also did well; he then turned to the American vernacular literatures.

Patricia's arrival meant that the historical side took off. The hiccough of Jack Street's departure and Joslin's death did not affect the Cambridge series for long, and it is now near its ninetieth volume. There also began to be an input from the New York Office. The name of a recent Professor of Latin American Studies in Cambridge, David Brading, first appears in a note from Miriam Firestone to Ronald Mansbridge as a contact she had made while he was researching in the USA. He was later visited by a Cambridge Editor (I think Patricia), as well as a New York one. He became a valued author, the first book appearing in 1971. The major achievement was the *Cambridge History*, on which I remember helping Patricia in the early stages. The extraordinarily effective General Editor, Leslie Bethell, was her choice, and was one of a group of distinguished historians she found. In the very long term I set up a *History of Literature*: the Editors were all from America, North and South, but they were found through my contact over a number of years with Peter Russell, Professor of Spanish at Oxford, an engaging ex-intelligence type, pleasantly non-academic in manner, though he was an expert on both the history and the literature of Spain and Portugal, in touch with scholars in the Americas, and a first-class series editor and contact man.

Asian studies also grew from a Cambridge root back in the 1950s. We published, on commission for the Cambridge Department of Oriental Studies, a series of very scholarly monographs. In those days 'Oriental' covered everything from Casablanca to Yokohama, and the Department had a small number of very distinguished senior scholars who were world experts on topics like political philosophy in medieval Islam, the Avestan Hymn to Mithra, the T'ang dynasty and politics in Meiji Japan. The Secretary of the Publications Committee was the young Gordon Johnson.

The books were good, since the authors (apart from the over-prolific Professor of Arabic, A.J. Arberry) were authorities in the mode of the early to mid twentieth century, austerely pursuing their topic over years. But the subject was just waiting to be broken up into rational geographical and political entities. The University set up an Institute of South Asian Studies – headed at first by Benny Farmer, Syndic, and so we had a new series, announced in 1965, and a *Journal of Modern Asian Studies* in 1967.

In the end I set up a new *History of India*, edited by Gordon. By this time I had extensive experience of the problems of collaborative histories: principally that they took a very long time to complete, even when the contributors stuck to their delivery dates. When they didn't (and there was always a non-deliverer, who would go on to the retiring age and beyond if allowed), the time stretched out, and I had learned to be brutal and fire people, since the delay meant that chapters delivered on time were already going out of date, and if you took long enough the whole thing would have to be started again. With Gordon I worked out a plan under which the *History of India* became a flexible series of shortish books, each by a single author, which could be published when delivered: those with textbook potential could be paperbacked on first publication, and in theory all the titles could be updated and reprinted singly.

If we turn to Chinese and Japanese studies, while there were centres in England – mostly very small – which could be visited, the overwhelming strength was in the USA, which meant that a list could only be developed by editorial visiting over there, whether by Cambridge editors or those in the New York Office. This takes me naturally to the whole subject of New York editors. It will be remembered that when the Branch was founded, it was stated as policy that it would not seek US authors. Whether it was thought that the USA could be served editorially from Cambridge was not, I think, seriously entertained: it was a merely negative decision. But the attitude could not possibly be maintained for long, as one observed the way things were taking off in the late 1950s. In 1960 the Press published the first edition of Walt Rostow's *Stages of Economic Growth*. It was reprinted and paperbacked, sold enormously, and was politically and economically very influential. The phenomenon was repeated with David Landes's *Unbound Prometheus* in 1969. A best-seller by an American academic author was obviously some sort of indicator that the policy had to be changed.

But there was another issue, the personal-political one, which I touched on in the chapter on Dick's Secretaryship. While Kingsford was Secretary and Dick David was Manager at Bentley House, relations with Ronald

Mansbridge in New York were good. When Dick took over from Kingsford, Colin Eccleshare took Dick's place in Bentley House, and it is my impression that he started to pull rank on Ronald, seeing him as head of a selling-office under himself as head of the whole sales operation. It must have struck Ronald that if he had editors he could reply that he was not heading a mere sales office, but a real Branch, representative of the whole Press. So he appointed Miriam Firestone and Bob Adamson.

Whatever the underlying motive for what was actually a sensible move forward, it caused a momentary difficulty in Cambridge as well as London. We didn't then have a Chief Editor in Cambridge. I was by now the senior member of the editorial staff (if one were proleptically to use that term) in that I was Education Secretary and the longest-serving member of the Secretary's Office. I was beginning to enter into the role – had been since 1961, when I toured Africa with Philip Harris. I mentioned that in 1964 we also toured Asia, coming back via New York – so I suppose I met the editors then. When in 1965 I became Chief Editor I found that I had these two, later three or four, editors in New York whom I had not appointed, but whom I needed to direct, since acquiring books and journals in the USA was an obvious priority and an essential part of any editorial policy.

And it was not just that: acquiring the books and journals was part of the world-wide policy which Philip and I were working out together. We had an obvious term for it: we wanted to turn the Press into a world-publisher. To those who might reasonably have said 'Well, actually, you are already', the answer would have been: 'Without knowing it, and now we have to do it consciously, deliberately, consistently, with a plan.' I don't now have early forms of the policy document which was being formulated and developed over those years, but one later version sets out a full statement made in 1977–9, as we entered the next phase of the Press's history. The starting-point was the concept of the 'world-publisher'. By the late 1970s this must have seemed obvious; in 1961 it wasn't.

To go back a bit, I was by 1965 appointing and training editors in Cambridge, the aim being to grow a team which could eventually cover all the subjects, and especially the new ones we were entering, and to publish consciously and intelligently in them. We wanted people who were active, took initiatives and liked being self-propelled. Above all it meant not sitting in the office waiting to be approached: at the least one had to write to potential authors, and the obvious next step was to go and visit them, court them. And this had to be part of one's strategy for the list one was building.

That wasn't Ronald's strategy. As I pointed out earlier, this was partly a personal trait: he was himself very active and enterprising in the things he cared about (sales, mostly). But he also wanted to have people about him who were small, manageable and did pretty well what he told them. Miriam and Bob, as editors, illustrated the problem, since she was interested, intelligent, enterprising, liked getting about and knew some key people, while Bob had no idea what to do unless told, and even then had difficulty doing it. My recollection of coming to New York, as I now began to do every year, is that he welcomed me by bringing out of the drawers of his desk all the things that he didn't know what to do next with.

At some point after 1965 Dick exercised his authority and told Ronald that I was in charge of the Press's editorial policy and had to direct what went on. I also had, somewhat later, to be involved in new appointments. This went down badly: I remember interviewing a candidate with Ronald, who wanted to appoint him because he was obviously biddable. I refused to agree, and Ronald had to go and lie down (or so he said – perhaps a little joke).

Miriam and Bob, appointed in 1962/3, were joined by Adam Horvath and Jane Alpert in 1967: I don't remember being consulted about their appointment. Adam was doing a doctorate in English, and he and I got on well; Jane had been a Classics major at Swarthmore. Though at this stage I was still not involved in New York appointments, it had been established that I was the head of the whole editorial team and had somehow to get it working together, so in 1966 I set up an arrangement by which New York editors came to Cambridge for an extended visit in which they attended Pre-Syndicate and Syndicate meetings – after all, their proposals for new books had to go before the Syndicate to be approved – handled manuscripts, dealt with designers and subeditors, and above all travelled a bit with the Cambridge editors.

Miriam remembers her visit in February–June 1966. Bob's (was it at the same time or later?) was curiously productive. I wanted them to enjoy it a bit, and one nice spring or early summer day got into the car with him just to let him see some East Anglian countryside – in old service parlance a 'swan'. We talked shop on the way and somewhere near Lavenham hit on the idea of a *Cambridge History of China*. I knew Denis Twitchett from the old Oriental series; Bob, who had been to Harvard, knew John Fairbank. There were our two General Editors, who actually liked the idea.

The other vivid memory is of Jane Alpert, very much of her time as terrorist intellectual. The New York visitors stayed in the old Blue Boar Inn in Trinity Street – handy for the Pitt Building. I remember picking her up there one morning, and she told me she had gone into the dining room at breakfast time and was revolted (that must be the word) by the pervasive smell of cheap soap. Everybody was using the stuff provided by the hotel – but not her, of course. Related feelings led her and friends to deposit not money but bombs in bank vestibules, and she had to disappear and go on the run for years and years. So now and again Ronald did find an independent-minded person.

I made a serious editorial trip to the USA in 1967, lasting some weeks. From New York I visited Harvard, Yale, MIT and Princeton. I then took off with Miriam and together we visited Bloomington, Ann Arbor, Chicago, Berkeley, Stanford, San Diego, San Francisco, from where I flew to Vancouver, and back across Canada via Montreal and Toronto. In California we visited, among other people, the artist R.B. Kitaj, who was doing the jacket for John Searle's *Speech Acts*, which Miriam had brought to the Press. She drove us round California, seeming quite competent to me, but she now tells me that she had only learned to drive for this visit, and crashed a car soon after, and gave up driving. But I have pleasant memories of the coast and hills north of San Francisco.

Miriam left in late 1968. In January of that year she gave Ronald a paper, which survives, about the work of the department. During the previous year the Press had published five books by American authors which she had sponsored (not quite negligible, since the whole annual output of the Press was then only 150-plus). More significantly, she listed twenty-four authors whom she had visited or was in contact with, and who were good prospects (we did publish most of them). They included expatriate Englishmen like Brading, some of whom were Press authors already, and some contacts which Patricia Skinner had visited – so Patricia was already visiting.

Ronald appointed Elizabeth Case as Miriam's replacement and effectively head of the group. She was more an administrator than an editor, but was sensible and diligent, did in fact produce one best-seller (Pollitt: *Art and Experience in Classical Greece*) and married the author of another. No New York editor of the time stands out in memory as really productive until Colin Jones – an expatriate Welshman – and that is partly because he stayed and got on with it. One thing I was learning is that it takes at least five years to get visible results, a crucial consideration which I must deal with below.

It was in the 1970s, and with Geoffrey Cass's reorganisation, that the New York and Cambridge editorial teams were really co-ordinated. In 1972 I was part of the group which interviewed and appointed a new editor, Luther Wilson; another member was Tony Wilson, who wrote a formal report to Geoffrey Cass on that aspect of New York's activity.

A brutal estimate would be that there had been ten years of tinkering and dabbling. But actually the mere notion that New York had to be editorially active was an important step, and it had been taken. And visiting had started, contacts been made, some good advisers found. But the real effort had come from Cambridge editors on editorial visits, who were becoming more like trained professionals. This had supported the small and intermittent local effort and was turning it into something effective. In the long term the best device, which as usual started as a one-off and was then seen to be a policy, was to support New York editors not just with editorial visiting from Cambridge (which always had the potential of seeming to trespass on the other group's territory, unless carefully handled) but to station a Cambridge-trained editor in New York either for a significant term or permanently, working alongside the New York editors, who had to become a longer-serving professional group under an Editorial Director. So, for instance, Adrian du Plessis, who had begun to revolutionise our ELT publishing with a crucial paper in 1973, later spent a substantial period in New York.

In Geoffrey Cass's time he, Tony Wilson and I, with Jack Schulman, appointed Walter Lippincott Editorial Director, New York (another opera enthusiast: he went off to direct the Princeton Press). The number of US acceptances rose: indeed by 1980 it had shot from 40 to 100, produced by six editors, including Colin Day and Richard Ziemacki from Cambridge. But this produced strains – for instance, the production department in New York found it hard to deal with the number – and I found myself arguing with the Branch, which wanted to rein back when we in Cambridge wanted them to keep pressing forward.

It is significant that later New York Editorial Directors – Colin Day, Alan Winter, Richard Ziemacki – started in Cambridge as editors, and the last two became Directors of the Branch.

But now I have to go back to the beginning of the chapter. What I have been writing so far is about starting all over again as a 'real' editorial department, professionally organised and trained, and entering new subjects. What I have been ignoring is something which I had been learning from experience since, say, 1960. If you are just publishing what people offer you, this year's accepted manuscript is next year's printed book – or the year after, perhaps. The new thing being slowly learned was that if you are commissioning books, have a good idea today and find a good author tomorrow (you won't, of course), he/she will take at least a year to write it (actually always more), and then you will take at least a year to get it out, and then need another year to see how it has done. In fact you are working over a five-to-ten-year-and-upwards cycle. Add in contingencies like having to appoint the people to do it, training them, replacing the ones who leave early – you are working long-term.

I have been writing as if some things changed overnight in 1965. Some things did, of course, but only as the initiating elements of what has been happening ever since.

The other strange thing about my own activity is that from the beginning I was always doing what would now be thought several jobs (that was the beauty of it, I came to realise). When I became Education Secretary I went on looking after some things I cared about, especially in literature, and was unwilling to be confined to schoolbooks. And when I became Chief Editor after another four years, the things I had been doing – as well as the things I had been doing previously – were just beginning to appear. In particular the African projects which went back to Oscar Watson's time, or even to Charles Carrington's, but had been intensified by Philip Harris and myself, became quite a little flood in the mid 1960s: at the upper level West African Language Monographs, history monographs and social studies of topics like urbanisation, and at the school level a French course for African schools, a lot of little readers, including French readers, by African writers, a science course by devoted missionary teachers at Mfantsipim, Hindmarsh's English course for East Africa. At the same time my Cambridge Bible Commentary started to appear (seven volumes in 1965, six in 1967), Selected Tales from Chaucer (six volumes in 1965 – the equivalent Milton texts began to appear in 1971), Understanding Shakespeare (a little series meant for overseas students), the first books in the SMP flood and in the British Authors series, Holbrook's edited texts, then his course *I've Got to Use Words*, then his Hymnal and his books for teachers. My efforts to enter ELT produced Trim and Kneebone's *English Pronunciation Illustrated* and a couple of course-books. And the Cambridge Latin Course began to appear in 1971 – but handled, by then, by a junior editor.

This flow was joined by the new initiatives. The journals: *Linguistics, Religious Studies, American Studies, Modern Asian Studies, Latin American Studies, Political Science*; the second linguistics journal *Language in Society*, the third, *Child Language*, the *Journal of Social Policy* – all these were started in the years 1965–76. So were the monograph series Latin American Studies, South Asian Studies, *Sociological Studies* (a yearbook), Studies in Linguistics, Yale Classical Studies, Studies in Society and History,

Studies in Early Modern History, Soviet and East European Studies, Publications of the Contemporary China Institute, Studies in Social Anthropology, International Studies, the yearbook *Anglo-Saxon England*, Cambridge Textbooks in Linguistics (an offshoot of the first series), Themes in the Social Sciences, and Past and Present Publications.

Meanwhile we had published, with Oxford, in 1970, the complete New English Bible, which meant that my editors of the Bible Commentary could now start on the Old Testament, which duly began to appear in early 1971, and went on, three or four a year, until complete (and that meant driving up to Nottingham twice a year for editorial progress meetings; there were fifty volumes in the completed series).

In 1970 there also appeared the *Cambridge History of Islam* (a neat two volumes: I had had the idea of commissioning some Cambridge Histories which could be shorter, and so easier and quicker to complete) and a volume of the *Cambridge History of the Bible* which I had set up before becoming Education Secretary (I think). The Reformation-and-after volume of the *Cambridge History of the Bible* had appeared in 1963, with my chapter on the printed Bible. The 'real' big Histories took a year or two to plan, and then several – or indeed many – to complete. For example, Philip Harris's *Cambridge History of Africa* began to appear in 1974, second volume 1976, long after he had left (was he even alive?), and my *History of China* is only now sort of complete (it begets supplementary volumes) some thirty years after conception.

Another example of these time-scales: in 1965 appeared Norman Rich's biography of Friedrich von Holstein, which linked all the way back to one of my very first jobs at the Press in the 1950s, when I had to produce several volumes of *The Holstein Papers*, with a very German red-white-and-black jacket in Albertus. Berthold Wolpe, designer of Albertus, had done the Holstein coat of arms for the title-page, and that too came out looking *echt*.

Anyway, I was still doing, or was landed with, many things which either just came along and had to be dealt with or which went back into my own previous activities. For instance, John Styan had become a friend as well as a best-selling author, and with my school interests in mind, which included the preoccupation with making things visually interesting and not just a chunk of type, he had written, and I got David Gentleman to illustrate, his *The Dramatic Experience*, so that it came out in 1965 looking like a book which was not just illustrated, but planned as a sequence of words and images which got as near as a printed book could to a dramatic experience. (And of course John Dreyfus had guided me both to Wolpe and to Gentleman, as well as to Peter Kneebone, and had designed the *Holstein Papers* magnificently.)

I have been giving lists of journals and series more or less in order of their announcement and first publication. As they move through the late 1960s and into the 1970s, the contribution of other editors becomes evident, most notably Patricia Skinner (now remarried as Patricia Williams) in history and especially social history and its relationships with economic history, demography, political science. Certain names begin to recur in the lists of authors and editors: Jack Goody, Geoffrey Hawthorn, Quentin Skinner, John Dunn, John Elliott, Peter Laslett, S.J. Tambiah, Anthony Giddens, W.G. Runciman, E.A. Wrigley. Colin Day had professionalised economics. Jeremy Mynott took over philosophy and produced the leading list: Charles Taylor, Arthur Danto, Hilary Putnam, Stanley Cavell, Bernard Williams (Patricia's second husband), the Australians Armstrong, Smart, Singer; a European perspective provided by Montefiore – one could go on: Hacking, Nagel, Lakatos, Gellner...

I have not said anything about the sciences: I entrusted them to Alan Winter – Anthony Parker had now moved out of editing – and Alan began to build up a team of editors with skills in botany, mathematics and astronomy (for instance), so that that large element of our publishing was taking off in the same way. To follow the announcements in the old seasonal lists is to begin to see the operation of incoming editors with specialist interests and qualifications; to trace the building-up of subject lists; and to imply the operation of groups of editors, with juniors working under seniors who were responsible for that systematic growth. Cambridge was beginning to be an impressive academic publishing house – it always had been, but it had also been in danger of becoming out of touch, and now it was setting the pace.

In short, the mid 1960s had seen the start of an expansion of output which became steadily steeper: so that Geoffrey Cass took over the Press in 1972 at a moment when one aspect of its activity needed no reform and indeed speeded its recovery. When Dick David became Secretary in 1963 he wanted growth. I began to secure it, first in schoolbooks (which at that time included ELT) and then by beginning to enter new subjects, and then by finding editors who would multiply this Sorcerer's Apprentice effect, starting with Patricia and Alan Winter.

Less obviously, but shorter-term, the number of units published in a year had begun to be swollen in the 1960s by other effects. In 1958 or 1959 Ronald Mansbridge effectively initiated the programme of 'egg-head' paperbacks – that is, reprints of classic back-list titles thought to have acquired a general intellectual interest. We had started a bit gingerly with half a dozen, and repeated the process, so that it was producing a dozen or so a year. What we had gone on to pioneer as a consequence was the paperbacking on publication of monographs thought to have undergraduate potential. As we published more and more of such books, the bare number of acceptances, itself slowly rising, produced a sharper rise in the number of publication-units. And at the same time Bentley House initiated a series of reprints of other classic back-list titles, doing short-run photolitho reprints. There could be a dozen or more of these a year. The figures seem small now, but if you add that three dozen or so to a mere hundred or so, you have increased publications by one-third without adding to your acceptance figure.

As the 1960s went on – or rather, post-1965 with the inauguration of an editorial department – the acceptances themselves began to rise. We hit 200 before Geoffrey Cass arrived; by 1979 it was 511. The rise began to turn exponential, and it needs to be remembered again that titles accepted meant – even allowing for books not delivered, a factor which increases as you commission more – a sharper rise in numbers of units published.

In the 1960s we had also been responding to a bullish market by printing larger impressions. In fact we overdid this, partly because we were at first inexperienced, and then got hubristic, and partly because the market began to turn down in 1969, and it inevitably took a couple of years of watching the sales of new books to recognise the phenomenon. So that did give Geoffrey Cass something to control – and he did it by putting Tony Wilson in charge of all print-numbers and pricing. The economic circumstances became quite daunting: the market – theoretically – continued to grow, in terms of student-numbers and academic staffs and subject-twigging. But the flow of central funds to universities did not keep pace, so academics – and especially librarians – had relatively less to spend. Inflation put up prices – especially in Britain – so that the price relationship between Britain and the USA was reversed. Average sales per title began to drop, and we found we were having to publish more for partly negative reasons – running hard so as not to fall back. That has gone on ever since.

Partly because we were becoming a team, partly because even a single operator has to be systematic, I began to work out operating rules, which derived from my own experiences, at first almost single-handed. My activity had been based on getting out of the office and visiting potential authors. It was a bad idea just to drop in unannounced – one might be taken for a sales-person trying to sell the latest textbook. I fixed on a university or department which housed several potential authors – or indeed advisers – and I wrote to them well in advance, saying I was going to be visiting, and could I come to see them at a time suitable to them? This gave me a timetable of visits, where I could be sure the particular person was there and expecting me. When I got inside the door I could say what we were doing in the subject, ask for names of people doing good work there or elsewhere (the 'intelligence' part of the operation: one built up a list which guided future visits) and then get round to what the host was writing. This might produce an actual typescript there and then, or might lead to my writing, when I was back in the office, a letter inviting a proposal on particular lines. The visit might also lead me to write to one or more of the names I had been given, or to note them for a future visit to their university. It was an economical use of time to take several days out of the office, driving in my car to a group of universities in an area, and making as many visits as possible. When I got back I wrote a report, initially for my own use as a reminder. When the other editors began to visit, I required a report from them. Some of these survive, including reports on visits to the USA and Australia, and they are impressive.

As the team grew, I encouraged them to go and do likewise, saying that as an objective they should have eventually visited every university in the UK where important work in their subject was carried on, and met all the principal academics, as advisers or potential authors. Nobody actually achieved all that – I didn't myself – but it was a rational objective. As time went by it increased to cover the English-speaking world, which was even more ambitious, and forced one to set up priorities.

And we weren't just acquiring authors, we were building up a 'list' in the subject. Again, as time went by, this acquired a discernible shape. A list – for instance in linguistics – consisted of one or more journals, a monograph series, individual monographs, undergraduate and graduate textbooks, and popularisations for the general reader, all of which might feed into each other. In a developing subject one might be ready to take on volumes of conference papers, to help things on, though this was a kind of book we were suspicious of. In an area study most obviously, but also in other subjects, it would include a *Cambridge History*. We had also invented in the 1950s the 'good' Festschrift – the planned volume on a well-defined topic where all the contributions were commissioned in order to produce a coherent and useful book – so now and again one could do one of these. One should aim to have all these in relationship, so that the project cohered.

It all involved steady cultivation. A monograph series, for instance, needed to be watched and steered. The editors were appointed by the

Syndicate for a five-year term. They were given a specific annual quota of recommendations to the Syndicate. One watched the sales of the monographs when they eventually came out. At the end of the five-year term one reported the results when recommending (usually) that the editors be reappointed for another five years, sometimes with a modified brief. I used to call formal meetings of the editors, with an agenda before and minutes after, and I used to run the meetings as secretary. It kept things moving along, but under control. In particular the five-year review gave both the in-house editor and the Syndicate a crucial instrument of control.

As the young editors appointed in the late 1960s grew in experience, they became the seniors running a group responsible for related subjects, and the effect of two or three people all being active was to get the snowball running along faster and larger. At first the junior editors were given the results of senior activity to administer – which meant seeing the delivered typescripts through the press. But I didn't want that division too seriously enforced; I only really wanted to appoint people who would take initiatives themselves and would, so to speak, shake me off as a purveyor of what was obvious already to them. I was also concerned that all editors did the serious part of the business – which meant actually reading the books one had commissioned, to make sure they were what had been agreed, and if necessary to recommend revision. This was essential if you were taking the risk of commissioning books on the evidence of a synopsis and a specimen chapter. And I didn't want the division into roaming commissioning editors and stay-at-home pen-pushers which was too likely to establish itself. I can't say that I read every word of every book I published, but I did read enough to make sure that that was not necessary in many cases. In others I did read every word, wrote quite a few of them myself and often sent authors careful notes for a revision which would make their book more effective, sellable or useful. That is what editors are supposed to do. It meant that one took the MSS home and worked on them in the evenings.

All in all, though, that made for a wonderful job and a satisfying life.

CHAPTER II

Migration

The removal from the Pitt Building to the Edinburgh Building in 1978–80 was in an obvious way a physical upheaval, but it was also a significant move into a new period, a new world.

The whole operation was master-minded by Philip Allin. It was in two stages, so that the Bentley House staff (or those of them who were both willing to move and wanted by the management – and some were not wanted) came up to Cambridge first and were for quite a while disposed in offices in Trumpington Street as near to the Pitt Building as possible, while as many people as could be packed into the old building found themselves sharing offices there. It was a strange experience; in the triangle Botolph Lane–Trumpington Street–Pembroke Street every little office room was occupied, and you almost felt that if you went into the shoe-shop or Fitzbillies you would be served by CUP staff, who would also cut your hair in the barbers'. Those of us in the Pitt Building were like sardines; for the migrants it was curiously like the gathering of swallows in late summer: they weren't actually on the telephone wires, but there were a lot of them clustering about. In 1975, a surviving telephone list tells me, there were eighty people in the Pitt Building – a lot, already, and more in those offices in the buildings across the road.

It was a major event in the obvious sense that the Press, which had had three rather self-consciously separate elements in three places – the Printing House, now in Shaftesbury Road, Bentley House in London, the Pitt Building surviving on the old site – was now beginning to reunite in Cambridge, and was on the way to a single site, and ultimately a single entity (though that was not at all apparent yet). But of course the separation had produced self-consciously different communities, with some mental distance from each other to match the physical separation. In particular, being in London at the centre of the old world had produced a strong sense of superiority in Bentley House, and finding that they now had to leave, to become part, and a subsidiary part, of the organisation was traumatic. And not all of them were wanted in Cambridge, if they were going to go on with old attitudes.

But now people got to know each other better and to work together, and this was in itself a good thing. Some joined the editorial staff from London – Sarah Stanton and Bill Davies, for instance. And then in 1980 we made the next move, into the new building.

This enforced another sort of culture-change, for we found ourselves suddenly transformed from denizens of a traditional building where you could shut the door of your private office, and people had to knock, and might not enter until invited in. We were now in an open-plan building where everyone worked as a member of a group, with their desks in working-areas such that the whole group was like a parish in a large town with other parishes around. You could look around almost the entire floor and take in the scene of activity – all the groups: not quite ant- or bee-like, but certainly quite unlike what we had known. It suddenly became clear that we were now a large organisation. It also became clear how much the groups themselves were now the dominant organising principle. We did not then occupy the top floor of the building, which was left vacant for the expansion which took place in a very few years, but even so, just to look around was to take in the fact that now we were one body – it was already a big one, with well-developed specialist functions, and the move made even more sense.

But it was a painful shock for some: I remember a subeditor who went around with a sun-visor permanently on her forehead, like the editor of a newspaper under the fierce arc-lights in an old US movie. This was because we were in constant artificial light, and she didn't like the lighting – or so she said. But I think she didn't like the building or the life, and she left. But it was now difficult either to be completely idle or to have a row, and my devoted secretary had to go to the ladies when she wanted to have a cry or a smoke or a cursing-fit.

We were seriously on the way to what I can now call 'modern' office life. And that is the end, properly speaking, of this section. But I allow myself a postscript. It's worth a moment's pause to reflect back on the old life in the Pitt Building which I had known since 1951, and others had since ... well, say 1918.

It was not just a matter of having a door which could be shut, and an office to oneself, with a window one could look out of while thinking (or not) and two telephones, one internal one external, but no computer. These were aspects of a very traditional life of fixed hours and inherited behaviour. There were the then-modern telephones, certainly, with an

Figure 16. The Edinburgh Building

internal exchange and a private line to Bentley House. Day-to-day operational instructions and exchanges were done down the line, but serious business requiring a record – which included memoranda to other staff, especially in London and New York – was done by typed messages on an internal memoranda-form with printed heading, copied to interested parties, with a carbon copy for the file (filing was a serious business, and took a lot of time and space). Every day the Bentley House van would arrive with the 'Bentley House mem.', a sort of contents-list of the bunch of attached papers. This would be annotated by the Secretary (capital S), who put your initials opposite the items you were to deal with. A similar memorandum went back, itemising the replies or our initiatives. I mentioned in a previous chapter the destructive memoranda-wars which could break out between the offices, with copies to interested parties, who could hardly not join in.

My secretary would put the day's letters and memoranda, with the files, on my desk at 9 a.m., and I would come in and study them. For important matters I would draft a letter by hand and put the draft in the out-tray. The secretary would come in after coffee (which she had brought me) at say 10.30, and I would dictate the other letters which did not need careful drafting, and she would take them down in shorthand. During the term-time cycle of Syndicate meetings I would also draft Syndicate papers and she would type them. After a meeting I would have to write the consequential letters, accepting or declining books. All this was typed by hand on old-fashioned machines by secretaries who prided themselves on their speed and accuracy. They slowed down as they approached the end of long letters because a mistake would mean doing a whole page again. And making copies meant feeding a sandwich of white paper and carbon paper into the machine: the more copies, the thicker the sandwich. As you went past her room you heard her rattling away, with the occasional shout when a mistake was made. You got the letters to sign after 4.30 p.m., when you had been down in the Syndicate room having tea.

When we got into the Edinburgh Building there were electric typewriters – which reduced the noise-level a lot and increased the speed – and also increasingly effective and rapid xerox machines, which reduced the horror of making multiple copies or copies of long documents. But the system depended on devoted and in its way skilled female labour for transcribing, transmitting and filing the enormous number of pieces of paper. In the Edinburgh Building still – for a while – the previous day's correspondence-outward was circulated the following day in a big folder and read by the whole department, so that everyone saw what was meant to be seen – not the most confidential stuff. It was a way of keeping in touch with what was going on. I was told once by a former subeditor how he had enjoyed reading my most carefully composed letters – it made his day.

People still write letters, of course, but – partly because of email, partly because so much is now done by telephone – they must be fewer, and have changed a lot in style. I had had to learn the old conventions: I came into office life without any idea how to begin or end a letter. 'Dear Mr X' was easy, but how do you address the Dean of York? (Dear Mr Dean.) How do you end a letter? If you are a colleague, Yours ever; if you have begun the letter Dear Mr ..., then Yours sincerely; if Dear Sir, then Yours faithfully. If he is a senior member of the University, and you are an MA, then you can call him Dear Black even if you haven't met him. Otherwise Dear Professor X or Dear Master. If you know him very well, then you may just call him Dear Michael, but very little of that went on. As for starting Dear Michael Black, it was not now unheard of, since the

Americans did it, but on the whole we didn't. I sum up that universe by remembering that when the NEB New Testament was published I read the Foreword and innocently asked who was Alwyn Winton? Kingsford smiled; there was a full-point after Winton., so he was Alwyn Wintoniensis, or Bishop of Winchester: My Lord, or, if you had met him, Dear Bishop. I remember sighing when, much later, I saw a copy of a letter by a staff-editor to a parson beginning 'Dear Reverend X'. No: he is just Mr, but at the bottom of the letter he is The Reverend.

I came in towards the end of all that. I still have the little silver pocket-case in which my father kept the day's supply of visiting cards. Brooke Crutchley told me that when he was first appointed it was quite normal still to go round leaving one's card at all the houses where one hoped to be received – and that could mean every married Fellow of every college.

So, oddly enough or naturally enough, the move to the Edinburgh Building was a sudden crucial stage into a new present. The telex was followed by the fax; the PC, the email were natural sequels. The essential basis was the open-plan, the absence of doors and the sense that there are as many flickering screens as people. If you went back through that absent door, you were in the nineteenth century, to all intents: a world of Misters saying 'Come in' to a world of Misses.

What only a very prescient person could have predicted in 1980 was that the two divisions of the Press now close together on the Shaftesbury Road site but still separate and more or less equal in staff-size – printing and publishing – would in little more than twenty years become once again a single entity. It had been one – a printing house – from 1584 until the 1850s. It had then become a printing house with a small publishing house sort of attached. Then the publishing house had established a London warehouse in 1873. This then became the London Office, where the books were published (effectively, though the place of publication was given on the title-page as Cambridge). Now, from 1980, the place of publication really was Cambridge once more.

At this time the printers were struggling, with a series of interim technologies, to make use of the computer for photo-typesetting, and printing by lithography. It was becoming clear that hot-metal letterpress and the Monotype composing on which our reputation as printers was based were dying, and the industry with them. I found myself finally taking in the process after I had retired and lost immediate track of what was happening. In March 2002, while I was making a little speech at Jeremy Mynott's retirement, it became clear to me that he had now become in one person the old trinity: Chief Executive, University Printer and Secretary to the Syndicate, and that where once the printing business had sort of given birth to the publishing business, it had now been taken back into the organism it had given birth to. John Dreyfus's successors as head of design for the Press's books had first of all become the designers in Peter Burbidge's production department in the Pitt Building in 1963, and then the designers in the Edinburgh Building who had progressively to deal with the computer-generated texts which replaced the old typescripts which authors had laboriously and not very competently tapped out themselves – or had typed for them by their secretaries or an agency. In those days any mark on a typescript was made manually with a red pen or pencil, and one tried as far as possible not to have to retype much, if anything. A total retyping would create the need for a total re-reading. And now – in theory – hard copy could be revised almost at will on the screen, and the printers' task was significantly changed – complex coding and tagging taking the place of old preparatory operations. What they were saved were the original text key-strokes, but this was not as substantial a saving as it had once seemed, partly of course because authors were no more supremely competent than they had ever been, and a lot had still to be done for them.

Nonetheless, moving to Shaftesbury Road was the way to a kind of apotheosis. In 1978 the people in the Pitt Building would have been as astonished at the thought as those in Bentley House, and the old-style printers would have been reduced to despairing incomprehension.

CHAPTER 12

Scrutiny *and after*

Scrutiny ceased publication in 1953: it was reissued photographically by the Press in 1963 as a uniform set of twenty bound volumes, the last one containing an index to the whole and a 'Retrospect' by Leavis (also issued as a paperback pamphlet). The Press also published, in cloth and paperback, a two-volume selection, chosen and edited by Leavis, in 1968. He died in 1978 and Q.D. Leavis in 1981. In 1984 we published a collaborative volume of reminiscences, called *The Leavises*, edited by Denys Thompson – a step towards a biography. I wrote in it a chapter about my dealings with Leavis as his editor at the Press, and what follows is a somewhat amplified version of parts of that chapter: other parts have been cut. For the record, I add here that we also published a volume of his uncollected papers in 1986, and three volumes of Queenie's papers in 1983, 1985 and 1989. These were edited by the literary executor G. Singh, an Indian professor of Italian in Ireland, and an enthusiast for Pound and Montale: a nice man but an unskilled editor (I had to try and stop him writing introductions which were simply a summary of the contents). We also reissued one or two of Leavis's books as paperbacks when Chatto had allowed them to go out of print.

And of course one advantage of having done these things was that I could, as the editor running the English list, develop relationships with his ex-pupils and others in English departments who looked in his direction. This was important for me and I pursue the theme below.

Since I looked after these publications I came to know Leavis through them. I had not been taught by him as an undergraduate at Cambridge, had not even met him then. But as a boy in a small and remote country grammar-school sixth form in the 1940s, making my first attempts to understand the poetry I was reading for the Higher School Certificate, I had come upon the copy of *Revaluation* which my Cambridge-trained headmaster had put in the school library. It helped me to see what might be said and gave me words to use – his, of course, at that stage. I went up to Cambridge to read English in 1945. Like generations of Cambridge English students I went to Leavis's lectures on Practical Criticism. At that period he always had a big audience, but you had to sit in the front rows if you wanted to hear him, for he lectured in an unraised conversational voice, without oratorical tricks. He looked like a ruffled bird in his black gown, and the very imitable voice was hung upon, for various reasons. We all did him, trying to catch the characteristic phrases, the little gasp or sniff before a sardonic joke, the pondering tone. We also listened for the latest technical term: it was 'realised' at that time. I remember Maurice Hussey, the Billy Bunter of the Leavisites, and eventual compiler of the Index, squealing over coffee somewhere about images not being 'realised'.

It was much later that I grasped what a superb reader-aloud of poetry Leavis was, especially of Eliot. It was the rhythm he conveyed – not just the word-to-word phrasing but the sense of the whole meaning being born and animating the movement. Nobody else could read like that: yet the voice was the one we imitated, slightly nasal, seemingly flat, with faintly Cambridgeshire vowels (he was a local: it was not the 'Cambridge' of Dadie Rylands and the Marlowe Society).

By 1945 he was one of the few surviving figures from the founding of Cambridge English: Chadwick and Forbes were dead, and Richards and Empson had gone. Those remaining from the early days were, apart from him, mostly embattled mediocrities, the politicians. He was coming into his period of critical dominance: we knew it and rather revelled in it. But it was contested. I had had a sobering glimpse of that bitter feuding when, quite unexpectedly in 1946 or 1947, I was sent for one evening, just before Hall, by Tillyard, then Master of Jesus. As Senior Tutor he had admitted me as an Exhibitioner the year before, and perhaps saw me as one of his bright young men going wrong. I had no warning what it was all about. It seemed he had read one of my essays (I think, an entry for a college prize; I had won one the year before). Pink, and trembling with rage, he told me at length that if I went on like that I would come to no good. I had no answer: white and trembling with shock I went into Hall and ate my dinner in silence. I don't remember what I had written, but of course it must have been callow and derivative. And it was the case that I wrote some of my weekly essays with the Faculty Library's copy of the relevant issue of *Scrutiny* on the desk before

Figure 17. F.R. Leavis in his garden at 12 Bulstrode Gardens

me. I got to know the contents of the early volumes quite well, and I was one of many. Cambridge supervisors must have sighed as they read this week's permutation of the message from Downing. Some must have become angry, like Tillyard. But it was not the reaction of a good teacher.[1]

Some years later, Tillyard met Dick David in the street and asked how young Black was getting on. By this time I was one of his bright young men again – or so he thought. He told Dick complacently that he had once given me an almighty row, but I didn't bear him any ill-will. He was quite wrong about that, I told Dick. Anyway, his outburst shook me out of an innocence. Before I took Part II I took the trouble to discover who the examiners were for each paper – not a thing I would have done before. I became a subscriber to *Scrutiny* when I went down, and I bought and read – and re-read – Leavis's books as they came out, and reviewed the later ones. I began to see what he was about, and it became my settled conviction that he was the greatest critic in the language and the greatest living Englishman. As long as he was alive, it was a comfort.

It must have been Leavis himself who approached the Press about the reissue, and it must have been in 1960 or possibly early 1961, because Boris Ford was still there: Kingsford asked us both what we thought, and of course we were in favour. As I have said, Kingsford was a modest and open-minded man, transparently honourable – in short, a gentleman. Leavis respected the type, and the two were impressed with each other. Leavis in his formal role could be a persuasive advocate: in fact he had great social address. Kingsford was persuaded that there was a serious case for the reissue, even though it was quite unprecedented as a publishing venture, certainly for us, and I think absolutely.

I wasn't present at the Syndicate meeting at which the proposal was accepted. Was I in Africa? Nor was the Chairman, Stanley Bennett, who was on sabbatical leave in the USA, I think. This was perhaps a fortunate chance: when Stanley returned I remember him being genially rueful, perhaps thinking he had been spared one embarrassment at the cost of a slighter one – that his friends might ask him how *that* had happened during his chairmanship.

---

[1] Tillyard was not, like Lucas, anti-modernist. I still have his hand-written card inviting me to the Master's Lodge in Jesus to hear Eliot, on one of his visits to Magdalene, talk about Poe. Tillyard was pleased to be the sponsor, showing he was in with the advanced people.

It was my job to administer the publication, which was a long and quite complicated affair. Maurice Hussey was engaged as indexer, and his first task was to give me a complete list of contributors, whose addresses I had to get from Leavis so that I could write to them, show them the list of their contributions, get their consent and pay them a fee, which was a first charge on the royalty, the balance going to the Leavises. I discovered then what a wide range of contributors there had been – at any rate in the early days – and how distinguished they had been (by the end it had contracted to pupils, colleagues and allies). Wilfrid Mellers, the composer and writer, had written more than anyone else, except the Leavises.

I got agreement from everybody except W.H. Auden, who thought that *Scrutiny* had been a bad influence, did not think his own contributions 'were any good' and withheld permission. I consulted Kingsford, who advised me to wait until I had permission from everyone else and then ask him to reconsider. He did so, making it a condition that a note should be included, saying that republication was 'with his consent but against his will' – a curious notion. I failed to remember to do this, and Auden presumably failed to remember he had asked for it, which was discreet of both of us. (Or so I said in 1984, when this was published. Actually Auden's executor, noting the publication of *The Leavises*, asked for a photocopy of Auden's letter, and I had to sophisticate it, eliminating my own immediate annotation refusing to do what Auden asked.)

The technology of the time was photolitho reprinting and binding, in the USA. We ordered 2,500 sets, in the hope that half might be sold over there and half in the rest of the world. The printers supplied a lot of 'overs', so we had initial stock of nearly 3,000 sets. The published price was £2 a volume, or £35 a set. The USA never took Leavis seriously, so we sold fewer there than expected, but more in the rest of the world, especially in Japan. The reissue went out of print in the mid 1970s – we had a small number left.

By commercial standards the reissue was a success, and for some years it supplied the Leavises with a useful supplement to their royalty income. Our initiative led Faber to reprint *The Criterion*, and Frank Cass *The Calendar of Modern Letters*, which *Scrutiny* was intended to succeed. In historical terms, these three journals marked the approaching end of the British tradition of serious quarterly periodicals moderately priced for a subscribing general public which was not conceived as entirely academic, but in some sense 'cultured'. Indeed the journals were themselves a very important part of the culture: their heyday had been the late nineteenth century.[2] So it was appropriate that Auden made that largely symbolic contribution as representative contemporary writer, just as Lawrence had made his début in Ford's *English Review* and published one or two of his later essays in Rickword's *Calendar*. Between the two dates – say 1910 and 1930 – the medium had started to decline, though there were quite a few short-lived contenders. Leavis could never pay contributors, so that the Press's reprint-fee was the first payment they received. On the other hand, several of them had been able to reprint their contributions in books of essays – for Chatto in most cases. And that produced another problem.

When the reissue was accepted, we had suggested to Leavis that in due course there should be a selection for those who could not afford the whole set, and he agreed. But when the time came to think about the contents, he found there was a difficulty. He did not want to duplicate what was already available in book-form, whether his own writings or those of his colleagues. But actually, that should not have been the main issue: the ordinary reader simply wanted the best, whether it was available in a number of other books or not. We should have gone for that. However, there was still a great deal not so collected, and of high quality – though a good proportion of it was by him and by QDL. This was a chance to do justice to her, and his own material was important, but he still felt sensitive about it. It was my function to get him to suppress this feeling, and now my familiarity with the contents came in handy. He gave

---

[2] This needs some qualifying. It was not a Golden Age which came to an end; rather a continuous evolutionary change which leaves us with some highly specialised survivals. The *English Review* in which Leavis first encountered Lawrence (Lawrence and the Chamberses clubbed together to buy it, and Jessie sent in some of his poems) had in 1910 monthly parts of about 200 pages numbered serially through 12 issues, and selling at half-a-crown an issue or 25 shillings a year. It could be bought at newsagents or railway bookstalls. It had advertisements for Gentlemen's Furlined Overcoats, the *Times* Book Club, De Reszke cigarettes and Atlantic passenger liners, table-water, typewriters, hotels and other journals. The contents included poetry and fiction, essays and articles on current affairs. Contributors included Conrad, Belloc, Wells, James Stephens, Hugh Walpole, Frank Harris. They were paid: Ford overpaid them and got the *Review* into difficulties. In 1929 *The Calendar of Modern Letters* was also monthly, had fewer than 100 pages per issue, numbered serially, cost 1 shilling and sixpence, or 18 shillings per year, or £1 direct. It had a few advertisements, for books, bookshops and other journals. It contained poems, stories, and critical essays and reviews (including music criticism). It had become almost purely literary-critical. It paid contributors, which is one reason why it collapsed quite soon. It showed how the formula had narrowed, but had not yet become academic. *Scrutiny* started with a wide range of contributors, and even had a few poems and one chapter of a novel. Quarterly, it had 400 pages a year, and started at 10 shillings a year post-free. It had no advertisement revenue and did not pay. It started very small and never had more than 1,400 subscribers (constrained partly by wartime paper-rationing). The Leavises subsidised it themselves, but in the end had supporting subscriptions from the British Council. One could say that, at first, it remained of general interest to an educated, culturally aware public. Its successors – for instance *Essays in Criticism* or the *Cambridge Quarterly* – are really for academics and English teachers. The more general cultural periodical still survives in the USA.

me a generous acknowledgement in the preface for my help, and I was very grateful for it, indeed proud of it – while knowing that he was in a sense displacing on to me any residual criticism that there was more by the Leavises than by anyone else. When he had put it together, his own doubts were partly overcome. Indeed he said in a letter to me:

> I've tackled the fitting in, etc., and now suddenly (immodestly perhaps) see the whole thing as very impressive – irresistible – *ktema es aei* – a classic, etc.
>
> The trouble is that FRL and QDL preponderate so unconscionably. No, not really unconsc.: we did the work, wrote more than anyone else, gave our lives to it (*not* for money or the world's love), and have left there so much unreprinted.
>
> That brief preface is a delicate job.
>
> [...] If anything has to go it must be something of mine – *Under which King?* I think.
>
> At any rate, I hasten to put the upshot in front of you.

I was anxious that the piece he mentions here, 'Under which King, Bezonian?' – an editorial written in 1932, one of the most intelligent texts of the literary politics of the 1930s – should go in, so I pressed him again. I was also very keen to include the exchange with F.W. Bateson on 'The Function of Criticism', first published in 1953. 'Under which King?' examined the supposed necessity to take up a political position;[3] 'The Function...' contested Bateson's view that you only 'understood' literary texts if you had the 'background' or as we should say now the 'context' at your command. Leavis had been trained as a historian, was more sophisticated about history than Bateson and knew that history provided no automatic insight – was as much a construction as anything else, and the appeal to it usually concealed an unacknowledged determinism. He anticipated much of more recent theory, and dismantled it in advance.

These pieces gave two of the best statements of Leavis's critical position, though they are less well known than his very mild exchange with Wellek. The second item produced an unexpected complication. Bateson, asked for his permission to reprint his side of the exchange, wanted the opportunity to have a last word. It was a mistake: he should have been content to have occasioned a valuable debate, in which the issues were well brought out. Actually, his new piece did not change the ground of the

---

[3] 'Under which King?' mentions D.S. Mirsky, who had contributed a review on Soviet literature, somehow posted from the USSR, where he was sent into the Gulag and died (see *A Russian-English Life 1890–1939* (2000) by G.S. Smith). When I asked innocently for his address Leavis cast up his eyes to heaven.

discussion, merely stating that he thought he was right. I urged Leavis to let it go in, and with the equivalent of a shrug he did.

The selection did not sell very well, partly for the reason I have given: the contents were too much decided by the then availability of other publications, and so – from the general reader's point of view – did not contain the most essential pieces. It came either too soon or too late. Another ten years, and one could have chosen from the whole range. But then again, Eric Bentley in the USA had done a one-volume selection, appearing in 1948, and much reprinted in paperback, which sold well for a number of years and pre-empted the American market.

The *Scrutiny* reissues opened a relationship with Leavis which I greatly valued – inevitably, since he was the greatest man I ever met. There were also opportunities to extend the relationship, though I was careful not to poach on Chatto's territory. (I once in a clumsy moment pointed out that I had not done so. 'You wouldn't have succeeded', he said bleakly.) It was my idea that he should be invited to edit a *Cambridge Book of English Verse*. I remembered from the days of his lectures how he would occasionally produce a really bad bit of Victorian verse from the old *Oxford Book*, and exclaim with amused affection about old Q's standards and taste. So it was a natural challenge to ask him to do better. After some pondering he wrote in September 1964:

My conviction is only reinforced by the intervening opportunity to revert to the matter of the anthology, and to reflect on it. I'm all in favour of the Oxford Book's being ousted by something better, but still can't believe that a massive, would-be inclusive anthology is a good thing – could be, I mean. All my considerations of the critical problems that would be involved in deciding what was properly anthologizable and what was not leave me there. The temptation to ensure that what I know ought to go in, given an anthology, and probably won't, has kept me reflecting. But any bent towards yielding has been inexorably checked by the confirmed realisation that the undertaking would be a major one, and that I'm now nearly a septuagenarian, and am so much distracted by my responsibilities on what I may call the Robbins front that the unwritten books most important to me don't get on except slowly.

. . .

An important initiative had come from his side in 1962. The Press had published in 1959 C.P. Snow's Rede Lecture on *The Two Cultures*. It had an extraordinary reception. Normally we would sell at most 1,000 or 1,500 copies of such lectures, even semi-popular ones, and over some years. Snow's lecture had reprinted and reprinted, and I stopped counting at 100,000 copies. It had been extensively excerpted in magazines, and rumour had it that the President of the USA thought it an important statement which ought to influence national educational policy. Leavis has recorded that when it came out he picked it up in the Press showroom, saw what it was and decided not to put down his money. But when he began to find it quoted at him in scholarship papers as received wisdom, he felt it was time it was unreceived as unwisdom: and he chose to make Snow's piece the subject of his Richmond Lecture, also given at Cambridge.

That lecture was normally a domestic occasion at Downing (Admiral Sir Herbert Richmond had been Professor of Imperial and Naval History and Master). But guests had been invited – I was one – so a public occasion was in the making. I turned up not knowing what to expect, and was surprised to find the hall packed tight with people, some of them perched in the window-embrasures – including a couple of the Downing hardline bully-boys, Wolf Mankowitz (I think) and Morris Shapira, in beards and leathers.[4] There was a tension of great excitement.

Lectures are an absurd way of communicating. Only an athletic listener can carry away a long argument of any subtlety – I can't. I don't know what other listeners made of it. We were all aware that an onslaught had been delivered; and I listened glumly as the hardliners laughed triumphantly at the mockery of Snow (very skilled, since Leavis was determined to make a mock of Snow). I went off in a daze, only knowing that it had been a great occasion, of some sort.

Among the audience was Patrick Wilkinson of King's, the *Times* Cambridge correspondent. He must have been invited by the organisers in the knowledge that he was that, and that he would think the lecture should be reported. He did so, and the domestic occasion became a national one. The terms of the report meant that the text needed to be made available, and quite shortly the *Spectator* (Literary Editor Karl Miller, ex-Downing) printed the lecture. This was good, since the outraged could now discover what they were being outraged by; it was bad in that the *Spectator* illustrated the text with little caricatures of Snow, as if his worst offence was to have dewlaps and wear pebble-lensed glasses. This

---

[4] Extraordinary pair. Mankowitz became a figure in the world of musical comedy – wrote a hit show – and an expert on Wedgwood, as antiques dealer. Morris was the occasion of Leavis's final breach with Downing, since Leavis wanted him as successor – very bad judgement, proved when the two finally fell out over the Leavis Lectureship and Morris became abusive and was excommunicated. He was the spoiled son of a very rich father, and once gave me an elegant lunch in his well-appointed lodging in Canterbury. Shortly after, he was murdered.

hardly looked like argument, and outrage was compounded. There followed in the *Spectator* and elsewhere all those letters from such as Edith Sitwell (paying off an old score) saying that Leavis was a nasty man and had been nasty to a nice man – a classic case of the English gift for turning an intellectual issue into a social friction, so confirming one of Leavis's grievances. It was often urged against him that he had a paranoid feeling that the literary establishment of London was a conspiracy. But that was not his point, which was that if you have a herd you don't *need* a conspiracy – for, in Snow's words about scientists, without thinking, they all react alike. Hence some of Leavis's thematic imagery about 'flank-rubbing' or 'swimming, shoal-supported, with the tide'.

There was a sad inevitability about his whole long struggle, epitomised in the Snow affair. The sequence of events was not predictable, but once it had unfurled one was tempted to be wise after the event. How else could it have gone? What was ignored in the row was what Leavis had said and what it really meant. Even when the text was printed the angry reader would at first see it as a gratuitous attack. My experience always was that I had to read Leavis three times. The first time left me asking 'What has he actually said?' The second time I asked 'Is that all?' The third time I said 'Now I see.' That difficulty is the obvious mark of an original mind, and ought to be expected: but most people hadn't the patience, and I have not read much criticism of Leavis which starts from the position of comprehension, of elementary homework done. That too was one of his problems: he was always ahead of people. He was also courteous in that he wouldn't condescend or talk down: speaking or writing at his own level, he paid his audience the compliment of assuming that they were keeping up. They weren't, and were mostly not willing to make the effort.

So it was with apprehension that I learned that Leavis had approached the Press, proposing that it should publish the Richmond Lecture. I was at the Syndicate meeting at which the proposal was discussed. There was quite a long debate, and at one moment I thought the answer was going to be yes. But then the sentiment tacked the other way because of a feeling that the remarks about Snow might be actionable. Judgements in English libel cases are unpredictable enough, and there was stuff in the lecture which made this a reasonable fear. The Syndicate then had a lawyer as member – Jack Hamson, the Professor of International Law. He was a pleasant, intelligent and cultured man with one wildly squinting eye which seemed to appeal to heaven while he was addressing the world. If he wanted to help you in your case he would cover it, so making you look into the one which was looking at you. On this occasion the eye roamed about the ceiling while he did his lawyerly humming and hawing about the chance of an action. Some innocent asked 'Do you mean that it is suggested that Snow is not a very good scientist?' and Brian Pippard in his cool Cambridge scientific voice answered 'Oh, he won't sue on *that* count', and there was a roar of laughter. But they took fright all the same: the answer was no. Austin Robinson, the economist, as he made for the Fitzbillies almond ring at the tea interval, said to Richard Braithwaite 'I think we are going to regret that decision.'

The lecture was published by Chatto under the faithful Ian Parsons, though I understand that they contacted Snow and got his word that he wouldn't sue.

I had to convey the decision to Leavis. I usually found myself conveying polite regret on such occasions. For the only time in my professional life I used the formula to suggest that I thought it was the wrong decision. I made the mistake of trying to convey to Leavis that he had what we now call a communications problem – his audience needed more help if it was to keep up with him. Things in the lecture struck the naive reader as simply unfounded. I was wrong, but it is the sort of thing editors say, and was meant to be helpful. He replied on 1 May 1962:

Many thanks for your two notes. I've been too driven to reply before.

Of course, we neither of us expected any other decision from the Syndics. Merely, I have a deep piety towards Cambridge, and should have liked the imprint of the Press to have been on the anti-Snow lecture as well as on Snow's. And I know from my American correspondence (voluminous) that America takes note. It isn't pro-Snow!

There could be no question of enlarging the Lecture – tampering. It was addressed to the occasion: its point and edge and 'attack' are inseparable from their functional quality. There would be no point in my trying to 'explain' to the classics (who are the resisters). If one had to concede that the Lecture didn't explain itself, then there would be no point in trying to do educational work with less than a volume – or a set of volumes. And then no point . . .

I've looked at the lecture again and am bound to say that I've done better than I should have thought possible.

The reprint of *Scrutiny* was going forward meanwhile, and with that experience to digest I found myself being asked to brief our American office about Leavis, the journal and his work generally. Leavis at that moment would have seemed to most people an obscure academic who had caught attention by making a waspish attack on the Olympian Snow – at best parochially English, a small Cambridge eminence. So I wrote a long brief for my American colleagues, and then saw I had material for an article. I developed it, and it was published in 1964 in two parts in *The Use of English* which Denys Thompson had founded and was still editing. I called it 'The Third Realm', borrowing Leavis's own phrase, which encapsulates his 'theory' as we should say now. I was the first commentator to see the importance of the term – the sort of thing he threw out in a seeming-journalistic plain-language way, and meant comprehensively.

Actually it came from the Richmond Lecture – a crucial passage in which Leavis develops the notion of an intellectual meeting-ground which is neither the public knowledge of scientific 'fact' nor the private realm of the subjective apprehension of one person, but is created collaboratively when one person approaches another with a report of his/her experience, implicitly saying 'This is so, is it not?' (wonderfully 'period' greeting). The other person typically responds with a qualified agreement, saying from his/her apprehension 'Yes, but …' The ensuing exchange may bring in other people, and so over time there builds up something 'conventional' in the etymological sense: an agreed estimate of cultural values. This can become *too* conventional in another sense, so a revaluation may be called for. But Snow had proposed of his scientific culture that its members 'without thinking about it, respond alike. This is what a culture means.' It was an insult really: defining a herd, a tribe.

'The Third Realm' had been deliberately proposed as a metaphor, implying that figures of speech were necessary in the discussion, which had better be kept naturally a-logical (in the Russellian sense of logic and its claims). Leavis's occasional and opportunistic development of the idea was also deliberately confined to an aside here or an interpolation there in his main business of the discussion of this or that specific text – except for the last two books, where the preoccupation becomes an organising principle, and previously in the dazzling performance of the debate with Bateson. The main body of his work seems to be so specific that you overlook the implicit epistemology, so that theorists of the coarser sort can deny that he had a 'theoretical' underpinning.

And despite the apparent implication of the debate with Bateson, he had a strong historical sense – or rather he and QDL had absorbed from Chadwick a sense of the historical-cultural forces which inform literature. One stage of historic culture produces epic; a later phase, in cities, produces theatre; a third produces romance, which in early modern times transmutes into the novel. In all these phases literature is a form of the society's self-consciousness; and Leavis's overall if unstated ambition was to indicate and assess this. In doing so he was aware of his own place in an English tradition – the 'Condition of England' debate. You can also infer the moment, after *Revaluation*, when it struck him that it was an extension of Victorianism and classicism to go on giving poetry and tragedy the primacy, and that it was the novel that he should be attending to, as a modern society's prime set of formulations.

I could only start to bring out all this in my article – for one thing, he had not yet produced the important last books – but I was on the way. I also realised that I was wasting his time urging him to 'explain himself' at this lower level. If I could understand him, he had done it – but then there were the other people who did not listen. There was a role for a commentator. After a time I plucked up the courage to show him the article. 'I am very far from deploring it', he said, and I was very far from discontented with that.

I see from the letters that he wrote me from time to time – usually on business, but he often dropped a friendly word on other matters – that he regularly maintained what he called his 'anti-philosopher' stance, which was a paradoxical ploy, or a provocation to think what philosophy was, and why he was doing something else.[5] Of James Smith, a contributor to *Scrutiny* whose work I admired, he said 'James was apt to be maddeningly philosophical and, in his interpretations, fantastically allegorical.' He was opposing the imposition of an 'approach' and the dogmatic consistency that went with it: also the unwillingness to let the text do its work on the reader rather than the other way round. The systematic or ideological pushing of a basic position into merely logical extensions was alien to him – and yet the consistency of his own position was agilely maintained over a wide front, and people sometimes said to him, as I did, 'Come, now, you are some kind of philosopher yourself.' He got a mischievous amusement out of this, I think, as when he wrote to me in June 1974 a comment on the forthcoming *The Living Principle*:

It's anti-philosopher – merely more explicitly so than my work of the last 40+ years; *needs* to be, now that Philosophy Depts tell me that I don't do myself justice: I am a philosopher. (A friend of Sir Karl Popper's wrote to me from the London Sch. of Ecs. sending me his last book by way of justifying the bracketing of me with *him*.)

---

[5] I now think that the sort of thing he was against was Russell's determined effort to make everything in language relate to formal logic: to arithmetise, as if there could be no other kind of meaningful mental enterprise or communication. But, following Lawrence, he was also against domination by the mind itself or by accepted conceptualising. It comes out in the last two books that he was pursuing, in Eliot and Lawrence, their effort to formulate something which the intellect had not pre-processed, and to evolve linguistic forms in which the effort worked its way through to a hitherto unfound expression: not a formalisation or a conceptualisation but what he had long been looking for in the word 'realisation'.

But he had the last word:

I can't help wondering whether I haven't given you a false impression of my book, and whether your conviction will survive a perusal. If it does, I shall take that as a confirmation that my method of trying to enforce my intention has justified itself. It's the intention, with the attendant 'logic' (or dialectic) that seems to me, in my innocence or non-modesty, not to be a philosopher's: it's too inescapably intent on practice – expository in that way. I'm not saying that no philosopher is of any use.

It is a reduction of language if the logician's analysis of it is taken as anything but a specialist account of a narrow range of uses. His moral stance was anti-analytical for related reasons: for him the philosopher's 'empty choosing will' was a reductive fiction. But that phrase comes from Iris Murdoch: who must have known that the human case that Tolstoy, say, poses in its specificity, its complexity, and its extension and complication over time, its place in the life of the individual and the related people, is quite unlike the simple examples that philosophical writers had tended to use. One now sees philosophers taking examples from literature, which is an advance, and it would be good to find them writing at his level.

. . .

I have placed my letters from Leavis in the archive, and am left with the fading memory of visits and conversations. He would sometimes consult me about business matters. With great courtesy and formality he would telephone to make an appointment, because I was, he thought, a busy man. I would show reciprocal regard by going down to the Pitt Building showroom to meet him and afterwards conduct him back downstairs. He was increasingly lonely, and increasingly driven by the thought of what he had to do in the time left to him. 'I would like a brief colloquy', he said on the telephone, but it turned into a long monologue, and there were obsessive elements in it towards the end. In one of these retrospections he told me that he had known two geniuses in his life: one was Wittgenstein. The other – though he did not explicitly say so – was his son Ralph, who had indeed been a prodigy as a child, but whose life had collapsed and who had been expelled from the home by QDL: a re-enactment of the way her parents had treated her. This was a grief to Leavis: he would loyally take the long bus-journey to Oxford to see Ralph. I offered to take him by car but he refused, saying that he used the journey to think, or just to repeat poems to himself.

As he sat in my office on the other side of the desk, I watched the lean brown left hand on my desk, playing an unceasing accompaniment. I also remember him standing there, having dropped in on his way by cycle to the hospital where Queenie was critically ill. He wore a black oilskin cape, and had half a dozen eggs in one hand and a half-pound of butter in the other. It was raining hard, and there was a drop of rain glistening on the end of his nose. He conveyed without words his anguished preoccupation. He ought to have looked comic, and he looked awe-inspiring.

I also remember some relaxed anecdotal moments. I listened, to pick up some sidelights on literary history – about the relationship with Eliot, for instance. 'There was something wrong with him down there', he said, ostensively striking himself well below the belt. He told me, as he told many others, of the occasion when Eliot, staying at Magdalene in the late 1930s or early 1940s, had crossed the road to Chesterton Hall Crescent, where the Leavises lived, and spent a long evening pouring himself out, while the pile of cigarette ash in the grate grew and grew. And when he left (in a Jamesian narrative style, where intense significance is conveyed but not defined, and the reader has to grasp the point) 'My wife said to me "You know what he *wants*, don't you?" and I said "Of *course* . . .!"' After these oral italics and suspension points it would have been crude to say 'Well, what *did* he want?' (He had this gift of italicising. 'My wife's a *scholar*, you know', he once said. Impossible to convey all he packed into the word, but respect, amazement, amusement and reprehension would be among the ingredients.)

Lighter moments were provided by his visits to York, where he was reverently regarded, as a visitor from the Old Testament: impressive, indeed venerable, but a sort of extra. But for him it was different, a new hope. He was not naively hopeful about all new universities as such – could not be, given what he had said about Robbins – and there were things he was sardonic about – the social sciences, for instance, as represented on academic committees, and paying political regard to the supposed national interest. '"We *are* the nation", I said.' He was scornful of the professional unionised student of the time, and could not see herd-behaviour, drinking, noise, promiscuity, untidiness or other manifestations of basic self as anything but that. He had a practical turn which enabled him to meet most situations. 'So I opened the door, and said "What the BLOODY . . ."' Before the rare expletive I imagined the young rioters falling back, abashed. He was also aware that as a notorious figure he was the object of idle curiosity. He needed small classes, but many people turned up for the spectacle. 'I *bored* them. Next week there were only twelve.' 'How did you do that?' 'Oh, I gave them a long analysis of Mallarmé's best poem.' 'Oh, which is that?' 'You know: the Toast to Gautier.'

There were also passing aphorisms – '*De mortuis nil nisi verum*', for instance. Or, pausing as he was going out, and tapping his chest: '*Cet *animal est très méchant ...*', leaving you to complete the quotation. And I remember with embarrassment that, meaning well enough, but being obtuse, I asked him how it was possible for him to maintain his 'deep piety' towards Cambridge, having been shabbily treated for so long. How could he have such faith in the idea of the university? Any university would be staffed by human beings, a specialised form of the herd. His face changed, perhaps it fell. I don't know whether I had said something which he was used to hearing, or the opposite. He replied that one did have to have the sense that in the end one belonged to, was working for, a community, with a common end in view. It was, as he said of other things, a necessary faith.

But his loneliness weighed upon him. He had not sought it, yet he had created it and had to accept it, but it was a grief. He had Queenie beside him, but had to spend much energy reining her in or accepting the results of her extraordinary nature. She alienated more people than he ever did, and out of sheer animosity. Noel Annan once wrote 'But is Dr Leavis *kollegial?*' It was a question, but could merely mean 'Is he clubbable?' I remember that in Hall where I ate my dinner, shocked, after Tillyard's admonishings, I could have looked up and read over the High Table *Ecce quam bonum et quam iucundum fratres habitare in unum.* I also remember Leavis's look when I put my question to him, and his answer, correcting my simplicity or rebuking my cynicism. The collegial ideal did exist for him: painfully real if seldom realised. He and his colleagues and pupils at *Scrutiny* were initially and at moments examples of it – except of course that he and they finally fell out with each other, thus sadly refuting the opposition's claim that they were a cosy coterie.

He conceived an ideal community, a community of the nineteenth-century mind, the Cambridge that Sidgwick and Leslie Stephen represented – and that he represented in his time. It was the type-case of his system or faith. Because he effectively represented it, it was to that extent true, and confirmed every time someone responded to his 'This is so, is it not?' by saying 'Yes, but...' But to a positive mentality or a modern systematic relativism the answer was increasingly 'True for you perhaps, but not for me.'

And in his own time, since the 1920s, the ethos of Cambridge had ceased to be represented by Sidgwick and Stephen, residual puritans who had kept a faith in faith. Their successors were the circle, with their conscious group-spirit, which took Moore's *Principia Ethica* and converted it into the authority which sanctioned a group ethos of 'personal relationships' above any other ideal. At its lowest the Bloomsbury mentality fostered the coterie, even the political cell: it prolonged into adult life the herd-loyalties – including hero-worship – of the public school, but displaced them from the sanctioned corporate enterprise on to the private loyalties of the group that selected itself as an élite. But it was a specialisation of the herd-mentality, complimenting itself for being superior to the rest of the herd, and this accounts for Leavis's detestation. Yet something like this was what the opponents accused the *Scrutiny* group of: they were not *kollegial*, like us, but a puritanical sect.

He did have his answer to those who, like me, with good but mistaken intentions pressed on him that the world is as it is and he was simply seeing the consequences. That was cynical or despairing, and he had thought his way through it. He was the only man I knew of whom in that lonely posture it could not be said he was an egoist or flawed personality: and this was a matter of intellection, of reading and meditation. In the last books, from the one on Dickens to those on Lawrence and Eliot, he was also constantly exploring the moral problem of being a self, and a self at odds with others and tempted to assert its absolute self in opposition. Like everyone else, he needed a way out of that threatened impasse: remission from the prison of the ego postulated by Eliot, from which Eliot himself could only escape by a vault into faith. For Leavis this had an element of inconsistency in that it pre-posed a creative human capacity which Eliot elsewhere denied, and of course it left most people outside the closed door. Leavis found his alternative in Blake's and Lawrence's notion of the identity which grows to become its fulfilled form: a concept which brings its own set of difficulties. There was also his rephrasing of the classical and Eliotic notion of the common pursuit of true judgement, which re-places him in the tradition of English criticism since Johnson.

He did also when necessary just let fly and hit out (but very intelligently). But I have the clear impression that he hated rows, tried to avoid them and only did it when he felt he must. It was the ulterior aim that guided him, and I think he managed to prevent his passions or his personality from misappropriating or deforming his ideal. Nobody could say that they did not affect it at all: he was human, and there is no pure distillate 'integrity' that can be run off and displayed in a bottle like an essence, uncontaminated by anything else in the personality. His anger and obsessiveness were the obverse of his earnestness and courage, and part of his integrity. So: the aim he had set himself, and his long pursuit of it; his evident lack of worldly wealth and the little store he set by that; his willingness to accept personal privation, to accept also a galling notoriety instead of proper respect and gratitude, to be a scandal and a stumbling-block to fellow academics when he ought to have been an inspiration – all that had purified his will when it might merely have soured his temper, so that when he spoke out he spoke with unique weight.

...

My contact with Queenie was slight and intermittent. I steered clear of her, on the whole. There was an occasional tart telephone conversation or brief note. When he died I wrote her a letter of condolence, saying he was the greatest man I had known – that sort of thing – and she sent me a photograph of him, and of his portrait by Robert Austin. I was an ally if not a friend. She did also invite me to dinner one evening at Bulstrode Gardens – a dinner for male admirers which she cooked and served with her daughter Kate, a nice, level-headed and interesting person. The admirers included one who talked the most amazing Baconian nonsense. QDL received this in the most courteous manner, saying things like 'Oh, do you really think so?' as if she were some mere upper-class hostess. Plainly in that role she was willing to be more than just polite. In her role as intellectual and prophetess she was prepared to say almost anything, and I had letters or saw others which were brutal and scurrilous – indeed mad. She shot between extremes: was always nice to ordinary people, especially mothers and children (she was also motherly to male homosexuals). But in the intellectual world she went in as a privateer with all guns blazing at friend as well as foe. She burned as many of his letters as she could, but Kate told me that she had kept her father's letters to her, which were precious. I urged her to hang on to them.

The Leavises had a strong prejudice against biographical approaches, wanting to be judged solely by their work, and forbade their children to authorise any such study. When in due course Ian McKillop was commissioned by Penguin to write a centenary biography I drafted a letter for him saying that while one knew they could not officially support him they had no obligation to forbid or to stand in the way of something which was actually desirable – even necessary. Ian had been a pupil, was sympathetic and would produce something preferable to much else that was likely to be done (there were already two or more superficial books). He had to work too fast in order to meet the centenary, but the book is not bad, and served the cause well enough – for the time being.

There is more to do: this was a major movement in twentieth-century English intellectual and literary history, and it needs appropriate treatment. For one thing, there is no sustained treatment of Leavis's own work of any substance, apart from Michael Bell's brief monograph. For a collection about him which McKillop and Storer produced in 1995

I wrote a long chapter analysing Leavis's work on Lawrence from 1930 to the last book in 1976 – almost fifty years of thought and reading, which produced an evolution not only in his understanding of Lawrence, but of language and literature – his theory, to use the current preoccupation. It struck me then that the same work needed to be done on the work on Eliot, on the novel, on his social-historical preoccupation and so on. For that matter, the whole *Scrutiny*-and-Downing phenomenon and its place in the Cambridge English movement are now ready to be historically treated.

I made a start with the set of personal recollections which Denys Thompson edited for the Press in 1984 – the source of the first version of this chapter. Its production caused some tensions – Denys by this time had a heart-condition and wanted to avoid the sort of row that the group specialised in. He had to turn down an article by Christopher Parry on the relationships with the schools the Leavis children went to, and my recollection is that David Holbrook's chapter had to be edited. The quarrel about the F.R. Leavis Lectureship trust also caused tensions, with the group splitting into those for and those against H.A. Mason.

Denys's presence in retirement in Cambridge until his death meant that I had a substantial adviser and potential author. I was Education Secretary until 1965, and as former teacher and Editor of *The Use of English* he helped me in that role. He edited Sampson's *English for the English*, collected a volume of *Readings* for school assembly and wrote *The Uses of Poetry* (the Chadwick strain in the movement: the book fitted the programme on oral and folk poetry I re-started). He also collected a volume in the Sturt tradition: *Change and Tradition in Rural England*. (I might mention here that Denys's former collaborator in the writing of schoolbooks on English, Raymond O'Malley, who had taught the Leavis boys at Dartington, had once actually lived out the tradition by working a croft in the Highlands with his first wife until she died. He recorded it in *One-Horse Farm*, which should be a little classic. It makes him a real, not a merely theoretical, proponent of the ideal – but then some of the authors Frank Kendon edited were also people who worked with their hands and lived the life they wrote about.) Denys deserves a chapter in a book, as an influential and active figure. I mentioned earlier his apparent persona as prophet-of-doom: he was actually mild and gentle, hardworking and earnest. He wanted me to write the Leavis biography, and I have a letter from him giving me a good deal of sharp insight. (When as a young man he had told Queenie that he was going to get married to his first wife, she sent him a ruthless letter telling him why he shouldn't. Actually she was proved right, but it was a characteristic performance.)

The other surviving member of Leavis's original collaborators was D.W. Harding, the psychologist, who brought his professional training to bear on criticism – productively. He gave the Clark Lectures in 1971, and we published them as *Words into Rhythm* in 1976, giving a companion to his *Experience into Words*, published by Chatto in 1970: two books of permanent value. He contributed a chapter to *The Leavises* which was both critical and sympathetic.

A later member of the group was Leo Salingar, who turned into a respected scholar of Elizabethan drama, for whom we published a couple of solid books. I mention him because I found myself persuading Ian McKillop not to publish part of a letter from Queenie in which he was mentioned in brutally derogatory language – vulgar abuse – for no reason that I know of.

But this is getting desultory. I need to reach a summing-up, and when I get there face a lurking feeling about all this – not so much a doubt about the *Scrutiny* movement as about being involved in the end of something without realising it. But there is a little more to say about influence and consequence.

CHAPTER 13

The English list – 2

The reissue of *Scrutiny* confirmed that the Press was now a publisher which the more radical members of the English-teaching profession could approach, and indeed I made it my job to approach them, or as many of them as I could identify. I found I had to travel far and wide. Few of Leavis's pupils had posts in UK universities at that time: I have mentioned earlier Robin Mayhead, who had moved to Accra, where I met him, from Colombo, where he had had pupils of his own. He edited my British Authors series, using people who had taught overseas. It was like the old English Men of Letters series, but written by authors who had taught outside the UK, and it was addressed especially to students in ex-colonial territories. As it turned out, that intention simply made it suitable for all students below a certain level of sophistication. Then there was Walton, whom I met in Makerere, Enright in Singapore.

There were also like-minded teachers heading groups as far apart as Natal and Melbourne. So Leavis-pupils like Bob Jones and Roy Littlewood had once joined Christina van Heyningen in Natal. That group was far too liberal for the regime in South Africa, broke up, and some members went on to Australia and Canada, where I met them. Jacques Berthoud came to England and ended up at York, with Jones. Those who went to Australia joined Sam Goldberg in Melbourne, and became part of the important group of colleagues and pupils who contributed to his journal *The Critical Review*. (I admired it and wrote for it.)

That is to touch too briefly on an important topic. I can fortunately quote a long letter solicited from Jacques Berthoud, which makes clear what a significant international movement this became over time:

the key figure in all this was Professor Christina van Heyningen whom I knew as a small, intensely responsive, occasionally combative, very artistic and morally uncompromising lady, with an extraordinary gift for awakening students to the life and quality of the literary classics ... As an Afrikaner she was born ... in a

British concentration camp ... Her distinguished family (one of her brothers, a scientist, eventually became Master of an Oxford college) like many other Afrikaners of that generation, were open to the world. She was educated at the University of Stellenbosch ... and later for two years at Oxford ... where she studied Spenser, Milton and Dickens ... and discovered D.H. Lawrence for herself. When she returned to a lectureship at Stellenbosch ... she discovered the early Leavis, whose critical approach she supported passionately ... for the rest of her life ...

Her discovery of *Scrutiny* ... had a decisive effect on her sense of the moral-political relevance of the study of literature. This certainly played a part in motivating her fierce opposition to nationalist racism. For instance, when she got to Johannesburg, she formed a group of academic teachers dedicated to diagnosing the vacuity and indeed the perniciousness of the doctrines of 'Christian National Education', a post-1948 Nationalist blueprint ... In this task, or more properly this vocation, she had a major ally. This was Geoffrey Durrant, today [Autumn 2002] at ninety-five still wonderfully articulate, incisive and vigorous in Vancouver BC ... A Cambridge student in the early thirties under Tillyard at Jesus, he was on the margins of the new Cambridge criticism, although he too (especially after a visit to Germany in the late thirties) was swiftly awakened to the ethical dimension of literary studies. Shortly before the outbreak of the war, he was appointed to Stellenbosch, where he quickly established a rapport with van Heyningen. Following the outbreak of the war, he served in military intelligence, under Colonel Malherbe who ... became Vice-Chancellor of the University College of Natal, and ... appointed Durrant Head of an English Department that was intellectually *in extremis*. In a very short space of time this new professor transformed his department into the most challenging and desirable location in South Africa for the study of literature. Durrant's essays, on Wordsworth and Shakespeare and other topics in the early issues of *Theoria*, a journal which in a minor key sought to do for South Africa what *Scrutiny* was doing for the UK, made a huge impact on the likes of me. Durrant's other publications, especially his two little books on Wordsworth which you published [one in Robin Mayhead's series] were for me full of incisive insights, though they did not please the reviewers, but I shall never forget his first revelatory essays. Even in Canada, where he finished his career, his command of issues and principles at academic meetings became legendary ... In a very different style, but as creatively as Christina van Heyningen, he helped for some unforgettable years to make literature even more immediately central to public life than Leavis himself.

In general there were three English departments that could be said to have registered the impact of *Scrutiny*, though always under the proviso that this group of South African academics interacted personally ... with creative writers, and that they brought the perspective of international literary studies to bear on Afrikaner nationalism. In South Africa the teaching staffs of these three departments included Afrikaner, Jewish, European as well as English intellectuals. Moreover, that movement lost some of its potency, for though it survived ...

there occurred an early diaspora ... This loosely-related group of academics ... was beginning to break up by the early sixties. Christina van Heyningen remained in South Africa, but in Natal; of the exhilarating Wits Department, among several Zoe Girling and Thelma Philip (the best close reader I have ever encountered) emigrated respectively to Canada and the UK, and they were in due course followed by the exceptionally gifted and influential Fred Langman ... who in the mid-sixties emigrated to the Australian National University, where he exerted and still exerts, an indispensable influence. The leader of the Natal group, Geoff Durrant, ended up on the Pacific coast of Canada ... Two of Leavis's students, Bob Jones and Roy Littlewood were drawn by van Heyningen to Pietermaritzburg and Stellenbosch respectively: both made a great impact on South African students ... but after a few years both were driven out by *apartheid*, Jones to a very influential career at York, and Littlewood to Bristol. Most dramatically, Derek Marsh, an academic protégé of Durrant's was swept up in a police swoop on the Liberal party in Natal, and imprisoned for about four months. When he was released he sought refuge in Australia, where he held senior chairs at two universities.

A sad little postscript: Christina van Heyningen did offer us a book – on Milton, I think. I showed it to Leavis, and he advised against publication.

I mentioned Robin Mayhead's series British Authors as tracing and using some of these talents – people who had taught outside the UK and were used to addressing students who did not have the 'background' notionally possessed by English students. But, as I have explained, we came to feel that this was not a real distinction once UK universities widened their intake, though it was still a valuable qualification to have taught outside England. The books served well enough in all markets. In particular Geoffrey Durrant did the book on Wordsworth, Bob Jones the one on George Eliot, and Jacques Berthoud, whom I met as Lecturer in Southampton under Frank Prince as Professor, the one on Conrad – the last still in print, with Alastair Niven on Lawrence.

Jacques also mentions Fred Langman as the link between the South African group and the Australians at ANU (the Australian National University). Australia did not have the political-cultural-racial problems of South Africa, but the colleagues and pupils of Sam Goldberg did have the academic-political embattlement familiar in Cambridge – were indeed stigmatised as 'Leavisite'. Though none of them had been immediate colleagues or pupils it was noticeable that some had spent sabbaticals in Cambridge, or done a Ph.D. under the supervision of Lionel Knights at Bristol before he came back to Cambridge (by that route Wilbur Sanders and Heather Glen actually joined the Cambridge department and became valuable authors). But for the traditionalists back home the term was a handy abuse.

The group was initially centred at Melbourne, but there had been an odd 'grand old Duke of York' moment when Goldberg led some colleagues to Sydney (bigger, richer, more prestigious) but found it unwelcoming and led them back again. When I got to know him he was at Canberra, at ANU, but it was the original group in Melbourne which had unity and thrust and made the impression.

In his letter Jacques makes the important point that the journal *Theoria* had a key role: it provided an intellectual centre or mouthpiece, rallying sympathetic readers and contributors in departments elsewhere. The equivalent Australian journal was *The Critical Review*, founded in the late 1950s in Melbourne by Goldberg. I became aware of it in the late 1960s and found myself using it as a source of potential authors and advisers. I also wrote three or four articles for it. Sam was still editor when he died in 1991, so that the issue of 1992, to which I contributed, turned into a memorial volume. I believe it still appears, but I can't think that it now has the drive and coherence he gave it, the width of application or the international appeal.

Sam wrote an excellent book on Joyce's *Ulysses*, published (of course) by Chatto in 1961. I made it my business to get him and members of his group as authors for the Press. I first visited Australia in 1971. To some extent it was already a matter of renewing and extending acquaintanceships, since their practice of taking sabbaticals in Cambridge meant that I had met some previously – had published one – and had been given names of others. This visit was I think the first serious editorial initiative from Cambridge (unless Alan Winter had already visited as Scientific Editor) and was the beginning of a regular traffic, since Australia was being recognised both as a significant market for our books and a good source of authors. What we didn't get, the Americans would – eventually if not at once. I was also supporting the developing local branch, which was growing out of an old agency arrangement, which had been a purely marketing thing, and run from Bentley House in London.

I secured both Goldberg and his wife Jane Adamson as authors, both writing on Shakespeare. They became friends of mine. Sam's last book, *Agents and Lives*, had an odd fate. It was published as he was dying at 65 of heart failure. It showed a move from English towards philosophy at the moment when philosophy was looking towards literature, but most of English had retreated into its relativist cul-de-sac where ethics had no place. But I think it is correct to say that Sam's death left a group of competent colleagues without a leader. Movements end.

Another kind of post-*Scrutiny* endeavour: one of Leavis's most impressive contributors had been James Smith. Articles of his in *Scrutiny* which bowled me over when I first read them were his 'Wordsworth: A Preliminary Survey' and 'Mallarmé: Life and Art'. He seemed to have that European outlook which I valued and looked for: it is still rare for an English teacher to be genuinely free of other literatures. (Enright was another: he wrote well on modern German writers in *Scrutiny*.) Smith had had a chair in Switzerland and retired early to Cambridge. I went to see him and was depressed to find him an old pussy-cat and not at all the bold, free-ranging person I imagined. But I persisted, and we were discussing a collection when he died. Unfortunately the collection was then put together by his friend Edward Wilson, Professor of Spanish and Syndic, and also now an old pussy-cat: his selection went heavily for Smith's rather boring later work on renaissance drama and left out some of the more interesting stuff.

There was a sort of history here. Wilson and Smith had been undergraduate friends at Cambridge in the pioneering days, friends of Empson, admirers of Wittgenstein. Leavis had a sardonic story about Smith striking the ground by the banks of the Cam with his stick and saying '*That* was where I realised Wittgenstein was wrong.' 'He was their Doctor Johnson', Leavis said. However, Wilson himself had at the start of his career been one of the pioneers in modern languages – there were others in Classics – who were transforming the study of those literatures to echo what was going on in Cambridge English.[1] Wilson had translated Gongora into English verse – one of the 'creative' contributions to *Scrutiny* (I later got the Syndicate to publish his whole volume of the *Soledades*, in English verse, and don't regret it). But he had become a mere scholar – a routine transformation that Smith had also undergone. So it was a lesson in how one's enthusiasms, quite solidly based, can turn into disappointments.

I mentioned another former colleague of Leavis's: Lionel Knights, whom I first met as Professor at Bristol, and who followed Basil Willey as King Edward VII Professor at Cambridge and became a Syndic.[2] To an outsider this might have looked like a triumph for the Leavisite cause, but

---

[1] The predecessors, F.C. Green in Cambridge French, who was Professor when I did the Tripos, and J.B. Trend, Professor of Spanish, had been literary men of a sort. Green published a book on Proust with the Press, and Trend had been a close friend of Lorca and also music critic of *The Criterion*. The sort of thing they wrote was of the generation of the more up-to-date men of letters in English higher journalism and must have looked amateurish to the next generation. I wonder now if it wasn't to be admired in its way.

[2] I met him on an editorial visit of the kind I had introduced. The Bristol English department contained Knights, Henry Gifford, a talented comparatist, and Christopher Ricks, as well as Littlewood. I went to a lunch in which Ricks addressed Gifford as 'Nuncle' – playing the Fool to his Lear.

Knights was no crusader, indeed very moderate (Leavis quoted him as saying 'I am no moral hero' – and quoted it enraged, because he took Knights to mean that he, Leavis, was setting himself up and acting the part of moral hero). It helped me a little to have him there; we reissued some books of his in paperback, and he brought some good pupils to the Press as authors.

When he was succeeded by Frank Kermode, I was at first alarmed, since Kermode was a hate-figure among dogmatic young Leavisites, especially Roy Littlewood, a colleague of his at Bristol, and Morris Shapira, who took care to review his books and did it maliciously. I hadn't read the books then – they seem inoffensive now – but I wondered what it would do for my own efforts to have him known to be there, and to have him judging my initiatives at the Syndicate table. Actually, I found he wanted to be liked – as Lionel Knights did – and they were both likeable. It was not difficult to get on with him.

I made it my business to do so, and I think he did the same. In this sort of deal, he did bring some of his own projects forward. I remember a book on tragedy by the French psychoanalyst-critic André Green. When the translation came onto my desk I had my first experience of the jargon produced by the modern theoretical movement. Laboriously, I edited this into plain English, which Frank and his wife had laboriously to convert back into theory-speak – or Discourse. They must have found me lamentably behind the times. Like George Steiner, Frank was at that time one of those who watch for things coming over the horizon, and feel it a pleasant duty to hail them. He was a convert to heavy theory for a while, but recanted spectacularly when he saw what it was all doing to criticism. I do remember saying to him early on that the main effect of the new movement was that it was as if deliberately cutting off the discussion of literature from general intellectual life: it was like a renewal of scholasticism, and a game for insiders and sixth-form epistemologists.

A diversion here – well, not really. I remember also coming across terms like 'foregrounding' in Jean Franco's general introduction to Spanish-American literature – still in print after many reprints. Wasn't this an awkward kind of formation, I asked? I wanted to rephrase it. No, she said, it was now a term of art, and one had to use it. It came from one of those critics like Bakhtin, whom I hadn't read. But I did then remember, much earlier, two young Research Fellows in my office who had been bitten by the 'rhetoric' bug of the 1950s, initiated by Rosemund Tuve in her *Elizabethan and Metaphysical Imagery* (1947, reviewed in *Scrutiny*). They tossed the OK terms to each other in a game of 'I know this stuff too, can you beat this?' It had struck me then that in the Middle Ages young clerics could display to each other their command of the terms they had learned from the leading Schoolmen, and feel secure and above the common herd as members of an in-group.

Rhetoric didn't take off then (but see Quentin Skinner's authoritative deployment of it on Hobbes, where it suddenly becomes authentic). What did take off later was the mostly French-derived theory which I had bumped up against in André Green. It moved quickly from being the latest interesting fashion to a deep-seated orthodoxy for the second-rate who wanted both to be part of the orthodoxy and at the same time to pat themselves on the back for being avant-garde. Green displayed the dogmatic Freudian element (the French discovered Freud later than we did, and typically made their late-coming look like a revelation). In due course the psychoanalytical strain joined up with feminism, anti-colonialism and general political correctness to become a persecuting self-righteousness, a natural puritan extension.

Hang on a moment, you may be thinking. Wasn't Leavis the source of such an orthodoxy, and weren't his less interesting pupils and people like me just such disciples? Yes and no. The supporters and followers of any important, innovative and charismatic figure are in that position – cannot escape it – will for a time think of themselves as similarly innovative and combative, and then fall into a conventionalism. But what was unfolding in Cambridge English in the mid twentieth century was not imported at second hand: it started as a sharp local debate among differing viewpoints; and Leavis's colleagues and pupils began as conscious innovators who were helping to create something coherent and put it to use. There began to be an orthodoxy post-1945, and it was basically more Leavisite than anything else. But the main source, Leavis himself, went on developing his thought until he died, so it was not an unchanging thing, was personal to him and original, and in my view people, including ex-pupils, have not caught up with him – have not effectively absorbed and developed much that remains implicit in his work.

That interim orthodoxy has been replaced by the French-derived, American-enforced theory, and my objection to it is that it is an unexamined set of assumptions and a routine set of moves assembled at second or third hand from a number of questionable authorities and expounded as scripture by a horde of mediocrities: became the majority view.

So it appears a shrewd move that Leavis did not make his 'theory' explicit – though I have suggested he had one – so it could not so easily be fastened on as a doctrine; rather it was a method. But actually he did not have a specifically personal method. Though he practised 'close reading', and did it more effectively than anyone else, it was a common element in all Cambridge English, and for that matter was the basis of American New Criticism and is still alleged to be a prime element in modern theory. What he had, apart from sheer critical ability, was the crusading spirit based on his historical and social perceptions – his sense of being the continuator of a tradition going back to Arnold and beyond. It was never a matter of just producing an 'approach', a set of tools, a jargon.

True, the mere epigones in the movement echoed his words and judgements, and it was they who made it look like a jargon and a doctrine. The more influential members went into the world, became theatre directors, publishers, civil servants, high-level journalists and academics, not just in English but in Modern Languages and Anthropology, or teachers like David Holbrook with an element of that crusading attitude.

The most obvious distinction is that Leavis produced all those essays and books of real discussible criticism, while the present theorists have not produced a comparable body of criticism, still less the sort of thing which is read outside the profession – indeed their primary aim is not to produce criticism as such, but to brood on method, on approaches – on the mere possibility, one might say.

I have read more Ph.D. theses than most people, and came early-on to dread that first chapter – the appearance of novelty turning into the guarantee of orthodoxy – in which the unfortunate candidate has to demonstrate command of the latest secondary-reading and the latest instruments before going on to use the instruments on some painfully familiar topic. In English, the laugh – or the ironic cheer – used to come when the new analysis was used on Marvell's 'Coy Mistress' or some other ancient favourite.

But that is something about academic work generally. I come back to my main, my professional preoccupation by saying again that in the period from 1935 to at least the late 1960s a book of literary criticism had a real chance of being reviewed in the weekly press, and being bought and read by people who thought of themselves as general readers. It hardly happens in the 2000s: Kermode – who renounced literary theory in his long and effective prologue to *An Appetite for Poetry* in 1989 – and Ricks, who always dismissed the movement as a waste of effort, are the only English academics who have this audience still: all honour to them. The trade in literary biography has taken the place of criticism. At least it keeps people interested in particular authors.

I am gloomy about this partly because reflecting on it now leads me to think that in the subject I cared more about than any other, where I tried over a longer time to do something effective, I don't look back on the whole subject as a particular success, though there are some areas which give me satisfaction. I started to write these chapters because Sarah Stanton, former colleague and respected successor, innocently asked me to put down something about what I had done for the English list. I felt a real qualm then, which has accompanied me throughout. What did it amount to, and was it worth while, and if not why not?

Of course, any publisher looking back forty or fifty years is surveying a cemetery of dead books, forgotten books, haunted by the ghosts of old enthusiasms. That is inevitable, and reinforced by the observable, painful phenomenon that books die very quickly now: when I started, they used to have a life of twenty years or more. The standard comfort has been that the individual book, the individual author, have to be seen like ants or worker bees, or, better, medieval architects and builders, working for their lifetime on something which never gets completed as first planned but is nevertheless recognisable as a continuing cultural endeavour. Knowledge and education get served, and it goes on. The books are there in the libraries, and some of them go on being used because they made a contribution to this topic or that. But the argument doesn't work easily for me in this case.

One possible reason, only clear to me now, is that I was simply too late. Ian Parsons at Chatto was the right man in the right place at the right time (he even went to the right school, Winchester). He did a wonderful job, but he had that element of luck on his side: he was there at the beginning; he was there at the end. The relationship with Leavis which I had was valuable and instructive for me, but Parsons had published the original books in that extraordinary list of Chatto's. I was, without knowing it, ringing down a slow curtain or at best trying to prolong the act. English studies were entering what I now recognise as a decline, not at first in the numbers studying or teaching, or the number of books published, but in the intellectual force, the influence outside itself, of a subject which for a time had been alongside the most interesting of the humanities, and was so because 'literature' started as what every educated person reads, thinks about and talks about to other educated people.

However, back in the 1960s, even in the 1970s, there still seemed a lot to play for, and I had what I thought was the advantage of representing the side which seemed to have won. The competition was still dominated by Chatto; but Routledge, Edward Arnold, Faber, Macmillan, as well as

Oxford and Cambridge, had lists of some worth and were active – most general publishers in the late 1950s began to pursue the suddenly expanding university market, and English was the easiest subject to enter, precisely because it spilled over into the general readers' interest.

Also there were the little movements which seemed to offer stimulus and hope. I have mentioned two: significantly they were outside the UK, and it seems to follow that insofar as they were correctly described as 'Leavisite' they were bound to be an after-effect. The group in England which was most lively, and might stand comparison with the South African and Australian movements, centred on Ian Robinson, who had been a pupil of Leavis's and became a lecturer at Swansea, where he worked with sympathetic philosophers and theologians. I came across him as the author of a Cambridge thesis on *Chaucer's Prosody* which had twice been refused a Ph.D. My recollection is that I helped it to become a book (1970) by pointing out a contradiction: it seemed to be arguing two opposing viewpoints because it could not bring itself to adopt a sensible middle position. In all his books Robinson characteristically moved between a remarkable, almost micro-surgical interiority and a very shrewd general critical-historical position. He is also a committed Anglican. So one of his later books demonstrates how Tyndale's New Testament and Cranmer's drafting of the prose of the early Book of Common Prayer[3] mark a foundational stage in the development of a natural English spoken and written prose – preceding the conventionally accepted origins in the seventeenth and early eighteenth centuries. The book of his which made most stir, in 1973, was *The Survival of English* – at first called *The Decline of English*. This was sharp about the language of, for instance, the NEB or *The Times* or politics or what Robinson generalised as pornography. It was reprinted and paperbacked, and I remember sitting through a meeting of the Literary Committee of the NEB at which the members shook their old heads at the hard words addressed to them. Another book, *The New Grammarians' Funeral* (1975), addressed the imperialism of Chomsky's Transformational-Generative Grammar, and its claims.

Robinson edited his own quarterly journal, *The Human World*, which ran for four years, from 1970 to 1974, and then mutated into a little offshoot, well named *The Gadfly*. I wrote a number of pieces for *The*

---

[3] Heard not just weekly by large congregations every Sunday in church, but daily, for instance in schools which used to have morning assemblies. So pious agnostics like me have this prose, its phrases, structures and rhythms, in our blood, so to speak. We can still recite the main elements. But we are the last generation of such people. Now this is a tradition scholars have to recover, giving footnotes in the once-obvious places in the texts.

Human World. It was a brave venture, with interesting stuff in it, but now looks like a brief after-shock or postlude. It did print two pieces by Leavis, one of them his recollections of Wittgenstein; and it did provide a rallying-point for a group of youngish activists. It was also pretty general in its interests, and that was a problem, for Ian himself had sharp political views which he expressed editorially. They were not exactly eccentric, but they put him on his own and made the journal look too much like one man's mouthpiece. I found myself writing letters of protest about the treatment of the Irish troubles. There was an object-lesson here, in how not to keep a group together. The result was that a remarkable man found himself on his own, became a voice crying in the wilderness. The voice was impressive, and the wilderness is real, but he did not have the effect he might have had. The contrast with *Theoria* and the *Critical Review* is instructive.

One thing I learned fairly soon is that no sensible editor pursues a single line, even if he or she must have a positive set of preoccupations. My sense, now, that I had come too late, should be added to my other sense that I was, like it or not, continuing something which had started long before me: the CUP English list which went back to the early 1900s and is still in some ways massively moving along. I have mentioned in the previous chapter what struck me as its out-of-dateness, or how it seemed so to me in the 1950s. But it had its silent slow momentum – still has: so books come in, solicited or not, to join the uncontentious solidity.

It's true that I started the drama list (now renamed Theatre and Performing Arts Studies) – if unconsciously, by accepting John Styan's first book, forming a friendship with him, commissioning at least one book from him and just helping him with the others, which naturally flowed from him. At first this was 'English', but his interests were wider, for 'drama' is more universal, and it became clear that this was becoming a subject in its own right. Diane Speakman and then Sarah Stanton took it over and developed it systematically, and the Cambridge list is now by far the best, so that is something positive. But in the beginning it was there alongside Shakespeare and the Elizabethans and the Restoration dramatists in England. Here too I had the luck to accept and support a good author: Andrew Gurr, whose *The Shakespearean Stage* and *Playgoing in Shakespeare's London* are standard works, regularly revised and reprinted.

Here we were taking a traditional strength and bringing it up to date. The venerable *Companion to Shakespeare Studies* was revised and reissued under successive editors – and will no doubt continue to be revised and reissued until the end of time. It set the pattern for all the Cambridge

Companions which have followed. On the other hand the reliability, in publishing terms, of the old annual *Shakespeare Survey* suggested that the yearbook, with its faithful subscribers, has most of the publishing virtues of the journal. A tip from H. P. R. Finberg, a medieval historian, led me to propose to Peter Clemoes, then Professor at Cambridge, that there should be a yearbook on Anglo-Saxon. Peter wanted the Cambridge department to be the main centre of study, and so we convened a meeting of English, European and American scholars, and *Anglo-Saxon England* was born – now in its 30th-plus year, and an originating source of the best list in a nice safe subject, with its origins in late nineteenth-century scholarship and then the Chadwicks. Medieval English literature also did well, with Tony Spearing, Peter Dronke, Jill Mann and Piero Boitani as fruitful authors. I take my share of credit for sponsoring all that, but it was altogether conventional or uncontroversial.

A key figure in the world of English and Shakespeare, until he died early, was Philip Brockbank, whom I had known since he was a research student at Jesus, and who moved to the Shakespeare Institute in Stratford from York where he had imported Leavis as visitor and helped to set up one of the best English departments in the country. The department there provided good authors, such as A.D. Moody, the Eliot authority. Diane Speckman and I set up the New Cambridge Shakespeare under Philip's General Editorship: the first volume appeared in 1984 and it is now near completion. It was founded in the era of Fredson Bowers as textual authority: the Press had published his *Textual and Literary Criticism* in 1959 and undertook massive editions of Dekker, Marlowe, and Beaumont and Fletcher of the kind he advocated. But the doctrine changed, and it was a Cambridge book, Peter Blayney's work on the text of *King Lear*, which dominated the argument from the 1980s onward. In theory, everything needs to be edited again every time this happens.

I won't list all the individual titles in English studies which seemed to me at the time to be good and interesting enough to publish. I do however have some favourites which I can't entirely overlook, and I mention them below.

But first I can make some general points. The story I have been telling was at important moments about groups linked by allegiance to a teacher and by access to a favoured journal. Some journals had a distinctive agenda; but there were others which were lively and successful without being in that sense political. One important genre in literary publishing was the collection in a volume of one's essays (not at all the same as academic journal articles), adding, as insurance, one or two unpublished pieces, and linked perhaps by an introductory essay, but much more by a personal style or approach. Reputations were made this way – for instance, by the Leavisite group – and the books were reviewed as part of the literary output of the time, and might sell well and reprint. A good deal of the Chatto list consisted of such books.

The main alternative, going back to the days of the old English Men of Letters series, was the book on a single author, with perhaps a brief biographical introduction, something about preceding criticism, and then a survey of the whole work arranged by titles or genres: ideal lengths about 250–300 pages, or 120–60 pages for a more elementary treatment. The hidden theme I am discovering in these pages is that though I was indoctrinated against the old 'men-of-letters' group or ethos, I was unable to do without characteristic elements of it. These were forms which those people introduced, and I and everyone else took them as natural, and adapted them.

Both kinds of book suited the general reader: the first kept you in touch with what was being written by interesting critics in influential journals, the second suited readers making a way through an *oeuvre* who wanted a convenient guide or set of reflections. I look at my own shelves, and see Leslie Stephen's studies of Swift and George Eliot (Swift 1882: reprinted, pocket edition 1909; Eliot 1902) – 200 pages of skilled handling: more worth reading after 100-plus years than much that has followed. These books were supreme examples of how to treat any author; and I simply accepted the model in various series that I instituted, as did my contemporaries.

It also occurs to me that, for instance, Sam Goldberg's best-known two books are on a single work of literature: *Ulysses* (1961) and *King Lear* (1974); Jane Adamson's was on *Othello* (1980). Of course, *Ulysses* had just become classical in 1961, but it seems unthinkable now that a whole book – even a short one – should be written about a single work, except as a brief, low-level, exam-oriented guide. It's possible that the lecture course, the set text and the Ph.D. thesis were already showing an effect on these and similar formats, but those institutions have themselves changed.

When I started, there were virtually automatic assumptions about such kinds. These were the books which the ordinary reader could hear about from weekly reviews, and think of buying so as to feel in touch with what was coming out of the literary world. The annual output was not enormous, though it was growing, and keeping up was becoming a problem. But that world was already being contested by the university world. When, for example, I adapted the second form – the monograph on the single author – for students in the British Authors series, the length had to be maintained at 160 to 200 pages simply because the books had to be cheap enough for students. They also had to be carefully edited for sequence, knowledge assumed, coverage of examination requirements. Something rather gritty and useful was produced by a practised teacher, something lively or elegant for a wider audience was being lost.

That form is virtually dead, and the general reader's interest is not now specifically catered for. The Cambridge Companion which fills the gap might be thought to meet that need as well as the students', and certainly the chunky work of reference contains a lot of information; but the approach is remorselessly academic: one can sense the need not only to give the information but to incorporate the currently fashionable approaches. This is actually dangerous in that when the fashion changes the book looks more dated than a much older one. But then you just do it again to the new prescription.

If I turn to the books which remain in my memory as better than standard productions, I can relate them both to the old genres and to a new one which was emerging. This was the Ph.D. thesis revised to become a book – or in the best cases always intended to be a book. So my first example, Tony Tanner's *The Realm of Wonder* (1965), is an instance; also of the influence of his teacher, A.P. Rossiter of Jesus, who taught Philip Brockbank, Tony Spearing, Jeremy Prynne – and me. It was also the foundation of our list in American literature, which was becoming a subject in its own right. I added books on William Carlos Williams and Lucy Beckett on Wallace Stevens, and there was Dorothea Krook on Henry James, and it began to be clear that here was a list in the making: Andrew Brown took it on, and it is now substantial and important. Another plus, to cheer me up a bit.

The book which I have the softest spot for is Norman Sherry's *Conrad's Eastern World* (1965); Denis Enright, then Professor in Singapore, directed me to him when I visited with Philip Harris, and I came back with it in my bag. It has every virtue: it is a well-told detective story, hunting out the extraordinary real-life incidents which Conrad came across in the course of his own life and travels as sea-captain; it is set in exotic surroundings at a legendary time; it is well told and uses the documents well; and it makes a substantial point about Conrad – that he had to have real experience, related to his own, as the base of his apparently romantic story-telling (an important element of most early twentieth-century fiction). The book ideally suited both the scholar and the general reader. Norman went on to write (inevitably) *Conrad's Western World* (1971), which has the same virtues but is not quite so captivating. He was then diverted into the massive biography of Grahame Greene (a Conrad fan who decided he wanted Norman to write the authorised life). This too was the start of something, like my next choice, Keith Sagar's *The Art of D.H. Lawrence* (1966). It marked an advance in the study of Lawrence by providing a much more detailed chronology of the work, revealing a writer who was a compulsive reviser, working, nearly always, simultaneously on a number of pieces in different genres, and using successive spontaneities to produce the ultimately realised effect (Leavis's term, itself realised here). With Lawrence one has to consider something which was as if always there, waiting for him to get it out entire over a lifetime – a short one. Lawrence had once been seen as a slapdash improviser, mostly concerned to get across his 'liberating' view of sexuality, not in any sense an artist. It was immensely important for me to find myself introduced to this revision of the standard view. Keith also did much to establish the reputation of his friend Ted Hughes in his *The Art of Ted Hughes* (1975).

I make the link with Conrad by saying that Norman Sherry's books made my mind work in similar directions. Having set up the Lawrence edition, I thought that a similar service could be done for Conrad: there was a much-needed and very complicated textual job to be done. It turned out to be a disappointment, because it is taking so long – though the edition of the Letters is complete. But the editions both atttracted other books. There was Conrad's son John, for instance, simple elderly gentleman, bringing into the office his reminiscences of his childhood and the family; and there were important works on the Polish background by the Polish scholar Najder (a political activist who had been condemned to death by the communist regime for making propaganda for the USA). The leading British scholar was Ian Watt, whose classic study had been published by Chatto. I had made a contact with him through the work on literacy he co-edited with Jack Goody (they were both at St John's). We got two books from him in the end, one on Conrad, the other his long-meditated book on myth in literature.

An absolute one-off – in my view a classic – was Elinor Shaffer's *Kubla Khan and the Fall of Jerusalem* (1975): the title links Coleridge and George Eliot, and the book is about the element of romanticism in England which links it with – is mostly derived from – the German tradition in philosophy and criticism. Elinor was a pupil of Trilling's at Columbia, and a friend of John Searle and Miriam Firestone of the New York editorial staff.

Another author who became a friend was John Fraser, who wrote for the journals I read and sometimes contributed to. I admired his work, and liked him. His *Violence in the Arts* appeared in 1974, reprinted that year and was paperbacked, with illustrations, in 1976. *America and the Patterns of Chivalry* appeared in 1982; and in 1984 a collection of essays called *The Name of Action*. This was dedicated to me (I didn't know until the book appeared). It was, I thought, a good example of that now old-fashioned kind of book, with essays from respected journals in the UK, the USA and Australia (Sam's *Critical Review*) on Shakespeare, Scott Fitzgerald, Mark Twain ... a characteristically wide range, with one group giving a new aspect to the idea of the organic community (one Cambridge tradition of publishing being part of that). I was startled to see that it got a really malignant review in the TLS, which effectively killed it.

A similar book, Wallace Robson's *The Definition of Literature*, had appeared in 1982, but was not ambushed in the same way. I had courted Robson as Oxford's equivalent of Leavis, had visited him there and used him as referee. The essays included some serious discussions of theoretical issues – and also one on *The Wind in the Willows* which is of course a classic of a kind. And in 1978 we had also published a collection by Graham Hough (deadly enemy of Leavis) cheerfully called *Selected Essays*. For me the review of Fraser's book marked the death of such collections, even though Ricks and Kermode have been able to go on producing good ones.

The other kind of traditional study, of the single author, produced at least one book which gave me satisfaction – Anne Barton's *Ben Jonson, Dramatist* (1984). She had shot into prominence as a young American prodigy, called Bobby-Anne Righter (first husband's name) with a highly regarded book on Shakespeare from Chatto. I pursued her when she went to Oxford – even, you might say, sent her a daughter of mine to be taught by her at New College. The book finally came in, and was worth the trouble. I could mention also a little book on Hopkins: *In Extremity* by John Robinson (1978 – also a very beautiful book: until the 1980s we were producing books that Walter Lewis and his team would not be ashamed of). A book I enjoyed, by an author I liked, was Howard Mills's *Peacock: His Circle and his Age* (1969: Mills also edited a substantial selection of Crabbe's poetry in an extraordinarily well-designed book, also paperbacked: 1967).

As for the other old Cambridge tradition, I commissioned a substantial two-volume selection of the journals of George Sturt, edited by Eric Mackerness, which came out in 1967. George Spater's biography *William Cobbett: The Poor Man's Friend*, also in two volumes, was published in 1982. John Barrell's study of Clare, *The Idea of Landscape and the Sense of*

Place, came out in 1972, and has lasted well. It is also a beautiful book, in the Cambridge classical style.

Well, I am just picking favourites down off the shelves, and sighing over the past. I have been indicating as I went along what it all amounts to – not as much as I should have wished. It represented the time, which was a gentle descent into what we have now. What we once had was a lively subject, with elements of amateurism, almost, dragged along by serious innovation. What we have now is more professional, keeps the machine going along, promotes orthodoxies and keeps its head down. In English, I did one really big thing – the Lawrence Edition. I give it a whole chapter.

CHAPTER 14

Other literatures

I had read French Literature at Cambridge in 1947–8 – not merely because I was disappointed in my Tripos result in English but because it was a genuine interest and a talent (Tillyard once told me that I had got my Exhibition at Jesus partly because my French papers were so good). It had then been a bit of a shock to find how old-fashioned the lecturing was compared with the English Faculty at its best, but I never wasted much time on lectures in either Tripos. I had supervisions with the *lecteur* Robert Déaux, who was good and interested, and every week I wrote him two long essays in French (I had to do more or less the whole of French literature in one year, so I read and wrote like mad). Then in the Army in Austria on National Service I found myself using my schoolboy German, and just going round the country and taking in a sense of the culture also had a deep influence.

My own sense that the Cambridge English I had begun to pick up in school and then felt in full force as an undergraduate – that this movement must naturally affect the study of any other literature, was logical, shared, had begun to be felt even before the War and was now becoming a proselytising movement. It went back more generally to Eliot's essays and more particularly to *Scrutiny*, where Denis Enright had written interestingly about German, and Martin Turnell about French. Turnell was not entirely approved of by Leavis, who once told me, uncomfortably, that he had wanted stuff about French, and Turnell was the best he could find. Turnell made his *Scrutiny* articles the basis of three books, on French classicism, on the novel in France and on Baudelaire, which appeared in 1947, 1950 and 1953. I bought them all on publication and found them useful as a student: in publishing terms they were a pioneering move by Hamish Hamilton. They were sharply reviewed in *Scrutiny*.

The other senior Scrutineer, James Smith, had written those two or three essays giving the powerful impression of being able to command both French and English and their modern interaction. I have described

Smith as a friend of Empson and Edward Wilson, and how that group had an early influence beyond the English Faculty in Cambridge, which spread when college teachers like Wilson and his fellow Hispanist A.A. Parker moved to other British universities and then the USA and forwarded the modernisation of European literary studies. This was also being undertaken post-war by pioneers in two or three widely scattered French departments: Vinaver, Mansell Jones and Alan Boase, for instance.

This influence on the teaching of other literatures has not had the attention it deserves – English, naturally enough, took the foreground, especially for being contentious. It has also been forgotten that English studies in Cambridge began as part of the Modern Languages Tripos and were bound to reflect back on it, as well as being initially affected by it. The early teaching of modern languages in British universities was a grim discipline dominated by German philology – historical, etymological, morphological – and the dire teaching of the dead languages in schools: rote-learning of grammatical structures, which was how I learned Latin and French in school. The treatment of French literature was dominated by Lanson's *Histoire* (1894, 1,200 pages, Bible-shaped: I bought it for 6 shillings in 1943, and used it, and have it still) and the routines of classical *explication de texte*. Nothing could be less favourable to the kind of reading eventually promoted in English studies.

The Press's publications in the early years of the last century offer one record, primarily of what went on in Cambridge itself. There was a small but creditable list of books in literary history by pioneers like Arthur Tilley on the French renaissance and seventeenth century, and H.F. Stewart on Pascal. It was a sort of beginning.

Later, F.C. Green, still Professor of French in my time as undergraduate, moved into contemporary studies with his book on Proust. In 1941, bravely, the Press published Elsie Butler's life of Rilke, and Humphrey Trevelyan's *Goethe and the Greeks*. In my first years at the Press the extraordinary Gerald Brenan produced the second edition of his one-man *Literature of the Spanish People*, which joined his no less remarkable – indeed classic – study of the Civil War, *The Spanish Labyrinth*. In German studies there was Walter Bruford's *Germany in the Eighteenth Century: The Social Background of the Literary Revival*, a modest best-seller of 1935 which reprinted in 1939, 1952 and 1959, and was paperbacked in 1965 as a standard text. Bruford was a first-rate, old-fashioned (if you like) scholar who transcended movements simply by being learned and intelligent. During my time at the Press I handled two books by him which furthered my own education – *Culture and Society in Classical Weimar* (1962) and *The German Tradition of Self-Cultivation* (1975).

One can say of that period in modern language studies – say from the 1920s to the 1950s – that it was pre-modern, even that it was amateur. But if it was so, it was in a good sense: it was serious and disinterested and moving towards modernity; the work was directed by enthusiasm, even love, and there are seemingly out-dated books which bear re-reading for their solidity and the spirit in which they were written. And writers like Bruford were carrying forward a good tradition of academic literary history. But the rise of English studies, the influence of Eliot, with his critical interest in other literatures and especially the influence on him of French poets and critics, meant that modern language teaching had to come into the new era, and specifically it had to adopt the new tradition of close reading.

But when I talk of modern language teaching I indicate a set of problems. At least half the teachers in the academic profession were linguists, and some of them had a contemptuous view of literary studies, especially in the modern form. They too had moved in a sense: they were now studying and teaching the living language, which is more than their predecessors had done, but they still gave themselves disciplinary airs. I mentioned the case of Lewis Harmer, Professor of French and Syndic, who prevented the Syndicate from accepting the classic first book – published by Oxford in 1953 – by Odette de Mourgues, Leavis's pupil and the teacher who did most to transform the study of French Literature in Cambridge, precisely by adopting the approaches pioneered in English.[1] It became my aim to recover the initiative then lost, and to catch up with publishers like Hamish Hamilton, Edward Arnold and others who had seen the point and were publishing the pioneers.

Moreover, the fact that this was in origin a language-study, designed to produce the nearest possible thing to bilingualism, had the important effect on books on the literatures that all quotation had to be from the original text in the other language. There was a kind of abyss lurking here. Leavis himself had a remarkable command of French and knew the literature. He also read books about German literature: I recommended one or two of ours to him. But there was a purist doctrine associated with close reading: it had to be from within the language, and you could only do it properly for your own mother-tongue. The Leavises even

---

[1] Her preface also gives acknowledgements to the other people in the profession who were moving in the same direction, notably holders of chairs outside Cambridge and Oxford.

half-thought that Americans were outside the English matrix-culture, at least so far as the classic English tradition was concerned. There was a trap here, which could lead to modern relativisms, where chronology becomes another sundering dimension. Leavis wrote a classic essay on *Anna Karenina*, and quoted in English because he had no Russian, so he was willing for once to be inconsistent, but there was this silent reservation about working on other literatures: he couldn't do for them what he did first for English poetry and then for the novel, where he was working from deep within his own native language.

For everyone else, it was axiomatic that serious work on foreign literatures had to assume that you spoke the language like a native and paid the reader the same compliment. Since the English, even in those better days, were mostly inept at other languages, it meant that as standards of competence declined, academic books about those literatures catered for a dwindling and threatened market. For they still resolutely quoted in the other language; but if they were trying hard to win more readers, they also translated the quotations, which automatically increased the extent and the price of the book. But it remained genuinely the case that you couldn't analyse a poetic text in any depth if you quoted in English translation, so there was this built-in obstacle to applying the best method of modern literary study.

In that situation the only options were to give up or to go on. There were people prepared to try. One was Ronald Gray, who came back after War service and did a Cambridge Ph.D. on Goethe's esotericisms which we published in 1952. He became a Fellow of Emmanuel and Lecturer in German, and in 1956 we published his *Kafka's Castle*. I handled this and struck up a friendship, finding that we shared views on the way literary studies should go. He too was looking in the direction of Downing, and in 1965 we published his *Introduction to German Poetry* which I had commissioned as Education Secretary as one of a set of sixth-form and undergraduate workbooks on the model of Leavis and Thompson's work in English, notably Denys's *Reading and Discrimination* (I see that I chose that book as a college prize in 1946). In 1965 we also published Ronald's *The German Tradition in Literature 1871–1945*, an ambitious piece of literary history with critical underpinnings, though it was mainly historical, with philosophical and political implications (why the German literary tradition leant towards the national disaster). Gray went on to write, in my Major European Authors series, on Goethe, Kafka and Brecht.

I mentioned also another early book, Eudo Mason's *Rilke, Europe and the English-Speaking World* (1961). It was dedicated to the memory of

Henry Caldwell Cook, legendary English teacher at the Perse Boys' School, who set up the Mummery where the boys actually acted the plays they studied, and who taught both Leavis and Mason (Mason taught Leavis to swim). I know Leavis read the book, because he quoted Rilke in one of his essays, making Mason's general point. This was that Rilke spent his life denying any knowledge of English, though he read Lawrence's *The Rainbow* in translation and was profoundly impressed. But one whole drive of his poetry was to resist or lament the inexorable advance of modernisation – or what people once called industrialism, then capitalism, and now call globalisation – which has been remorselessly displacing traditional local cultures: and the source of the globally modern was first England and then the USA. I simplify, but the simplification would do also for the resistance recorded in the *Scrutiny* movement, and for *The Rainbow*. Mason's argument was ingenious in following Rilke's seemingly tortuous social and written tergiversations, but then coming round to the full force of the poetry. I had had a passion for Rilke since discovering him in J.B. Leishman's facing-page translations, where a comparison of the often odd-seeming English led one to something profound in the German. So Mason's was a book which seemed like a narrow professional literary study but opened out into the whole of modern life, as well as demonstrating the extraordinary mixture of profundity and apparent posturing in Rilke. Mason's early death was a serious loss.

It took a long time to find the French equivalent of Ronald Gray's *German Poetry*, but in 1976 we published a two-book treatment by a good team, Peter Broome and Graham Chesters: an introductory volume, *The Appreciation of Modern French Poetry 1850–1950*, and a companion *Anthology of Modern French Poetry 1850–1950*, both published in hardback and paperback, and both successful long-term. They were prescribed and used as course-books, but it was possible to feel that they were not just successful textbook-publishing but were advancing the teaching of the subject and the actual appreciation of French poetry.

I have mentioned my roles as Education Secretary and Chief Editor, and how my work on books for African schools led to books by or about modern African writers, including the important Francophone literary authors: we published editions with introductions and notes of texts by Senghor and Birago Diop and importantly Camara Laye's classic *L'Enfant noir*, which is the French-African equivalent of Achebe's *Things Fall Apart*. There were also introductory critical studies. I formed a long-term friendship with the extraordinary scholar Abiola Irele, who went on to be a series editor.

I have also told how Latin American Studies produced a change of focus, so that classical Spanish literature was as if elbowed aside by the dynamic modern study. You could see it happening when an author who had started with a book on Machado switched to Latin-American poetry and eventually to the indigenous literatures of the other continent. This movement too produced introductory books for students as well as monographs, and we soon found how much better they sold. An odd result was that the pioneer Hispanists who had developed modern literary studies found that they had turned into traditionalists by sticking to the classic Iberian authors: Wilson and Parker went on writing about Gongora and Calderón. I founded a series edited by Peter Russell, Professor at Oxford – Cambridge Iberian and Latin American Studies. This very shrewdly combined literary and historical studies from both sides of the Atlantic, as if to hold the subject together.

The project closest to my heart was my series on European authors on the traditional Men of Letters pattern. I was actually the General Editor, but not declared as such. There was an issue here which went back a long way. Before 1945 I think an Officer of the Press could easily become one of its authors, or, for instance, an Editor of the *Cambridge History of English Literature.* SCR and Charles Carrington felt no difficulty: they could write books for the Press. But later the ethos changed: the officers were now like civil servants – strictly functionaries, impersonal, anonymous. It had become customary for authors in their prefaces to thank 'the Officers of the Press' for their services, and the acknowledgement was appropriate since the authors were served by some people they never met, especially the compositors and readers, who could feel acknowledged by the phrase.

I started to change this, first by allowing authors to thank me personally in their prefaces for editorial assistance. Nobody said anything to me about this, but I know it was disapproved of by some colleagues, especially I guess Brooke Crutchley, and partly for the good reason just suggested – that it deprived anonymous others of their share of praise. But I had two reasons of my own. One was that I had supplied intellectual help, critical help, with the substance of the book, and academics are scrupulous about acknowledging such help. Since I wrote and published on the side, so to speak, I wanted my status acknowledged.[2] Second, and more important from the Press's point of view, I wanted readers and potential authors to know that if they came to the Press they could expect this very important

---

[2] And indeed went on feeling it would be wrong to offer my own publications to the Press. The 1984 *History* was written as part of my duties.

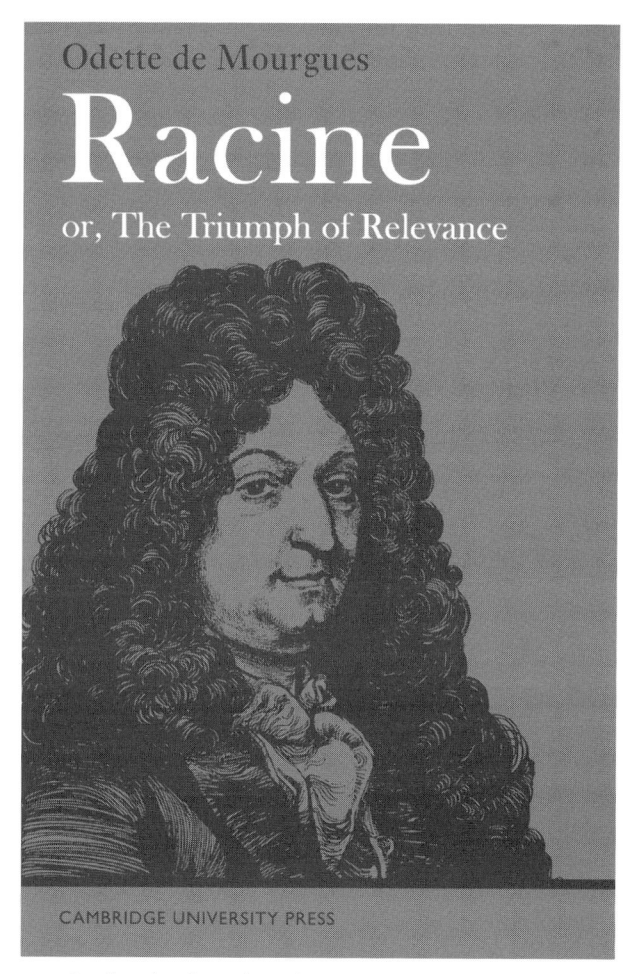

Figure 18. Book-jacket for Odette de Mourgues' *Racine*, by Peter Branfield

service, and not just from me, as we were now building up an editorial team, of people in some sense working within the subject.

But being sole editor of a series was another matter, and I never had the cheek – especially at the beginning – to go to the Syndicate and ask to be appointed official editor of a series to be called Major European Authors. I suspect that if I had, they would have said 'Oh, all right then', but I don't think they would have been comfortable with it, and I would have had to be re-elected every five years after a review of performance, like other series editors.

For that matter, I am not now sure that I planned a formal series as such: it sort of grew. The initial impetus was that Odette de Mourgues took the Cambridge chair, which was an important moment for the whole subject, and I made it my business to get to know her and to woo her as author. I wanted a book on Racine of the kind she would write. So in 1967 we published in hardback and paperback *Racine: Or the Triumph of Relevance*, a deft 180 pages of criticism. There was no series title or preface; it did have the characteristic jacket by Peter Branfield which gave a bold pen-drawing of the subject's head, rather like an engraving, and I used this device for later volumes.

My blurb starts 'This is a critical introduction to the work of Racine for the student and the general reader. It concentrates entirely on the plays themselves, and attempts to say what they are and how they work on the mind of the spectator or reader.' It ends 'This book is written for the reader who is looking for a "way in" to Racine. It provides an overall survey illustrated by a great deal of quotation and analysis. The more expert reader will find his[3] own impressions illuminated and extended.'

Most notably, all the quotation is in French, with no translation. I assumed that there would be enough readers and they would all have enough French – would probably have 'done' a play by Racine, as I had, for the Higher School Certificate, later A-Level, where they were set texts every year. I couldn't make that assumption for the obvious companion volume on Goethe, published in the same year, where I had turned to Ronald Gray as author. Here the quotations are translated in footnotes – and incidentally his preface says 'As on several former occasions, I am deeply indebted to members of the staff of the Cambridge University Press for help both in the composition and the presentation of this study.' The blurb begins 'This is a concise survey and criticism of Goethe's work for the general reader and the student. It is intended as a useful first book from which the reader can go on to more specialised studies. Here Goethe's work is seen as a whole and from the point of view of literary criticism.'

So in 1964–5, say, when these books were commissioned, I knew I wanted books of this kind, and was going to get them, but hadn't formalised them as a series. By the 1980s there were twenty-one books in what was now explicitly called the Major European Authors series: on Racine, Goethe, the Spanish poets of 1920–36 who could be treated as a

---

[3] In those days one said 'his' meaning 'anyone's'. One doesn't do that now.

group, Tolstoy, Dostoevsky, Pushkin, Rabelais, Grillparzer, Kafka, Ibsen, Stendhal, Brecht as dramatist, Pasternak, Chekhov, Nietzsche, Boileau and neoclassicism, Rimbaud, Hasek (author of *Schwejk*),[4] Valéry, Sartre and Molière. The books that I did not get were Lloyd Austin on Mallarmé – long promised but never delivered – and books on Baudelaire and Flaubert. To some extent I made up for this by publishing volumes of essays by the two other very distinguished and productive Cambridge teachers Lloyd Austin, the authority on Mallarmé, and Alison Fairlie, authority on Flaubert, Baudelaire and the nineteenth century generally. There was also a Festschrift for Austin, and monographs by Chesters, Malcolm Bowie and others, mostly pupils of the first two. By this time the Cambridge department was transformed from what it had been, and especially by Odette, Austin and Alison Fairlie, and the work produced was excellent.

The final form of my series preface ran:

This series was initiated within the Cambridge University Press in the late 1960s as an at first untitled collection of general critical studies. For convenience it was referred to inside the Press as 'the Major European authors series'; and once the prejudice against the useful cliché 'major' was overcome, the phrase became the official title.

The series was meant to be informal and flexible, and when the books are commissioned no strict guidelines are imposed. The aim has always been to provide critical studies which can be justifiably given a title which starts with the name of the author and then is not too seriously qualified by the subtitle: therefore to be general, introductory and accessible. When the series started the general assumptions were 'New Critical': there was a strong disinclination to start from a biographical, or even from a more general literary-historical approach. The general aim was and still is to address the works of the author directly as literature or drama, and to try to give a sense of the structure and effect of novels and poetry, or the way drama works with an audience. More specifically, writers of these studies guide the reader through the whole œuvre, being willing to make judgments about importance and quality by selecting which works to dwell on. Readers are helped to form direct impressions by being given liberal quotation and judicious analysis. Little prior knowledge is assumed; in some cases quotation is entirely in English and in others translations are given.

The aim is to keep classics of European literature alive and active in the minds of present-day readers: both those pursuing formal courses in literature and the educated general reader – a class which still exists, though it is smaller than it ought to be.

---

[4] *The Good Soldier Schweik* had been very popular in a Penguin translation.

I had to add to the volume on Valéry – and this shows the inherent problem:

Dr Crow's volume is conceived within the general framework of the series; but to serve its particular purpose it must quote the original French very freely, and the depth and complexity of the argument are imposed by the subtlety and originality of Valéry's thought. To simplify, here, would be self-defeating; but the reader who follows this careful study is given access to deep insights into the nature of mind and language as well as a body of brilliantly original verse.

The qualification leads to the heart of the topic. Here, as in English studies, I am looking back on a body of work where I have to ask, how successful was all that? Does anything remain? I can feel more positive because the story represents an upward movement in the subject itself and the publications it produced – but only for a time. The question is made more pressing because of my sense that this kind of publishing has almost entirely disappeared. English and American cultural parochialism, the dominance of English as a world language, mean that the European literary heritage is becoming lost to the general reader in the same way as the classical heritage was displaced by the rise of the vernaculars. But I look back on the books themselves with warm feelings. This was something worth doing.

Another now-vanished concern: my whole working life was spent during the Cold War. It began for me during military service where on a specially summoned parade one morning our CO told us that things were going badly in Berlin and we ought to be prepared for action. In occupied Austria my shoulder flashes – a yellow cross on a white shield – were those of the old Eighth Army, which had fought through Italy to get there, and my parents were instructed to address my letters to me 'On active service'. But the old war had so to speak turned over in its sleep – I spent most of my time in civilian clothes: having been trained to find gone-to-ground Nazis I found myself watching, or rather listening to the telephones of, Russian sympathisers as well as resurgent right-wingers. The Russians occupied the East of the country: to go on leave in Vienna I had to go by train through their zone, with the curtains down. The occupying powers played destructive games against each other, with the civilians paying the forfeits, which included deportation to Siberia. I saw and heard – took part in – some sobering things during military service, and had little reminders later.

In publishing, there was post-1945 this developing subject, Russian, with a built-in current political urgency. Russian language studies took off, especially in Cambridge, which ran an intensive crash course for servicemen, mostly conscripts, and also in London, and there was a quite pressing interest in the politics, the history and, not least, the literature. For Russian literature now divided into the classics and Soviet literature, which became a subject of topical interest. And Soviet literature divided into the conformist and the dissident elements. Those were the years of Pasternak's *Dr Zhivago*, which became an international best-seller, and then the work of Solzhenitsyn. These books leaked out of Russia or were smuggled out, and became best-sellers for political as much as for literary reasons. Actually, the authors were important and the books were good: it was as if the political situation itself produced a higher quality, an intensity. I had no hesitation about including Henry Gifford's *Pasternak* in my Major European Authors series: the book I wish I had included in 1973 was Clarence Brown's *Mandelstam* – one of the best books I ever handled. It did justice to the life, as recently revealed by Nadezhda Mandelstam, and the poetry, which it quoted in Russian, but managed to comment on it in a way the reader without Russian could grasp. We also got studies of Marina Tsvetaeva and Bulgakov in a good series of monographs – Cambridge Studies in Russian Literature, edited first by Henry Gifford and then by Malcolm Jones. In a sort of parallel with the series on literatures in Spanish, Jones included both the classical authors and the modern ones. The genuinely interesting subject of conformist literature under Stalin also produced good studies – how quite serious and talented writers dealt with a society they did not wish to undermine.

But the main drive, for us in the West, was determined by the *samizdat* authors, who created the stir and also happened to be important. The Medvedev brothers, one of them, Roy, a serious scientist, under intrusive surveillance in Russia, and the other, Zhores, an exile in London, were relatively minor writers, but acted as a channel for the dissidents, and posed a serious question. Zhores offered us a book by Roy called *Problems in the Literary Biography of Mikhail Sholokhov*. Sholokhov was an early star in the Soviet literary sky: his *The Quiet Don*, a study of the Cossack people in the first Soviet days, was very widely read as a foundational epic of the new era, got him the Stalin Prize and the Nobel Prize, but he wrote little else, and that little not good. The question arose: did he write the classic book entirely himself, or had he plagiarised the work of a White Cossack, Kryukov? We published the book in 1975. It was a gamble, because until it was translated I couldn't read it and so didn't really know what I was dealing with. But reading it in English I found it serious, scholarly and judicious – even academic in the good sense.

I dealt with Zhores in visits to London. It was interesting to hear him talk about Russian literary-political life. (I remember hearing that the editor of *Novy Mir*, the nearest thing to a dissident journal, which took risks and was an exciting read, was, he said, 'an elkogorlik'. 'Elkogorlik?' – oh yes: alcoholic.) Zhores was an author himself, and presented me with his book on Solzhenitsyn, who had been a friend of his. It was noticeable that in order to talk to me he led me outside the building where he worked and took me up to open spaces in Hampstead with nobody about – approved tactics for dealing with agents or informants. Certainly he had reason to be careful, but so did I. It struck me that the KGB knew all about this pair of dissidents and the channels they used, and had the choice of cracking down on them or tolerating them in order to slip in something useful now and again. The book on Sholokhov was very moderate, if dissident, and could be shrugged off. I was then offered a *samizdat* book on Solzhenitsyn by a group of authors. I got it accepted, but when it was translated saw that it was an attack – either the normal factionalism of dissidents and exiles or an inspired confection. I went back to the Syndicate and got them to rescind the decision to publish. Harry Hinsley was Chairman at the time, knew all about intelligence work and made nothing of it. The book was published in the USA. I was offered nothing more from that source.

As for the factionalism of dissidents, I met a striking instance which I can use as a neat conclusion. My wife Fay and I got to know Vera Traill, born Vera Guchkov, daughter of a Tsarist Minister of War, emphatic communist convert post-1917, and initially tolerated or used for advertising the cause in Western circles. Some of these intellectual adherents lived a kind of half-exile in Paris – like Tsvetaeva, for instance, whom Vera knew and disliked, but whom she claimed to have discovered as a poet – but they popped back to Russia from time to time, sometimes to disappear for good. Vera married Robert Traill, a communising English journalist, who had worked in Russia and later did the other fashionable thing: he went to Spain to join in the Civil War, and got killed. Vera took up with Mirsky, ex-Prince, White Army officer and very distinguished critic. I mentioned him as a *Scrutiny* contributor. They went to Russia together, and one day Mirsky disappeared. Vera went to Commissar Yezhov, the government Minister of the Interior, to say this was surely an administrative mistake, and then had a call one night to warn her to get out, since a similar mistake was about to be made with her. She took the next train back to Paris. Yezhov himself disappeared. She ended as exile in Cambridge, and was a source of much interesting gossip about the borders of literary-political life in the 1930s. She knew most people and claimed to have almost seduced Eliot, but all she said was romantic and self-promoting. Years later a more spectacular and quite noisy arrival was Stalin's daughter, Svetlana Alliluyeva. Fay taught her daughter briefly, and introduced her to Vera. They fell out immediately and violently: both Russians in half-voluntary exile; both daughters of autocratic eminences; both impossibly warped people, in no way united by their common fate. I think of them as like grotesque book-ends, one at each end of a long, sad set of volumes. Put them together and they can only press against each other.

CHAPTER 15

Getting the Lawrence Edition started

That familiar formula: 'It all started when . . .' comes naturally, and I do actually remember. For me the *Cambridge Edition of the Letters and Works of D. H. Lawrence* – to give it its full title – started with my failure to see a point and take an initiative.

It was at a party given by my old acquaintance the historian Maurice Cowling, who had a certain fame in England as the guru of the Tory right wing, since as college tutor at Peterhouse he once taught a fair proportion of the post-1980 Conservative cabinet when they were at Cambridge. It was at midday in his rooms at Jesus College, and I was invited partly because I was an old acquaintance (I had been an undergraduate there when he was a research student and we became friends, and he went on to become a Fellow) and partly because I was now an editor at the Cambridge Press, and was asked to parties so that people could tell me about this book they had written.

I was standing on the fringe looking at all these people I didn't know. Out of the corner of my eye I saw one strange figure, and thought 'What an odd-looking woman.' Looking again, I thought, 'For all the world she looks like Kingsley Amis in drag.' I looked again, and saw it *was* Kingsley Amis in drag. Why he was doing it I don't know: I suppose he thought it would be fun.

It's the sort of thing which stays in the mind. What stays even more in *my* mind is that a young woman, hearing I was a publisher, came up to me and said that she was a relative of Louie Burrows, and the family had inherited her letters from D.H. Lawrence, and were wondering what to do with them. Louie was the nice, uncomplicated and loving girl to whom Lawrence was chastely engaged from December 1910 until February 1912. She provided some of the family circumstances and early teaching career of Ursula Brangwen in *The Rainbow*, and is an important figure in Lawrence's life. She remained deeply attached to him and to his memory, and had kept his letters, which were bound to be interesting and important.

So I *should* have said, 'Let me look after this for you. Let's get them published.' Instead, I launched into a short talk about copyright, and how the copyright of these letters must be the property of the Lawrence Estate even though the physical objects, the letters themselves, belonged to the Burrows family, and the copyright period, of fifty years in those days – now seventy years – did not begin to run until they were published. All this was true, and among the issues which the family would have to face, but I presented them as reasons why it would be difficult to do anything, when I should have said 'Let me help you with all that.'

This must have been in the mid 1960s, since Louie died in 1962. The letters to her were eventually edited by James Boulton and published in 1968 by the University of Nottingham. One remembered then that Harry T. Moore had in 1962 edited two volumes of Lawrence's letters, and thought he was doing the world a service by making available many more than had been published in Aldous Huxley's pioneering volume in 1932. But already in the 1960s serious readers of Lawrence were aware how many others had been published here and there, mostly in books about Lawrence by friends and enemies, and how even more – at least 1,600 – were known to exist but were still unpublished in any form.

So when I look back to that party, I think it must also have been in my mind that another friend of mine, Andor Gomme, had been the anonymous writer of the scathing review in the TLS of Moore's collection, and had, in effect, made the case for a complete edition. Obviously the time had come to think of collecting all the letters.

And so as time went by and I thought about that exchange, my feeling about myself was 'You fool. What a chance you missed.' But it was not all loss, in that I had been made aware of this very large potential project, which needed to be treated in a more comprehensive and scholarly way than Harry T. Moore had managed, and I was well aware that a university press should have the commitment and the expertise to handle it.

I have recounted in previous chapters how I read English at Cambridge just after the War, that I admired and read F.R. Leavis. I had also as Editor of the *Cambridge Review* in 1956 got Andor Gomme to review Leavis's classic book *D.H. Lawrence: Novelist*, which had altogether changed the critical status of Lawrence. Later at the Press I sponsored the reprint of *Scrutiny*, in which his pioneering essays on Lawrence had first appeared; and in that way I had got to know Leavis quite well. I have described how that reissue was published in 1963, with important consequences for me. So I had a general sense of Lawrence's place, based on some undergraduate reading of the novels and short stories, and my awareness of these various things which were, so to speak, in the wind. For instance, at the Press I also worked with Keith Sagar on his *The Art of D.H. Lawrence*, published in 1966. This was another pioneering book, based on solid research into the writing-life, and began to create a new sense of the development of Lawrence's career, and his composition-practice.

Of course, there had also been even as late as the 1950s the problem of censorship, and this would come to mind because we had seen, in England in 1960, the spectacle of the great *Lady Chatterley* trial, where a government-inspired prosecution for obscenity had been thrown out by a jury. As a result Penguin Books had been left free to publish the book, and paperback it.

From my office at the Press, still in the Pitt Building, I had looked down into the street on publication day. Heffer's Penguin Bookshop was directly opposite my window, and on that morning there was a very long queue. There still used to be errand-boys in those days, and more than one had taken time off to join the queue and was standing there with his bike. I reflected mildly on the literary tastes and interests of errand-boys – but I suspect they weren't any different from other people's: sheer curiosity, a degree of excited prurience, and also, in the end, an interest in this strange book and its author. The *Chatterley* trial also reminded the well-informed that *The Rainbow* had been banned and destroyed in 1915, and that book had never been properly published in England. Was there perhaps a problem with that text?

The sexual issue preoccupied people in the 1960s, when Lawrence was thought of as an apostle of liberation, so this meant that any thought about the reliability or otherwise of the text was dominated by the question of censorship. It was generally understood that publishers, especially in England, frightened of a repetition of the *Rainbow* prosecution, were for ever asking Lawrence to tone things down – and even, now and again, snipped away here and there and took out little bits without his knowledge.

So much was true, but the textual problem in Lawrence does not reduce to that of censorship. In principle, censorship is mechanical and easy to deal with. You just put back the bits cut out (if they have survived). But to go back to Keith Sagar's book: its importance was that it had begun to give the ordinary reader a sense of the complications in Lawrence's writing-life considered as a continuous sequence in which he was engaged, not so much with one work after another quite distinct work, as with a whole network of writings which he was working on at intervals. And though each was, so to speak, itself and at a different stage from the others, they were not so much neighbours as interrrelated members of a group or family. Each chapter in Sagar's book is prefaced by a detailed list of these writings at each point in Lawrence's life.

This chronology of the writings, set in the context of the events of the life, was one basic instrument needed both for critical writing and for textual work. One began to see how the books which stand on the shelf as finished, bound, jacketed and completely ordinary-looking were in the course of Lawrence's writing-life drafted, redrafted, revised and rethought, so that most of them went through very different versions before they reached the printer. And as a publisher I knew very well what could happen to a manuscript as it went through the press: I was doing all those things myself, or getting others to do them. For most books these are simple improvements, but editing a genius – interfering with his work – is another matter. I also knew what could happen in error or by accident.

It is in this long process of redrafting followed by the modern publishing process that more complex textual problems begin. The editor of such a text has to follow its progress all the way through. At every stage you have to try to recover what Lawrence wrote, and to purify it by removing various kinds of interference. You have to look out for Lawrence's own failures to check what he was now reading (in typescript or in proof) against what he had written in the previous form, especially manuscript, since he hardly ever compared one stage with the previous one. If the second form seemed odd, he often substituted a third one. Where others had done the typing, he failed to spot their 'improvements' or errors. You also have to identify his late revisions in manuscript and typescript and his own proof-corrections, while eliminating – so far as you can – house-styling and publishers' interferences, including censorship. One rather startling thing you will come across is the existence of substantial or complete early drafts which are so different from the published version that it is impossible in editing the final one to incorporate notes relating it to the previous one: the gap is simply too wide. So you are faced with the First and Second *Lady Chatterley*, which enforce the thought about members of the same family – closely related but not the same identity. These drafts were already known about; but we came also on *Paul Morel*, which is a draft of *Sons and Lovers*, very different from the final version, and 'The First *Women in Love*'. They have had to be published as separate volumes.

The one thing you can't do is to take a printed edition as base-text, and just correct it. You have to go right behind it to the manuscripts and typescripts if you are not to overlook the whole procession of these sets of changes, so that what you eventually produce is like the first real publication.

I have jumped ahead to what I know now, having worked for all these years on the Edition. To go back to Keith Sagar's book, it had begun to give me and others this sense of the lifetime sequence of drafting and rewriting. I remember working on it as publisher's editor and beginning to form a dim sense that there was a complex matter here, and an important job to be done.

We remained in touch, and actually the first document in the Cambridge Press's huge file on the projected complete edition of the Letters and Works is a note from Keith to me in September 1968 reminding me that I had expressed interest in the idea of a Collected Letters. It is something we came back to in our correspondence over the next year or two. I gathered that Keith and other Lawrence scholars were trying to get the Lawrence Estate, in the person of the Literary Executor and Agent Laurence Pollinger – representing Frieda and her children, then still alive – to act on the suggestion of a Collected Letters. I had pointed out to Keith in 1968 that the usual publishers of Lawrence – Heinemann in the UK and Viking in the USA – were the people to approach first with the idea, but had also said that if they wouldn't do it, the Cambridge Press would certainly think about it.

Nearly four years passed in frustrating correspondence between these Lawrence scholars and the Estate, so that Laurence Pollinger became rather fed up with the steady bombardment about a project which he and the usual publishers felt to be unnecessary or impractical, and certainly a large investment which might not pay. Heinemann formally refused to publish in April 1972, so my half-promise fell due.

Early in June that year, Harry Moore, Jim Boulton, Warren Roberts, Gerald Lacy (the American scholar who had compiled a census of the known letters) and Keith Sagar invited me to a meeting in Nottingham – where Jim was Professor of English – in order to develop a plan for a complete edition of Lawrence's letters. I got into my car and drove up from Cambridge with the firm determination that this was something which had to be done, and this time I wasn't going to haver about the copyright problem. What I had to be, as a professional publisher who understood copyright and such matters, was a facilitator, one who brought the parties together and helped things to happen – if necessary, *made* things happen. The starting-point that was needed was the commitment of a publisher who said that the letters were *going* to be published.

If that was said, the other people concerned had a guarantee that they were not wasting their time if they embarked on a great deal of work.

I now met these leading scholars. Keith I knew. Jim Boulton had been trained as a historian, and had worked on the eighteenth and nineteenth centuries. And here was the famous Harry T. Moore, author of the current very popular Lawrence biography and editor of the two-volume Letters. What was good about Harry was that he had a kind of innocence, a boy-scout enthusiasm. He really wanted to make the case for Lawrence as great author. He wasn't a true academic: though he had a distinguished professorship he was more a gifted journalist. He wrote about European authors as if he could read them in the original, and I'm pretty sure he couldn't; and the work on Lawrence, popular in its time, served its turn but has not survived. Warren Roberts, on the other hand, combined real powers. As Director of the Humanities Research Center at Austin, Texas, he controlled, and significantly added to, the biggest collection of Lawrence material in the world. He had compiled the standard bibliography. For the Center he went to sale-rooms and courted collectors. He knew Frieda and the family, the beneficiaries of the Estate. He was a diplomat and an organiser as well as an enthusiast, and a naturally nice man, breezy and friendly. He and Jim had it in common that they had seen active service in the War. Gerald Lacy was a young researcher who had done that essential thing: compiled that census of known letters, which was an indispensable preliminary for future work.

We had a positive meeting. They wanted to have the project formally backed, so that it acquired status and would be taken more seriously by the Estate and by the owners of unpublished material, and I now wanted to be in an official position with the Estate. A week after the meeting, on 12 June 1972, I recommended to the Syndics of the Press that it should commit itself in principle to the publication of the Letters, and my plan was accepted. I needed to have that commitment so that I could start the long process of talking the Estate first into a similar commitment in principle, and then to a discussion of the terms.

The first volume of the Letters was published in 1979, and the seventh in 1993; a very full index followed in 2000. The architect, General Editor and high-powered motor was Jim Boulton, assisted from the start by his wife, Margaret, and by individual volume co-editors. It is a masterly edition of one of the great letter-sequences in the language; it ranks with Keats and Byron and Dickens.

Of course, a very great deal went on between that first meeting in Nottingham and the publication of the first volume. There was another important meeting, in Austin, Texas, in 1973, at the Humanities Research Center itself. It was hosted by Warren Roberts, and it brought together several generations of Lawrence scholars from a number of countries, including Emile Delavenay from France and H.M. Daleski from Israel, important pioneers. The primary purpose was to draw up a careful set of directions for the editors of the volumes of Letters, and this we did. The tangible result was an eighteen-page printed pamphlet for editors, briefly making the case for an edition, setting out exhaustive working-rules and supplying a sample edited letter showing all the conventions in use (350 copies printed, it says: I think Warren was aware of the future market for copies). It had become my practice to do something like this with any series or multi-volume project, so that as much as possible was laid down at the start. One had to try to think of all possible needs and problems, to save having laboriously to get things right at a late stage, and to maintain consistency. I came back from Austin with the draft, and got it set up and printed at the Press.[1]

Agreeing all this in committee was the main function of the meeting – apart from getting to know each other, which was important. But there was also a kind of carry-over, in that the presence of so many experts and the general discussion of the state of Lawrence scholarship led to the thought – if we can do the Letters, why not the Works as well? Now that really was an enormous leap. Eight big volumes of Letters are one thing, but a further thirty-plus of Works take us into another league altogether, and even for the Press, used to publishing multi-volume works over many years, it was a huge enterprise. But we had the bit between our teeth, as the saying is, so we made for the next fence, the big one.

I wrote to Laurence Pollinger in July 1973, saying that it was in my mind. He replied that he still thought it both visionary and unnecessary. The publishers of the existing texts would be mistrustful of anything which might cut into their sales. He added 'Personally, I have been against a "definitive edition" for the simple reason that the text of the published books was passed by D.H. Lawrence himself.' If a man in his position could say that – a man who knew Lawrence and had seen in his own office some of the complications in the publishing process – you can see how naive even experienced professional people were about such things, and how much talking had to be done.

---

[1] When in 1978 we produced the comparable twenty-four-page pamphlet for the Works, I was able to use on the cover the phoenix-device which I had commissioned from Reynolds Stone, which became the emblem of the whole enterprise and is used on jackets and half-titles.

It took me eighteen months of hard talking and letter-writing to break down that opposition – together with some equally hard business-lunching and a small amount of backstairs conspiracy. As I have suggested, my function here was that of middleman or diplomat or organiser. I had three important groups to deal with and to keep on side. The first was my employers, the Syndics of the Press. The Syndicate makes all the most important decisions of principle: and specifically what gets published. In all my time at the Press, and however high I rose, I never had the power that other publishers have, to say to an author 'All right; we'll publish. Here's a cheque as an advance.' I had always to go back to the Syndics, make a careful case on paper, and then at the all-important and quite intimidating Syndicate meetings, had to support that case with careful argument. In important instances, like the Lawrence edition, the stakes were high, and I sweated a bit. Often, I had to talk quite hard.

In particular the Syndicate had to be persuaded that Lawrence was now a classic, and that a classical modern author can, despite modern printing and publishing processes, actually require the same kind of editorial rescue-work that one needs to put into the text of older classics like Shakespeare; and that the investment of those years of work and those millions of their pounds would both be enormously to the credit of Cambridge University and its Press – and might even in the long run make it some money.

Fortunately there was close at hand a young Cambridge scholar, Carl Baron, then a Research Fellow at Trinity, who was working on an edition of George Neville's memoir of his boyhood friendship with Lawrence (we published it as *A Memoir of D.H. Lawrence*, with Neville's own subtitle 'The Betrayal' in 1981). I asked Carl to write me a long and detailed memorandum on the state of Lawrence's texts, saying what was currently known about the ways in which they had been corrupted before publication, and reviewing the then-known material – in the form of manuscripts, typescripts, proofs and other documents – which would have to be used as necessary aids in the reconstruction of the text. Carl produced a dissertation-length document in the autumn of 1973. I could use it as a mine of evidence, and really questioning Syndics could be given it to read if they needed to be convinced. So could Pollinger and the other publishers.

Their potential question had been bluntly put by Laurence Pollinger; it is the question that the ordinary reader asks, as an expression of incredulity: 'Do you mean to tell me that in the twentieth century, with modern printing processes and publishing organisations, there is nonetheless a serious textual problem? Are you telling me that the texts I am reading are seriously defective and need editing as if they had been written before the invention of printing, which we were all told in school made the production of accurate texts not just possible but inevitable?' The answer to all these questions is 'Yes'. And actually, more needed to be done than is now necessary for Shakespeare, since with Lawrence we were starting from the beginning. Furthermore, we have had to learn how to do it, since the circumstances of modern writing and the processes of modern printing and publishing produce their own forms of corruption. On the other hand, while there is no manuscript of a Shakespeare play, the wealth of Lawrence MSS, the survival of substantial widely differing drafts, of typescripts (often differing from each other) and proofs presents the editor with a body of evidence to be evaluated and sequenced. For instance, Shakespeare did not write in places all round the world, producing material which was typed by all sorts of people, and he was not published more or less simultaneously in England and the USA, with the printers working from typescripts which did not agree with each other, and editorial processes peculiar to each country.

The second group I had to deal with was the Lawrence Estate, and in the first place Laurence Pollinger. In his experience a collected edition simply meant reprinting all the works in a new format with a nice new jacket, perhaps correcting some misprints on the way. For a long time, he could not conceive that there was a need to do more. The case for doing the Letters was easy: there were simply so many unpublished and uncollected letters. About the Works he was sceptical.

I worked on him over many months, which meant going up to London quite often and talking hard. He was a very charming man, and too shrewd to dismiss immediately our visionary scheme, so he was willing to listen; I always enjoyed meeting him. He was a great believer in the working lunch, and had a table reserved for him every day at Quaglino's, a distinguished old eating-house just down the road in Mayfair. We used to repair to Quags, as he called it, and I soon learned that it was important to do the hard talking during the soup and fish, because by entrée-time the atmosphere had got so exceedingly genial that not much more business got done. Fortunately I was relatively young and strong; how Laurence survived years of that regime is a mystery to me. It was important both before and after these meetings to write, first setting the agenda and then recording the progress. Reading the files after all these years I am impressed by my own eloquence in those letters. Here is one, perhaps the most effective, in the sense that it convinced me. It didn't work with him, but kept the discussion going:

29 October 1973

Dear LP

It was nice to see you again, and I enjoyed your hospitality. Next time it really is my turn – though I suspect you would rather not be taken somewhere else.

About the critical edition of D.H. Lawrence, may I now write you a rather long letter, setting out the position as I see it? I shall send you two extra copies which you can send on to Roland Gant [of Heinemann] and Marshall Best [of Viking Press] if that seems right to you.

I am going to have copies made of the long memorandum I commissioned from Carl Baron of Cambridge, and will send them in a few days. He's a little fierce, as young scholars are, but what he says is, I think you will agree, conclusive. There is a real need for a comprehensive new edition. Baron makes the case for the most elaborate treatment of all, i.e.

a. carefully revised texts
b. the addition of scholarly notes, textual and explanatory
c. publication of all unpublished material.

It would be possible to limit oneself to (a); but (b) is probably necessary. The addition of (c) makes the whole enterprise more daunting, even to us, but it could be faced as the final stage in a long operation.

Now, as a university press editor, I am in the scholarly editions business, and having read Baron's memorandum I can assure you that an edition properly prepared would present a text sufficiently distinguished from previous texts for a new copyright to be claimed. If therefore a new edition is set on foot now, controlled by the Estate, it will prolong the copyright, and the Estate's revenue from copyright. If however the ordinary copyright lapses, the works pass into the public domain. If somebody *then* produces a new edition, he can probably claim copyright in it for himself, he will pay nothing to the Estate, and you will have no control over what he does. I really mean that.

If I were a fly-by-night or unscrupulous person, I should not be telling you this. I should have my team of editors working on the texts now: I should publish in 1981 [*the copyright was due to expire in 1980, 50 years after Lawrence's death, under the law as it stood*], and if reproached I would reply 'You had fifty years to do it in, and you didn't. I've now done it; it needed doing; the world will be grateful to me for doing it, since for many years scholars have been asking for a critical edition.' And he will conclude with some more or less derisive gesture. I don't think you could do anything about it.

Now I ask you to look at Baron's memorandum again, and the material he quotes. The memorandum shows that he and people like him are virtually in a position to edit the texts now. Much of the needed information is publicly available. Some of it is in US libraries like Warren Roberts's collection. During the period of copyright, Warren, who is a scrupulous person, will protect the interests of the Estate and the present publishers. In 1980 librarians like Warren, who is a scrupulous person in all directions, might conclude that the public interest demands a critical edition, and they can't stand in the way. They are under no legal obligation, except to protect unpublished material, which retains perpetual copyright, as you know. Their scholarly obligation is to make the other stuff available.

I don't want to be a scaremonger, but I put it to you that what Heinemann and Viking don't do, others will – sooner or later. And 'later' nothing can be done about it. The interest of the Estate is simple and obvious: some volumes of a critical edition ought to be published in 1980 or sooner. The world ought to know that such an edition is planned, and the pirates may lay off that particular target (not in any case the most lucrative one).

The interest of Heinemann and Viking is in one sense direct: a critical edition may offer unwelcome competition. Well, there are two things to be said about that. First, there *is* going to be competition, from 1980 on. I assume they recognise that. What will happen immediately is that paperback houses will bring out cheap editions of the present texts – no doubt further corrupted. Nothing can stop that. Second, the initial publication of volumes in a critical edition *won't* be direct competition. Such volumes would be like – to take a familiar example – the scholarly versions of the Boswell papers that Heinemann produced (I think). They would be expensive, for the library and the expert in the first place. They would not initially conflict with the sale of the present much cheaper popular editions. It's a different market altogether. There's no question of Heinemann and Viking and Penguin suddenly finding they have vast dead stocks on their hands.

On the other hand, if we do this edition, we shall be putting into it over a number of years a quite colossal sum of money. In the end, we'd want to do student editions in order to get some of the money back. We, however, would be prepared to recognise the interests of the present publishers, and would want to consult them about the sequence and the timing.

This letter is getting too long. Let me sum it up like this. If I were executor of the Lawrence Estate I'd be saying 'We must now protect the Estate by instituting and announcing a scholarly edition which will remain our copyright, and be prepared under our control.' I'd go to Heinemann and Viking as the obvious people, and say 'Will you do it?' If they wouldn't, I'd feel obliged to find someone who would. It would not necessarily be unwisdom on their part to say no, since an edition of this sort will be a large capital outlay with a slow return, and they have shareholders. We haven't, and it is in any case a university press enterprise. We are familiar with that kind of operation. Heinemann and Viking might perhaps agree that a university press is the obvious publisher for such an edition, but would ask you and us to see that their interest is secured as far as possible. I would want to do that – but a mere interloper wouldn't care two hoots.

My own interest is that I think Lawrence is the greatest writer of the century, and a proper critical edition of his works is something it would give me enormous pleasure to take part in. It would be an ornament to the Cambridge

Figure 19. A volume from the Lawrence Edition with Reynolds Stone's phoenix-symbol

list, Lawrence would be the first major author of the century to be treated this way, and I'd like us to have the credit – and in the long term some profit.

Of course, if Heinemann and Viking decide to do it themselves, nothing could be more proper, and we then have no standing in the matter. But if they feel they can't, I urge you to urge them to let us. Here it is, nearly 1974. If someone starts in that year it should be just possible to have something out in 1980: but there isn't all that much time.

If you, Heinemann and Viking are sufficiently impressed by these arguments to say 'Let's discuss it further', I will go to the Syndics of the Press at one of their forthcoming meetings, and will ask them for their part to agree in principle to publish the edition. I believe they will agree, but of course I haven't asked them yet since I'm not clear whether the Estate and the other publishers are prepared to discuss it.

Yours ever
Michael Black

Now that I re-read it, this mixture of blandishment and threat, or idealism and blackmail, seems at best a brave try. I can see why I said this and that – the letter was at least carefully thought out. In one respect the letter, written in 1973, was misleading because ill-informed. I did not realise then how much unpublished material there was, and how much it was bound to influence the editing and need to be incorporated, either in the text itself or in the apparatus. I was mistaken in saying that an outsider could step in and do a proper edition, since the Estate owned the copyright of the unpublished material and could refuse to make it available. That meant, however, that an interloper would have to do an incomplete job, but could dress it up as a serious one, as a spoiling tactic. It would cream the market, and make it difficult for anyone to do better later. This has happened, actually, with other authors.

But time was going by in these meetings, and there was no obvious progress. One trouble was that the other parties involved, especially Heinemann and Viking, would neither do the edition themselves nor move over so that someone else could. The mere multiplicity of interested (in one sense of the word, but not the other) parties was a recipe for stalemate. The whole situation, it gradually dawned on me, was one of trying to move the immovable. Roland Gant of Heinemann, it turned out, was dying. Marshall Best of Viking was writing from happy retirement a long way from the office in New York. These were the people in those publishing house who had always 'known about' Lawrence, and were turned to for advice. Laurence Pollinger was old, and was not going to make a move he was not sure about. Together, they were tottering towards 1980.

It became sensible to go round the backstairs, so to speak, and to exert an influence on the beneficiaries of the Estate, Frieda's family. Fortunately, Frank Kermode had become a Syndic. He had written about Lawrence, and he also had a line to some of the family. He gave me an introduction. In 1974 I wrote to and met Monty Weekley, Frieda's son by her first marriage, who was also charming, and I observed the handsome, wide-blue-eyed hawk-face he had inherited from her. He listened kindly as I explained about the text. Equally important, I met with him at a later meeting a younger member of the family – Richard Seaman – Frieda's grandson, Elsa's child, and I think an accountant. I rehearsed my old arguments. As I explained all this to my interlocutors I have the distinct impression that their expression changed from polite interest to something more thoughtful. It is my belief that once they had reported this conversation to the family they told Laurence Pollinger quite firmly that they wanted the edition to go ahead, and it was left to him and me to work out the terms. This is the letter I wrote after the meeting; I think it did the trick.

16 October 1974

Dear Mr Weekley
I am now back in the office, and was glad to get your letter.
As I see it, the position is this:

a. It is, if the truth were stated, disgraceful that there isn't a carefully edited Lawrence text.
b. Such a text could constitute a new copyright. We claim copyright in our main text of Shakespeare. A properly edited text of Lawrence would differ from the present texts more than Shakespeare texts differ between each other.
c. A new copyright would be of advantage to the Estate, just as, from another point of view, it would be a kind of public service.
d. When the copyright expires, anybody can embark on a new edition, without reference to the Estate, or anybody else.

The questions boil down to two. Is the edition to be started now, with the agreement and participation of the Estate, and with the Estate benefiting; or is it to be left for a free-for-all? Are Heinemann and Viking going to do it, or will they let us?

I will be frank in private to you, and say that Viking and Heinemann ought to have planned all this years ago. They have neglected both their duty and their advantage. They have just time to get started; but if they don't move it will be an additional scandal if they prevent others.

I write with some force because it is in my mind that dear LP, old and tired and rather frail, may be met with mere inertia by Heinemann and Viking, and he may accept their inertia and conclude that nothing can be done. I am hoping therefore that the beneficiaries of the Estate, having a clear view of the public interest and their own, will refuse to accept that answer. If they press, they are in a position to get what they decide to have. So I hope the family will *insist*. If I can help, for instance by talking to Mr Seaman (to whom I am sending a copy of this letter) do let me know.

Yours sincerely,
M.H. Black

That letter, and the conversation which preceded it, did it, I suppose. It was important that at this time Gerald Pollinger succeeded his father as head of the agency. I had an equally friendly relationship with him, and he took the view that the whole thing was at least worth trying, and so it has proved.

It is important to be realistic about the arguments I deployed, not cynical. The cynics are those who say that money and self-interest should play no part in life, and if they do then the result is corruption. It was quite often suggested in the early years that the Press and the Estate were simply using copyright as a way of making money that other publishers were not allowed to make. But people do have legitimate financial interests, and must be expected to follow them. The law of copyright protects one kind of legitimate interest: that of the producer of original work, and his or her family or heirs. When I first sat in Laurence Pollinger's office he pointed to a framed cheque on the wall. It was for the first year's royalties from Penguin for *Lady Chatterley's Lover*, and it was for a huge sum, well into six figures. Pollinger had the satisfaction of taking his agreed percentage from all the deals he was able to negotiate for the estate of his old friends Lawrence and Frieda, and he was not only serving his and their interest, he was doing his professional duty. The thought that this tap would be turned off in 1980 could give no pleasure, and the possibility of retaining some royalties for a further period was one perfectly respectable incentive for him and the family to go forward with the new project.

My reasons, and the Press's reasons, were quite different. We wanted the credit – the glory if you like – of producing what was likely to be recognised as a monument of modern literary scholarship. By doing so, we were implicitly suggesting to the estates of other great modern writers that it was not only to their advantage, but, properly considered, it was their *duty* in the same way to conserve what had been left to them. It was not merely a source of money during the copyright period, after which it could be abandoned to others who would simply exploit it: it was a part of the nation's literature, it needed conservation, and they could actually combine duty and interest in the way we have done. If what had been left to them had been a great house, or a collection of pictures, they would rightly be criticised if they did nothing to conserve them and make them available to visitors, as often happens now in England; the public for its part is perfectly willing to pay the equivalent of a royalty in order to see them. Nor does it resent seeing the family still living on what is after all their property. I have to say though, that my experience of the literary estates of great writers is that they have no real notion of their duties. Naturally enough, they are just lay-people, but they don't stir themselves and get good advice.

Finally we reached agreement. In January 1975 I was able to go back to the Press Syndicate and ask it to commit itself in principle to publishing the complete edition. It was the culmination of some four years of negotiation, and took us to the start of the practical work.

Once the Press Syndicate and the Lawrence Estate had committed themselves to the venture, I could turn to my third group, the scholars who were to do the actual editing. The two seniors were Jim Boulton, who had by now moved to Birmingham, and Warren Roberts of the all-important Humanities Research Center (HRC) at Austin. Warren was already an experienced editor, having in 1968 edited with Harry Moore the second *Phoenix* volume of material unpublished in Lawrence's lifetime, and in 1965 the then-standard edition of the Poems with Vivian de Sola Pinto. He had also compiled the standard bibliography. As Director of the HRC he controlled access to the unrivalled collection of twentieth-century literary manuscript material at Austin, including the most important collection of Lawrence material, and he was active in the market, looking for more. This led him to travel, to make acquaintances and friendships which were crucial.

As time went by, the supervisory Editorial Board of the Edition became Jim Boulton, Warren Roberts, myself, John Worthen and Lindeth Vasey, who had been a researcher at Austin and who moved to the Cambridge staff in 1979, becoming our resident textual expert and, like John Worthen, a substantial volume editor. The job of the Board was to set editorial standards and define methods; then to find volume editors. These editors were asked to produce a substantial proposal – essentially a draft introduction – for their volume, which meant surveying in detail the available manuscript and other material and proposing a way of using it to produce a text. When this had been done to its satisfaction, the Board recommended that a contract be given by the Press. Then it had to supervise progress, read drafts and proofs, and approve the final version. I wrote the first draft of this chapter in 2003; we had already published some thirty volumes since 1980, and this is an exceptionally fast rate for such editions. We are now, in 2011, virtually at the end.

Some of the volumes were so strikingly different from received texts that it had to be acknowledged that the Edition had a point – for instance, we published in 1984 *Mr Noon*, which had led an unregarded life as a rather sharp short story, but when we added the substantial unpublished part it turned out to be a very lively if unfinished novel in which Lawrence carried further and into his life in Europe with Frieda the semi-autobiographical account of life in Eastwood which he had started in *The White Peacock*, continued in *Sons and Lovers*, and then broadened and varied, with other characters, in *Aaron's Rod* and *The Lost Girl*. He is here being really funny about himself and Frieda. Another landmark was the publication of the full text of *Sons and Lovers* in 1992. Edward Garnett's cuts were restored, so that the novel is about 10 per cent longer – but conservative critics went on arguing that the cut and censored version was better art. The editors were Helen and Carl Baron; after his death she went on to edit *Paul Morel*, the strikingly different early draft of *Sons and Lovers*.

Our volume editors have been predominantly English; but Americans, Germans, Italians and Australians make them a truly international group. The amount of thought and detailed work which went into each volume is hard for the outsider even to conceive. To go back to the point I made earlier, the editor has to construct a sense of a growing, changing identity in the texts which Lawrence went on revising. We want *his* changes, but not those made by others: if they are to be admitted at all it must be because they have some authority, or simply because we can't now get behind them to the original. It is a long and complicated process, which I have compared to tracing the path of a stream, growing into a river, with tributary streams flowing into it, and a good deal of pollution from people living on the banks.

The scholars who have done that did years of hard and not very well-paid work. I come back to the question of money and copyright, which has been a contentious issue because superficial observers have written off the whole endeavour as an attempt by the Estate merely to go on making money, and by the Press to sell at a high price something nobody else can sell. My final argument is that copyright protects the editors' work as well. If there was no copyright in the new text, any opportunist publisher could take it and reprint it with no acknowledgement of the source and with no payment to anybody – and would start all over again the process of introducing errors by careless reprinting. Editors will not give years of their lives if they get neither payment nor credit, and serious editorial work would therefore cease. It is actually important that the main texts of our literature are properly edited and kept correct. The invention of printing, which theoretically made it possible to keep texts accurate, rather and for hundreds of years made it possible to corrupt them very rapidly by careless and inaccurate reprinting. The scholars who reverse this process are public benefactors, who deserve their modest reward, and proper credit. For my part, I am sure that the Cambridge Edition of Lawrence was the best thing, the most important thing, I ever undertook as a publisher.

CHAPTER 16

Lawrence and literary biography

Being involved with the project from the start as organiser and administrator, helping to produce the guidelines for volume editors, reading the proposals and typescripts as they came in, calling and attending regular editorial meetings (important), corresponding with the Board and the volume editors – all that got me deeply immersed. I started as in a particular sense an editor – a publisher's editor, not a textual editor: but that gave me a set of insights and experiences which were relevant. For instance, as a young man at the Press I had used daily for its publications the old hot-metal printing methods used in Lawrence's time and still in use at the Cambridge Printing House. Also as part of my work at the Press we had been producing for scholars editions of dramatic and poetic texts. Having talked to and published books for textual authorities like Fredson Bowers and his successors, having produced large series such as a whole Bible Commentary and the *Cambridge History of the Bible*, which was itself an introduction to the longest tradition of editorial work – through all that I had come to have some sense of what was going on in those related spheres.

It was a genuine interest. I had to drop my undergraduate feeling that textual scholars were just fiddling about with details, while the critics were the interesting people. In its quiet way the textual-bibliographical-printing-publishing-history movement is, or should be, profoundly important and influential, and underlies – in my view corrects – all theory. If I go back to Keith Sagar's work, it is also seen to underlie the sort of criticism I have been interested in and found myself pursuing.

There were also interesting personal aspects. One can't help being specially impressed by actually meeting people who are otherwise just names in the books. I did once see Eliot plain. I knew Leavis quite well. Now I was meeting people who had known Lawrence – old LP and Monty Weekley, for instance. Warren Roberts gave me the tip that Helen Corke was still alive and had written a memoir. I got in touch with her, and duly got into the car again and drove down to Kelvedon in Essex, where I met her.

She was the school-teacher whom Lawrence met in his time at Croydon, also as a teacher, and had a kind of affair with in 1908–9. It didn't go well, for reasons not clear to either of them at the time, but they were certainly very close – he pressed her to go to bed with him, and she wouldn't – and he came to know her story. She had just previously had another affair – a deadly serious one – with a married man, her music-teacher, Herbert Baldwin Macartney. They had had a stolen week at the Isle of Wight, where Lawrence had also – at exactly the same time – had a well-remembered holiday with his mother and sister. The week was crucial for Helen in that on their return, on 7 August 1909, Macartney killed himself. She had gone down to Cornwall with friends, failed to hear from him, got worried and came back to read of his death in the first paper she bought, at the station.

In her desperation Helen had written an account of the week in the Isle, and a long sort of diary-letter to the dead man. She showed these to Lawrence. They became, with her spoken acccount, the germ of his second novel, *The Trespasser*, which went through two drafts and was published in 1912. In basic respects – plot and characters – Lawrence sticks closely to her story. The book has been routinely neglected as early work, but it has extraordinary and uncomfortable power, since it takes off from that basic plot in order to become a sort of symphony – opera rather – in prose.

So there she was, a little old woman with a sticking plaster on a recent wound, scruffily dressed, living in a council house, and looking rather grubbby. She was tiny. But she was very full of herself, as the saying goes, had always wanted to be a writer and now saw her other moment coming.

The autobiography was in two parts, and we published the first, because it told of her early life and the relationship with Lawrence, which was what the world would wish to know. The second, unpublished, part made some things clearer. She had at some point come to realise that it was not men she was really interested in, though she had the power to charm them – not exactly entrap them, since she didn't know what she was doing, and got herself into serious trouble, but she couldn't respond fully to them. So Macartney was destroyed by the entanglement: he had wrecked his marriage and gained nothing. In later life, as a successful teacher, she had a female partner, and used to go on holiday with her, driving a motor-bike with the loved one in the side-car. I should have liked to see this tiny, powerful person on the road in her helmet and goggles, a bit like Mr Toad.

She had written useful school-history-books for Oxford, and several things about Lawrence. She had also written a novel about the affair: called *Neutral Ground*, it was written in 1918, based on her reminiscences of 1910–12, and of course on *The Trespasser*. It was not published until 1933 as part of the immediate posthumous interest in Lawrence which produced a number of biographical and critical studies, notably Jessie Chambers's *Personal Record*. The title of *Neutral Ground* suggested that Helen had recognised that she was, as the blurb put it, 'of Uranian temperament'. It is a powerful piece, by no means completely upstaged by *The Trespasser*. It completes a sort of circle. *The Trespasser* had been based on what might be called 'the facts' – the events lived by and later narrated by Helen. It was also written after Lawrence had read and been deeply impressed by Helen's own first two written documents (reproduced in the Cambridge Edition). It had then taken its own form as Lawrence's complete re-fashioning of 'the facts'. In its turn it had influenced Helen's later re-telling – also a fiction, and also a way of dealing with 'the facts'.

This is a big issue in Lawrence. Nearly everything he wrote has some antecedent in 'real life' or 'the facts' as something he lived, observed or was told about. It has become a complex area for scholars and critics. In the notes to the Edition we have, where we could, given a brief outline of 'the facts' – the places, the people – or have reproduced actual related documents, always knowing that in a note you can't do much more. But the mere outline fact is meant to suggest the distance between it and its treatment, its transformation. But you can't stop some people being literal-minded and treating the fiction as a dressed-up fact, or other people being offended by what seems like editorial simple-mindedness in offering a too-simple parallel.

In Our Infancy was published by the Press in 1975 – a slightly odd title if you only remember that the quotation begins 'Heaven lies about us …', but perhaps she implies that it falls away with adulthood – 'Shades of the prison-house …', the poem continues. She enjoyed her later moment: Malcolm Muggeridge, whom she had once taught, did a programme about her on BBC TV.

She was of my father's generation as well as Lawrence's. I enjoyed talking to her about the books people read then, and she presented me with her copy of Maurice Hewlett's *The Forest Lovers*, which my father loved. (Lawrence wrote an early short story in the Hewlett manner.) The copy is inscribed, in copybook writing:

"Nell"
with love from
Agnes
Jan 26th 1905

Agnes was Agnes Mason, who had been a colleague at her school and then moved to the other school in Croydon where Lawrence was a new, young member of staff; and Agnes had introduced them to each other. The two women used to play music together, Agnes at the piano accompanying Helen on the violin. *The Trespasser* opens with them playing together while a young man – the Lawrence-figure – listens. One assumes that Agnes loved Helen. Lawrence also introduced Jessie – on a visit to him in London – to Helen, and they went on holiday together and became remarkably close.

So, in meeting Helen and publishing her account, and then in 1981 publishing our edition of *The Trespasser*, I was gaining an exceptional – a privileged – insight into that extraordinary aspect of Lawrence's work – the relationship with, the use made of, what we call 'real life'. Related as mere plot-summary, *The Trespasser* sounds like the simplest re-telling of the Corke–Macartney affair, with that Lawrence-figure present at the beginning and the end, and seeming in some danger of taking the place in the woman's life vacated by the dead man. Read as the novel it is – that is, as a kind of prose-poem – the events are submerged, transformed, by an entirely re-imagined orchestration. (There is, as a matter of interest, a strong Wagnerian influence, perhaps the most successful adaptation in literature: the motifs are Lawrence's personal association-system adapted to the sea, the sky, the sun and moon of the remembered Isle. But then again, Macartney was a first violin in the Covent Garden orchestra, and in 1909 played in the whole Ring Cycle, to leave on the last night for the week in the Isle of Wight.) There is also that remarkable relationship with Helen's own writings – the 'Freshwater Diary', the 'Cornwall Writing' and *Neutral Ground* itself. So there is a kind of palimpsest or multi-layered relationship in all the writings, and the 'mere' facts are deployed and re-deployed each time in ways which make them works of literature.

But the ideal reader, the archetypal naive reader of *The Trespasser* in 1912, would have picked it up and read it simply as 'this book' – and probably found it strange in more than one way. A less naive reader might have remembered that this D.H. Lawrence had written an earlier novel – *The White Peacock*. There is no very obvious relationship between the books, except a remarkably 'poetic' (one might have said) handling of scene and a 'troubled' handling of relationships – a preoccupation with failure in love. By the time *Sons and Lovers* appeared, Lawrence had to be recognised as an author – for there were short stories appearing in journals as well. The reader ceasing to be naive might recognise themes and preoccupations. This author came from the industrial midlands, was disclosing a class origin which was welcomed by middle-class readers who wanted to know how 'the other half' lived (actually the other nine-tenths). He was closer to things middle-class novelists observed from a distance – he had lived them. And it was already possible to think he was using his own experience as well as his background, and this was a source of the emotional disturbance or conflict he was conveying. One wouldn't have known that *The Trespasser* came from 'real life' – that perception could come later when one realised that Lawrence nearly always based his fictions on something he knew about or had actually lived with.

To us now *Sons and Lovers* – like the second half of *Mr Noon* and the chapter 'Nightmare' in *Kangaroo* – might look at first sight like autobiography lightly fictionalised. It raises difficult critical questions, like the long-running debate about the treatment of the Morel parents and the Jessie-figure Miriam as they are portrayed in *Sons and Lovers*. Had Lawrence 'distanced' his own problems, and so on, and if he had not distanced them, is the book to be criticised for that reason, as not an adequate treatment of the real-life situation (which we only know about from the books)? One could look at Helen Corke's *Neutral Ground* and say that it is an only just adequate treatment, but that is not because it is biased towards the Helen-figure but because it is written by an author who had a less extraordinary gift. On the other hand, the gift, as I call it, would join an adequate art to an adequate grasp of the human situation, and it isn't easy to separate the two.

I don't myself doubt that, though it is an early work, *Sons and Lovers* is a masterpiece, and add that the complete text, published by Cambridge in 1992, makes this clearer than it was. It succeeds as a novel which, in its final draft, unedited by Garnett, is a handling of the basic family situation which both does justice to it and also re-imagines it – even manipulates it freely in certain respects. In particular, while Miriam is presented as revealing an aspect of the central male figure's 'problem' with women, it is also shrewd about Miriam's own nature and role, in which she reveals *her* needs and difficulties, her own problem. She is presented as a person, not a mere heroine: the kind of girl that young man, with that family background, and especially that mother, would be involved with and reject, and both things because she was so like the mother. The case is familiar enough in principle, but deeply understood from the inside, though presented as from the outside. It's one of the things novelists show an essentially dramatic skill in presenting.

The problem there is that 'Miriam' was based on the remarkable woman Jessie Chambers, and she has left us her own very impressive account of the relationship with Lawrence, published in 1935, after his death. Her letters have also been collected and published, and there was at one time a whole 'subject' or debate about whether Lawrence was 'fair' to her. She certainly thought not, which was partly why she wrote.

One can get bogged down in that sort of discussion, in which one is taking sides about people one didn't know, and most if not all of the evidence, one way or the other, is in the books themselves. Not quite *all* the evidence, though Jessie's *Personal Record* manages to be as just as anyone can be while still maintaining one's own point of view – and indeed Lawrence could be said to have used her and dropped her, and he knew it and felt bad about it. But it still means one is arguing from one book to another book – and did Jessie actually see the final draft of *Sons and Lovers* (perhaps not: her own account suggests not), and in any case she was writing her account long after the events, and he was now famous and dead. And she never seems to have said to herself: but this is a novel. Yet, to complicate matters, she did write her own novel in answer to his, and before she destroyed it he saw it and was devastated by it. One has to assume that it was 'fair' to her, whether or not it was to him. But it seems to have left her – and some of us – with the view that 'being fair' about the real-life relationship was the main point.

It was not a silly argument, and it is difficult not to join in, but it does fail to get to the essential issue. This might be best put by pointing out that the greatest early twentieth-century novelists all used personal experience. They were none of them writing autobiography. They needed a basis in real life so as not to be veering into romance or fantasy. There had to be, as starting-point, a solid relationship with what they knew first-hand and direct, something to be pondered. But they also had to make something of it, that is, to depart from it, and this was their art, and is in the end the point of the books themselves. One could play the same game with Conrad, with Proust, with Joyce, with Virginia Woolf, with Mann, Céline and so on. They were not being fair: they were writing novels, and were bound to manipulate the 'facts'.

On the other hand, I am beginning to make the case for serious literary biography. I am all in favour of naive readers, and of their remaining naive if they can. I think writers write for naive readers, and value them as ideal readers who just pick up this book and read it with no preconceptions, meaning to enjoy it. But it's hard to remain naive, if only because you may read the book again with more understanding, or become aware that you have read other books by this person, who is therefore The Author. It would be very difficult to go on knowing nothing else about him/her in our world, and the question sooner or later arises, how or why did he/she come to write these books? Is there some personal involvement? Questions like that.

Things take a further turn when you suddenly realise that some actual person may be being part-portrayed as a character in a novel. An awful lot of that went on in the 1920s and 1930s, much of it mere caricature. Lawrence was given to making use of people in that way – or aspects of them – and it happened to him as well. One key case is Hermione Roddice in *Women in Love*, where readers in the know said to themselves 'Ottoline Morrell, to the life'. Especially Ottoline Morrell, who had the right to feel injured. Not, on the other hand, Jessie Chambers, yet she saw beneath the surface characterisation that what is shown to be going on inside Hermione was like what Lawrence thought went on inside *her*. So doing shrewd or witty external Dickensian character-sketches was not actually the point, though many readers thought and still think it was.

A serious biography is not primarily designed to sort out these matters, but it is meant to recover as much of the actual fact as is possible, to present it in relation to the art, and to make it more difficult to treat the art/life relationship superficially. It's true that there has been a good deal of simple-minded biography which seems to say 'We all know about the books, don't we; let's just get on with the life-story, and especially the sexual life and the scandalous bits.' There will be some reference to the works, but mainly as being written and published at this point or that, and some simplifying comment may be added. That sort of 'mere' biography has been promoted by the post-Strachey impulse to say the things which could not be said in the nineteenth century, when a biography was a positive record of achievement written by a loyal admirer who may have known about the other things but thought they were diminishments and not the business of outsiders. And since the growth of popular psychoanalysis it has become conventional to think that sexual experience, especially early in life, is determining, so what might once have looked like nasty gossiping is what we now need to know in order to 'understand'.

Evidently, there's no going back. The only course is to go on and to make the biography as detailed, careful and sympathetic as possible – and to undertake the really difficult thing, which is to treat the writing-life as an intrinsic part of the whole life. That means being very careful about the relationship in both directions, since one obvious danger is determinism – the 'simply because' impulse. It was nineteenth-century determinisms, especially in France, which led to the twentieth-century New Critical impulse to block off the relationship between the work and the author – or indeed the world taken as source of determining agencies – to treat that as none of the critic's business and a source of irrelevant gossip or simplifying 'explanation'. That was the attitude I absorbed from Cambridge English – though not from Leavis, who was not naive about these matters. The work of art was to be treated as a free-standing structure whose elements were to be related to each other and not to anything outside them. There was a lot to be said for this purity of interest, since it produced close relevance in one kind of criticism (it underlies the 'death of the author' in more modern theory), but it can't be maintained for ever in the face of what we happen to know and what we go on learning. Literature is more complicated than that, and a good thing too.

It became clear as the Letters were published and the Edition proceeded that the background work on the writing-life was turning up, with each volume, a great deal of new information, and a deepening of what we knew about the life of the writer, and the experiences he was transforming into fiction. The idea of a biography presented itself as natural consequence and companion to the Edition, but it had to be one which did justice to the issues I have been outlining.

The form it took was unexpected – not just three large volumes, but each written by a different author. And they do face the problem, keeping both life and work related to each other but not in an easy sense 'explaining' each other. Published in 1991, 1996 and 1998, they ran the risk, while the Edition and the Letters were still in progress, of being outdated in detail by the continuing work – but there is no way of avoiding the risk of later knowledge. John Worthen, Mark Kinkead-Weekes and David Ellis worked successfully as a team, so that in some sense each volume has all three of them behind it. It will be a standard reference for many years. And it is a good and satisfying read.

But one thing implicit in what I have been saying did not really strike me for years. I can think of two examples which convey what I mean. When the first volume in the Edition was published, we had to devise a copyright notice. Copyright had been an important issue from the beginning, and we had to make the claim, and in the right terms. In an unthinking moment of euphoria and hubris I wrote:

This, the Cambridge Edition of the text of *The Trespasser* now correctly established from the original sources and first published in 1981 © the Estate of Frieda Lawrence Ravagli . . .

The word 'definitive' is hovering in the background. I should already have known better by then. For instance, I should have remembered the moment in 1978 when a hitherto unknown collector, Charles Smith, wrote to Gerald Pollinger from his retirement home in Bermuda to say that he had a considerable body of unrecorded Lawrence MS material. Gerald shrewdly invited him to the Lawrence conference being held in Carbondale, Southern Illinois that year. A deep impression was made on both sides. Smith was pleased and impressed by being made welcome by all the Lawrence scholars, and perhaps that made him more open than collectors usually are. The scholars were half-elated, half-depressed to learn of so much that they did not know existed. The one who had already got under way the edition of *Studies in Classic American Literature* realised he would have to go back to the beginning, and resigned. That volume was published in 2003, having turned out to be the most complex of all the editing jobs so far. And an essential part of the operation was a sort of privateering raid on Smith's home in Bermuda carried out by Warren Roberts and Lin Vasey, in which the essential documents were photocopied, while Mrs Roberts was entertained by the owner and his wife. The papers have since been sold and have disappeared again. Smith was perhaps momentarily distressed to find that the selling-price of his collection might have been reduced by the thought that the material was going to be published – or perhaps he remained silent about that, and the editing process certainly took years. The implication is that it will always be possible for some collector to emerge with hitherto unknown material, which may have important textual implications, so from that point of view there is no definitive edition.

Add to that the fact that the principles of editorial procedure are now a matter for quite bitter controversy. Consider the case of the edition of *Ulysses* carried out in Germany by the textual scholar Hans Walter Gabler and published in 1984. The Penguin Edition in 1986 is described on the cover and title-page as the 'Corrected Text'. In the original edition Gabler wrote a most important Afterword describing his method, which seemed to me to correspond with the one we had worked out for Lawrence. He was assailed in the USA by conservative scholars, who did in fact point out some errors of detail but did not undermine his general principles. The publishers felt out of their depth in this row, and did not know whether to support Gabler or his opponents. In my view he was correct and his work needed minimal revision, but the whole controversy suggests that editorial principles and procedures are not ever going to be established as a settled matter, so there are not going to be any 'correctly established' texts, only good ones carefully prepared on stated principles. We quietly rewrote the copyright notice some years later.

For all that, I doubt whether the Cambridge text can be easily impugned, and I should be surprised if any body of editors undertakes to replace it for many years, long after I have gone.